"Deeply personal and written ~~with~~ _Upon a Kentucky Farm_ shines a ~~light on many levels~~ of trauma. It's one of those stories that oozes vulnerability and courage, sharing some of the deepest wounds anyone could ever carry. Heartbreaking, inspiring, and told with a thoughtful tone, this memoir radiates a deep understanding of the importance of moving beyond our painful circumstances toward the boundless possibilities of healing. It is a book of truth, helping others to free themselves."

—Cherie Kephart, award-winning author of
A Few Minor Adjustments

"Connard Hogan's _Once Upon a Kentucky Farm_ gives readers a front row seat to a heartfelt search for truth, meaning, and healing in a world where the wounds remain unchanged regardless of the 'progress' generations of humans have made. The good news is the discovery of a cure that is also unchanged: unconditional love."

—Matthew J. Pallamary, author of _Spirit Matters_

"If you were to say _Once Upon a Kentucky Farm_ is a memoir about being raised in an abusive household, you would only be partly right. Yes, Connard Hogan's father was an alcoholic who physically abused Connard's mother and emotionally abused his two sons. But equally important was the counterbalancing effects of Connard's grandmother and grandfather and their farm where he spent many of his weekends and holidays. The farm was an oasis, an escape from the tough realities at home, where nonetheless he learned essential life lessons. This touching memoir is a testament to both the damaging and healing effects different family members can have on us. Particularly poignant is the ending where Connard fully realizes the weight of these effects and celebrates those who nurtured him while forgiving those who didn't."

—Dale Griffiths Stamos, author, filmmaker and
award-winning playwright

"Not only does Hogan's narrative show the insights of a young boy exposed to the harshness of alcoholism and spousal abuse, but it also transports the reader into farm life each time Connard visits his grandparents. The endless chores, constant need to attend to farming tasks, and the slow moving, lazy evenings with the absence of TV and electronics are all part of the story, bringing to life an era from long ago. One that few will recognize. But for those that do, the tale renders a step back into time. Into lazy dog day summers, quiet living, and nights without TV, devices, or electrical gadgets. The simple life."

—Martha Louise, author of *Married to Merlot: A Memoir with a Message of Hope*

"Connard Hogan's *Once Upon a Kentucky Farm* is a story more than "once upon" but one lived by many families who might find comfort and hope here. Hogan shows how family dysfunction can come around in time with courage and love. Told from Connard's perspective, growing up from age 5 through high school with all the usual childhood joys and pitfalls, we follow his awakening that something wasn't quite right, and how it changed him and his family for the better once he said 'Stop!' to his father's alcoholic rages. This is a gripping story where any reader will find parts of their own lives within and be glad for the eventual redemption."

—Perie Longo, Marriage & Family Therapist, poet

ONCE UPON A
KENTUCKY
FARM

Hope and Healing from Family Abuse, Alcoholism and Dysfunction

CONNARD HOGAN

ONCE UPON A KENTUCKY FARM
Hope and Healing From Family Abuse, Alcoholism and Dysfunction
by Connard Hogan
1. FAM052000 2. FAM001000 3. BIO000000
ISBN: 978-1-949642-95-7 (paperback)
978-1-949642-96-4 (ebook)

Cover design by LEWIS AGRELL

Printed in the United States of America

Authority Publishing
11230 Gold Express Dr. #310-413
Gold River, CA 95670
800-877-1097
www.AuthorityPublishing.com

Dedication

To Mom, Gramma Riggs and Gramma Hogan
(and to all others who are an epitome of unconditional love)

Table of Contents

Acknowledgments

My love goes to all those in my life who offered and provided their love, particularly the women who suffered my character flaws, poor judgment, and decisions. My gratitude goes to my mother and grandmothers who provided me their unconditional love.

I want to acknowledge all my family members for sharing their experiences, life skills, and humor, which helped contribute to who I've become.

Without excusing egregious behavior, I'd like to acknowledge that my father was also a victim of alcoholism and PTSD. I believe he did the best he could while struggling alone with his demons.

I'm grateful for all those who have guided me and offered constructive feedback on my writer's path: those in my critique groups, workshops and writing classes.

My appreciation goes to Rachel Sarah Thurston, social media consultant at "State of Sparkle," who assisted me in website and social media development. Without her assistance in designing my website, I wouldn't have had the courage to take the next step on my author journey.

Thanks to Dale Griffiths Stamos, author/filmmaker/playwright, who has been one of my writing instructors and editor on this manuscript. She provided me an important suggestion which helped bring the intensity of my childhood difficulties to life.

I'd particularly like to thank, Rebecca Robins, jounalist/author, who went out of her way to provide me invaluable guidance regarding development of a previous memoir manuscript. She recognized a potential and showed an interest in that manuscript far beyond what I could've ever hoped.

Lastly, but not least, my thanks and appreciation goes to my wife, Janet, who tolerates my flaws and idiosyncrasies on a daily basis. I'm assured she will remind me when its time for me to take a shower.

May my words provide solace, inspiration and encouragement to those who have struggled, are struggling, and are yet to struggle with trauma on their life's journey.

Walk in beauty.

Author's Note

This book was never intended to be a self-help or how-to book. Instead, it is a story, my story, of emotional hardship as a child, and written in a way as to bring to life the intensity of my difficulties without undue exaggeration. I've endeavored to share my journey as a healing exercise for me, while hoping to inspire and encourage others on their healing journeys.

This book was not intended to cast dispersion on others, including family members, nor generate or recreate emotional distress. I endeavored to portray my experiences as honestly and directly as possible, of course, all within the constraints imposed by the passage of time. In some few cases, names have been deliberately changed.

Lastly, I'll share a favorite quote from Carl Jung: "I am not what happened to me; I am what I choose to become."

Frank and Ada

1996

Another door had slammed shut.

"Your aunt Shirley and I went down there to look at the farm and the house," Mom had told me over the phone. "The new owner let us in. You should see it. They've re-modeled the inside. It's gorgeous. They put in a spiral staircase. . . ."

Was the glossy-white door to the secret passage that goes upstairs gone, too?

After we'd lost Dad, Mom and I talked long-distance on a weekly basis. We worked to shore up our relationship and make up for the years of sparse contact since I'd moved to California.

I'd witnessed a stream of changes regarding the farm and those there who had cocooned me in their loving care. Those changes had seemed incremental taken one by one. When grouped together, however, they led me to the realization—impossible to ignore—that, what I hadn't already lost from my childhood, I would do so in the not too distant future. And for me the farm, an oasis from the turmoil I faced at home, had been vitally important in my childhood, more so than I'd realized then.

* * *

After Mom and I had said our goodbyes, memories began to flood in and I recalled the last time I'd seen Gramma and Grampa together on the farm.

The farm had looked tired and unkempt, a lesser version of the one I'd remembered.

I'd checked the nearest of the two rain barrels that book-ended the front porch of the house. Had to. Looked deep into the barrel to see what little water remained, then picked up the well-worn footpath between the house and garage. That dirt path, a hard-packed shallow rut, had been there as far back as I could remember. Its gentle curve, carved through uncut grass, led me to the large, irregular marble slab that acted as the back doorstep.

Northbound in Mom and Dad's car, after a visit of haunts at my alma mater, Western Kentucky University in Bowling Green, I'd pulled off I-65 at the Upton exit. Now an interstate highway, we'd known I-65 as the toll road when the section between Louisville and Elizabethtown had opened in 1956 and you had to pay to use it. I'd not seen my maternal grandparents for several years, as I hadn't traveled back to Kentucky, money in short supply. And I'd decided I no longer needed to rely on Mom and Dad to visit Gramma and Grampa. Always called my grandparents that, on both sides. Always will.

I paused at the marble slab at the kitchen door. I never trusted that rock, a little tilted with a hump in the middle and wicked-slippery when wet.

The back door stood open to let in air, though the screen door was shut.

The kitchen was unoccupied. With a loud knock, I called, "Hello."

Gramma appeared through the doorway from the living room.

"Hi, Gramma," I said. Even through the screen I noticed she'd grown frail and I spotted a rag wrapped around her right ankle.

"Well, hi, Son. Come on in." She flashed that friendly, enthusiastic smile I'd always known. She'd always called me, Son, and I liked that. Made me feel closer to her, and special every time she did, even though she referred to all my male cousins that way, too.

I stepped inside. "What happened to your leg, Gramma?"

"Oh, I caught my ankle on the screen door the other day." She pointed. "See? On that corner there."

A sheet of the aluminum door, worked loose at the bottom, had curled into an unintended knife edge with an even more menacing corner.

"That looks dangerous, Gramma."

"I bled and bled. Thought I was going to bleed to death."

"Well"—and there it was, the possibility, no, the inevitability of her death and my loss of Gramma forever—"I'm glad you didn't, Gramma," I said as I choked back my sadness.

"I'll be alright now, I think."

"I hope so." *Would she?*

A tea towel, as Gramma called them, served as a bloodied bandage.

"Let me see if I can fix that door," I said, careful to give her a gentle hug beforehand. I bent the metal flap, all the while my heart breaking, though I didn't let on. I didn't have the courage to say, I'm going to miss you when you're gone. I'd never heard anyone in my family say that or anything near it. Just wasn't done. "That's a little better," I said, the result far short of what I'd hoped to achieve.

"Why don't you go sit with your Grampa while I fix us something to eat?"

"Okay, but watch out for that door," I said as I proceeded to the living room. Gramma best served by feeling needed, I figured. A vital reason for her to carry on?

I'd missed her kindness and gentle ease, the way she never got riled about anything that I recalled, the opposite of Dad's volatile temper.

Grampa occupied his favorite chair as I entered the living room. He peered over the top of the newspaper he held as I said in a raised voice, "Hi, Grampa." His hearing could've only grown worse. He sat pressed into his chair, as if losing his battle against gravity. His spectacles, as he'd always referred to them, rested on the mid-portion of his nose. His full head of ruffled white hair on display, the wrinkles on his face were deeper than I'd expected.

"Well, hello," he replied and put aside the newspaper, and after a brief pause, said, "Let's go out for a sit on the front porch."

Sounded good to me. That had been the custom on warm days throughout my childhood, when the air in the house had grown stuffy and uncomfortable.

With a grunt, he raised himself, then turned for the hallway leading to the front door.

I couldn't tell if he'd gained weight—he'd always been on the heavy side—but, with bent back, he leaned forward, which exaggerated his movements. His arms lifted as he bore down on his right leg, his limp more pronounced than ever. I'd always seen him limp, though now his steps resembled a shuffle.

* * *

With Grampa in his favorite position on the front porch swing, and me next to him, I'd provided an update of my life in California. After I'd graduated Western Kentucky University and migrated, my contact with everyone in Kentucky had diminished. My visits had grown fewer and farther between. Sparse phone conversations, mostly with Mom, and the occasional Christmas letters and cards provided me meager information to fill the gaps of everyone's daily life. All that, an immediate and continual cost of my escape.

"I don't understand how someone could move away from their family," Grampa said. "I could never do that."

Though not a question, his comment hung in the air and demanded a response. I'd gathered during my childhood, Grampa had been born and lived near Upton, central Kentucky. Then, after my mom was born, he'd moved his family to Highland Park, a suburb of Louisville, some sixty miles north. Mom had grown up there.

Not sure how to reply, I wondered if he knew the full story—I doubted it—or could appreciate what happened at my house as I grew up. The bits and pieces of details about Mom's relationship to Gramma and Grampa that I'd picked up, served as a bread-crumb trail suggesting direction, though without satisfactory end. I had little clue what Mom told them when I wasn't present. And every tidbit of new information led me to more questions.

I couldn't fully explain to him why I'd moved to California. Could've said I'd gone because I'd heard California graduate schools would be less expensive. I couldn't rule out the possibility, though, that Mom's desire to go to Hollywood to see movie stars, as she said repeatedly, hadn't played a significant role. I must've heard her say that a hundred times. Nor could I dismiss the likelihood I'd performed what's called a geographic cure, as referred to in Alcoholics Anonymous.

Not ready to be honest with the whole truth, as I'd understood it, I feared opening a deep gash. I wanted to avoid descending into an unknown labyrinth, like the unexplored sinkhole across the road. I searched for a plausible response. Some things hadn't been discussed in my family, at least not in my presence. Though unsettled, I concluded this wasn't the time to contradict the unspoken norm. Horace Greeley's words, "Go west, young man," came to mind, and I said, "I went seeking my fortune, I guess." When I'd deployed to Vietnam, I discovered San Francisco. The big-city sights reinforced my conclusion that Louisville, and all of Kentucky—though they held promise in some ways—were impoverished and that I wouldn't, couldn't flourish there. Nor did I mention the deep voice from within that had told me to break away and create the distance I couldn't achieve as a child. I didn't wish to acknowledge I'd hoped to avoid following in Dad's misplaced footsteps.

Mostly quiet then, Grampa and I surveyed the world beyond the front porch, interrupted only by short spoken bursts. I took opportunity to visualize my younger self engaged in activities around the porch, front yard, and beyond, until Gramma summoned us from the front door.

"You men come in for supper," she said. Everyone had always called our evening meal supper.

As Grampa worked his way to the kitchen table, I couldn't help but imagine myself acting as an usher, though from behind. *Don't fall, don't fall.*

Gramma focused on Grampa and me, offered us portions of everything she'd set upon the table. She doted on us, asked questions about what we wanted and ensured we were situated before she sat down. As she fussed around, I couldn't help but notice her slight forward hunch and the way her long checkered dress, covered by a white waist-length apron, hung loose from her shoulders as if she'd withered inside it.

* * *

I'd spent the night, steeped in the presence of Gramma and Grampa, their house, and the farm, before I said goodbye after breakfast the next morning. As I drove away, thankful I'd visited them, my grief, inseparable from my blood and bones, welled up.

Those two exchanges during that visit had been the most serious one-on-one adult conversations I'd ever had with Gramma and Grampa. Or would ever have? How many more times would I be able to visit them, talk with them, or see them alive? My relocation to California, in service of my survival, had nevertheless cost me countless opportunities to visit them, and all my other family members; a price I'd needed to pay, though painful.

As a child the farm seemed safe, changeless, and boundless, a predictable part of my life. There, I didn't have to contend with sidewalks, neighbors' dogs and cats, and most of all, Mom and Dad's terrible fights over his drinking. The farm possessed some magical quality, I'd believed as a child, since Dad never drank and never became a raging bull there, nor, as a result, did he and Mom argue.

But, I knew as I drove away that the remnants of my childhood refuge that hadn't already slipped away would soon do so, and I'd never again recreate my childhood days of innocence. The glory days of my play with cousin Billy couldn't be brought back. I'd never again have the thrill of the mad rush of Easter egg hunts. Never again experience the large, noisy, pleasant yet chaotic gatherings of family at Thanksgiving and Christmas meals, or the fun-scare rituals of Halloween. I'd never again experience hunts for rabbits, squirrels, and frogs, and picking fruit through the eyes of a young boy. But the role that my grandparents' farm played in my childhood and my growing into a young man, played a much more important role than I could appreciate then, and will ever forget.

* * *

Over the days and weeks, I recalled, reflected, and assessed my childhood memories, and how I came to be the self I am.

How had it all come about?

Root Cellar

June 1953

"Want to go with Gramma to the root cellar?" she asked me. Gramma always referred to herself in third person, at least to me.

I was five years old. Mom, Dad, and I had arrived for a weekend visit after Dad had gotten off work that Friday evening.

"Yeah," I said. Couldn't resist. I liked being around Gramma, knew she'd always do special things for me. Besides, I wanted to learn more about that mysterious cellar. Our house didn't have one, not even a basement.

Uncle James, the youngest and last of my aunts and uncles living on the farm, had told me things about that cellar.

"We used to take ice down there in the winter to keep things cool through the summer," he'd said.

I couldn't believe my ears. "How did you keep the ice from melting?"

"We covered it with sawdust and hay. And that helped the ice last longer."

Several steps behind, I followed Gramma to the tool shed about fifty feet straight away from the back door.

The weathered building, about three feet above ground level on one end, rested on stacks of flat rocks at that corner and in the middle. Rocks, no doubt, collected from the surrounding area, maybe from the hole now called the root cellar, located under one end. Tan shingles covered the sides.

"Are you getting excited about starting school?" she asked.

"I don't know," I said. Seemed everybody talked up school, which increased my curiosity. When Mom taught me numbers, drilled me about the difference between right and left, and explained how to tell time, she'd made that fun.

Gramma unlatched and opened the door, stepped up into the shed, and asked, "Can you get up?"

"Yeah." Using my hands to steady myself, I swung one leg up and followed.

Gramma turned left and headed down steps into the dark, while I paused.

The air smelled ancient and musty. An assortment of things, bathed in the light through the open door, appeared as my eyes adjusted. Covered with a layer of dust, nothing seemed disturbed for years, as if in a museum or time capsule. Objects large and small lay scattered across the floor, or leaned against and hung from the walls. I recognized harnesses for mules, parts of plows, and a knife-sharpening wheel. A pile of thick cast-iron wrenches lay in a loose pile. Assorted-sized boxes, lids open, advertised their contents of nails. I spied a square glass jar near me, noticed a gear and crank at the top connected to wooden paddles inside.

The sounds of Gramma's rummaging in the cellar drew my attention back to the business at hand, so I started down the steps to join her.

The wooden step under me creaked.

"I saw a snake in here last week. It might still be in here," Gramma said, "but it won't hurt you."

"Snake?" I whispered.

I had no reason to believe a poisonous snake, such as a copperhead, would end up in the cellar, but any snake could bite. I kept watch where I stepped as I descended into Gramma's grocery store, stocked every summer and fall with items harvested on the farm through her canning efforts. During winters, we'd eaten all kinds of vegetables, like green beans, and fruit, such as blackberries and apples. Anything and everything Gramma could cook and put into a jar ended up down there.

The air turned cool. I strained to see. Light, through one small window just above ground level, provided dim lighting. A bulb, dangling by its electrical wire from the center of the ceiling, added little more. One of Gramma's coal-oil lamps would do much better. Bits of straw lay on the dirt floor.

One hand against the rock outer wall to steady myself, I inched downward.

Creak! Another step moaned.

I didn't want a snake to sneak up on me, or worse, I didn't want to touch one, but I had no idea where a snake would rest in the cellar. Behind the open-backed steps? Gramma believed a snake in the cellar wasn't a bad thing, because rats were a snake's favorite food, though I wouldn't bet my twenty-five-cent weekly allowance on a snake not biting me.

Dusty cobwebs occupied the corners, while strings of them hung from the ceiling everywhere, and not the fake kind we'd hang at Halloween. The nearest thing to the inside of a grave I could imagine. I decided I'd never come to the root cellar alone.

"I asked your uncle James to come get that snake out," Gramma said.

Gramma never showed squeamishness about things like bugs or spiders, never seemed scared of anything, including death. She strongly held to her religion, and just shooed bugs away without fuss, but I gathered she didn't like the idea of getting bitten by a snake, either.

"Said he couldn't find it," she added.

Still here? I'd bet a snake couldn't get enough of that place.

A dirt ledge ran along two sides of the cellar close to the wood ceiling, where exposed beams supported the floor above. Wooden shelves lined the walls. Numerous boxes sat on the floor, some stacked two or three high. The lids of many of the boxes hung open at various angles. Single jars of canned goods ringed the cellar on the ledge and shelves, while a few sat orphaned on the floor.

"Now, where are those stewed tomatoes?" Gramma pulled a jar from one box. "No, not here." On to a nearby box, she said, "No, not here, either. Those are pears." She paused a moment. "Gramma will find one."

Some of those canned goods had been stored last summer and fall, and some, who knew when? Some forgotten, older than me? I couldn't tell. "I can help you, Gramma." Standing at the bottom of the steps, I scanned the dirt shelves and floor for signs of a jar of stewed tomatoes, and at the same time, that snake. Careful, I checked one jar. *No, looks like beets.* I checked another nearby, while Gramma widened her search. *Nope, corn.*

She moved the top box off a stack three-high, and peered into the second box. "Here they are. Gramma couldn't remember exactly where she put them." She examined the lid. "This jar looks good. You can carry it to the kitchen for Gramma."

I turned towards the steps, the light-switch chain rattled and the cellar grew darker. I heard Gramma's footsteps close behind me.

One, two, put on my shoe. Three, four, get out the door.

I pointed to the square glass jar as she topped the cellar steps. "What's that, Gramma?"

"That's a butter churn. We used to make our own butter in that."

* * *

Back in the kitchen, I asked, "Mom, did you ever make butter in the churn?"

Gramma twisted the lid of the canned tomatoes. *Click!* "I think they're good to eat, Bea. Would you get me a bowl?"

I loved Gramma's canned tomatoes.

"Yes," Mom said to Gramma, then to me, "A few times. It took a lot of cranking to make butter."

I couldn't help but picture Mom as a little girl. She'd just wanted to be happy, like me, probably, though her happiness had become a part-time commodity around Dad's drinking

In hindsight, what Mom had shared of her problems about Dad's drinking with Gramma or Grampa, I can only guess, since I never heard talk of that. When we visited the farm, where I considered Mom safe from Dad's rages, I laid down my burden of anticipating his outbursts and wallowed in boy-joys of discovery, though I could never escape my mental splinters.

Dad entered the kitchen, and without hesitation asked, "Miss Riggs," that's what he called her, "do you have any canned peaches?"

"Yes, Cecil, I believe we do. Go down to the cellar and get you a jar."

In a flash, without asking me if I wanted to accompany him, he was at the kitchen screen door, which shut with a *Clack!*

Gramma looked at me. "I'll bake a cobbler for supper."

We called our midday meal dinner. Our evening meal we called supper.

"Can you make a blackberry one, Gramma?"

"Yes. Gramma will bake you a blackberry cobbler."

To this day, I can't help but feel comforted by the smell of warm pie and cobbler, and whenever I pause at those times, images of Gramma come to mind.

* * *

Seated at the head of the table, Grampa delivered grace with hands together, head lowered, and eyes closed.

Without fail, he'd offer his rote prayer at every meal in the same manner, with softly whispered words that flowed like warm gravy over turkey. He could probably recite it backwards or in his sleep, and most often, he and he alone, offered that prayer at his table.

I'd noticed the small room off the kitchen before, but afraid of what might be in there, I'd never explored it. With a direct view, I couldn't help but look while I ate a leftover fried-chicken drumstick and a few green beans, followed by a slice of store-bought white bread smeared with butter. I wanted to know what was in there, torn between my fear and curiosity. Long dresses, coats, and sweaters hung from hangers on one wooden rod, and a few cardboard boxes sat on the floor. *What was in those boxes?* "What's that room?"

"That's used for storage," Mom said.

Well, that was about as clear as Grampa's pond water.

Why didn't Gramma have a bathroom? Everyone followed the custom and took a trip outside during the day or to a chamber pot in their bedroom during the night. I hadn't been asked to empty a chamber pot at Gramma and Grampa's; hoped it wouldn't come to that.

"I said, are you done?" Mom asked.

I guessed she'd asked once and I hadn't heard. "I want some blackberry cobbler."

After I'd eaten my part of the cobbler, I said, "I'm done now."

Mom took my dirty plate and I struck out for a cautious exploration of the storage room.

Yep. About the size of a bathroom, a window and a door, an overhead electric light, but nothing else familiar in a bathroom. No sink, no tub, no medicine cabinet, no toilet. The lids on one of the boxes hung open. I couldn't help but see something inside. Clothes. Looked like clothes, nothing special.

"Would you go draw a bucket of water for me?" Gramma asked Uncle James. "I need some to wash up the dishes."

Plumbing? What plumbing? We had running water in our house, but Gramma had none in hers and the communal water bucket often needed a refill.

My questions of the storage room were satisfied. "Can I come, too, Uncle James?" I asked as he rose from his chair.

With an easy way, he didn't try to scare me, didn't give me the evil eye, or prank me like Dad. Once, Dad had encouraged me to taste a hot pepper. "Go ahead, it's not hot," he'd said. Couldn't have been further from the truth, but I didn't learn that until too late. Uncle James didn't talk to me like I was a kid, either. He seemed more like a cousin than an uncle. Even some of my cousins, whom I seldom saw, had to be older than him.

"Sure," Uncle James said, "you can carry the bucket."

"Put on your jacket," Mom demanded of me.

Aw.

The empty, gray-metal bucket dangled from its wire handle as I followed Uncle James the few steps to the water shed, the overcast sky still visible in the dimming light.

Not that cold out.

About the size of our bathroom at home, the water shed, fitted with a long-handled pump, had replaced the well next to a back corner of the house. Warned by Mom with stories of kids falling into wells, I didn't want to end up in some story told to others. I'd always steered clear of that well, usually covered with loose boards, and had only looked into it when I went with Uncle James to draw a bucket of water.

Uncle James pointed. "Hang the bucket on the spout there."

"Okay. Like this?"

"Yeah, that's right."

The bucket swung from the spout as Uncle James pushed the handle down, *Squeak!*, and pulled it up, *Squeak!*

Down, up, down, up, each time another squeak.

14

Though I pictured dangling from the handle as Uncle James pumped, I knew he wouldn't want to haul me up each time.

The water poured from the spout as if by magic, and I said, "Where is that water coming from, Uncle James?"

"A bore-hole well we had dug here."

Down, up, down, up, until the bucket was nearly full, then Uncle James said, "That's enough. Want to carry it?"

I grabbed the bucket handle and tugged. "I can't get it off, it's too heavy. Will you take it off for me?" I trusted that Uncle James would never raise his voice or hand toward me. I'd never seen him do that to anyone.

"Yeah," he said, then lifted the pail of water and offered it to me.

It felt like a ton of lead ready to pull my arms off; I used both hands and swayed the bucket one step at a time toward the house.

"You'll have to take it in, Uncle James," I said as I stepped onto to the large, smooth, white rock that acted as the backdoor step.

"Okay."

Simple as that. No angry words, no yelling, no criticism; he took the bucket with one hand, opened the kitchen door with his other, and followed me into the house.

I stood alongside while he placed the bucket in its special place on the small table by the door. *Important work.*

Uncle James' willingness to show me things in his consistent gentle way always put me at ease and provided me a male role model in contrast to Dad's episodic displays of explosive temper. Uncle James was the next closest person I wanted to be around after Billy, my most favorite cousin, and so, when Billy wasn't there, I usually sought out Uncle James.

Billy and I shared some invisible connection, gravitated towards each other like magnets, and I considered us of like kind, set apart from all others. Our younger brothers, Bobby and Verlon, the next closest living beings to us, always there to play with as a last resort, could go play on their own when Billy was around, by my way of thinking.

"Here you go, Mom," Uncle James said when he placed the bucket next to the water dipper, as we called it, a metal ladle with a curl at the end of its handle. The communal dipper rested on a clean cloth next to the bucket.

"Thank you, Son," Gramma replied.

Uncle James picked up the dipper, scooped some water, took a drink, smacked his lips, and said, "Mm, that's good." Several drops of water, shaken loose, fell into the washbasin next to the bucket. "Want to try some?" he asked me as he wiped the ladle dry with a tea towel hung nearby.

That sounded so good I couldn't resist. Germs? Mom had talked about those, reminded me to wash my hands before we ate, but hadn't mentioned concerns about the water bucket or dipper.

In later years, I learned that many of my aunts had avoided the water dipper, though I had no idea how they dealt with their thirst. For the most part, I'd been trusting in my ignorance of possible contagion.

I sipped at a small scoop of water. *Cool and sweet.* "Yeah, it's good." I followed Uncle James' lead, drained the ladle and gave it a shake over the washbasin, wiped it dry with the tea towel before setting it down on a second tea towel next to the bucket.

All and all, that chore hadn't been bad, especially done with Uncle James.

Our House on Harding

August 1953

Dad, who worked as a carpenter, started building us a house on Harding Avenue before I turned five early that September. We lived in the attic-converted-into-bedroom of Grampa and Gramma Hogan's house on Tallulah Street. Their youngest daughter, Linda, lived there, too.

The backyard of Grampa Hogan's property partly bordered what would become our backyard, so we could climb the fence going from one to the other. And from our front door on Harding Avenue, we would have a clear view, across an open field, of the terminal and control tower of Standiford Field, Louisville's airport.

I observed Dad every chance I got. He oversaw the construction and put in his own labor when he could. I helped, but how much could I do?

Slowly, from digging the concrete-foundation trench to hanging the drywall, the house had taken form.

* * *

I stood next to Dad in the living room of our five-room house as he asked the electrician, "Where did we put the electrical outlet on this wall?"

"Somewhere around here," the guy said, with a circular motion to indicate a general area.

"I somehow forgot to cut the hole when we hung this piece of drywall," Dad said.

I'd seen it. Knew where it was. *No need to poke holes all over the place.* "It's right there," I said and touched the spot with my finger.

"Well, we can always test for it with a screwdriver," Dad said to the other guy.

I pointed. "It's right there."

"We could patch the holes, no problem," Dad continued.

"It's right there." I touched the wall.

"Are you sure?" Dad asked me.

"Yes, right there." I tapped the spot.

I'd studied that box and fixed it to my height. I knew where it was, and knew I knew it exactly. Well, maybe within an inch or two.

One poke, two pokes, Dad found the box.

Told you so.

"How did you know that?" Dad asked me.

"I saw it." I considered myself a pretty smart guy, though Dad didn't seem to think so, as he said nothing else. But at least, I knew I'd helped build our house, what little I could do.

* * *

My father held nearly everything in, other than his anger, which boiled over when he'd "had a few" and Mom confronted him. He seldom shared anything about his childhood, rarely talked about his troubles and disappointments, and never his hopes or deepest thoughts. He'd wrapped himself in a cocoon and I learned tidbits about him as if stumbling over unknown somethings scattered about in a dark room. He couldn't, or wouldn't, open up. He never used the word love with my brother and me. Nor did he utter the words pride or proud, until many years later, when he concurred with one of his brothers who'd done so in our presence. It was as if Dad had never thought of saying that to me until that moment. By then, however, I'd realized that Dad's inability to say those things was a reflection upon him, not me.

* * *

We moved into our new house in August 1954, just before I turned six.

Verlon and I got our own bedroom with bunk beds, and, as the oldest, Mom put me on top. I didn't mind. That meant she trusted I wouldn't try to fly like Superman.

Took me a few nights to adjust, but the wooden brace for my bunk served as a reminder when I moved up against it that I skirted disaster, and if broken, I'd plunge to the hardwood floor. And so, in short order, I learned not to roll around in bed with abandon.

* * *

A few days before my seventh birthday, Mom took me to my first day of school at Prestonia Elementary.

She accompanied me into my first-grade room and asked my teacher for my bus number. Then, Mom told me, "That number will be on your school bus to come home. Can you remember that?"

"Yes," I said.

Mom had tried to enroll me at Adair Elementary the year before, but the lady there told her, "You'll need to enroll him next year. His birthday is a few months late."

That first day everything was okay, not bad, until some minutes after the bell had ended our school day.

I waited in my assigned seat along with a number of other kids in my class for the next bell to signal the second wave of kids to board their bus. Someone came to my room and told my teacher that I needed to go to the principal's office.

What had I done?

"Your mother called and is worried that you didn't come home on the bus," one of the ladies in the office said. "Did you forget to get on after the first bell?"

"I guess so," I said. *My teacher didn't keep track of that?*

"You can wait here until your mom comes to get you."

Would Mom tell Dad? Would he come after me with his two-inch-wide leather belt? He'd threatened to use it on Verlon and me a few times. He'd fold it in half, hold it in one hand, and shake it at one or both of us. He finally had swatted me once on my arm. After that his stern looks and threats drove his message home. Seemed he could stare a hole through me whenever he wanted. But, no matter how good I might be, I worried he'd come after me with it. And I was never sure when, or if, he knew when I felt angry at, or afraid of, him.

When Mom arrived to pick me up, she asked, "What happened? You need to get on the school bus right away."

"Okay," I said. I'd remembered the number, which hadn't been the problem. Looking back, I can't rule out that I just didn't want to go home to face Dad, though I'd known school was a part-time thing and I couldn't live there.

"Are you going to tell Dad?" I said. She promised she wouldn't, this once.

* * *

My Ps and Qs minded the second day, I didn't dare miss my bus again. I knew where it would be waiting, got on right away, and got off at the right stop.

Mom greeted me after I exited the bus, "Hi, Hon, did you have a good day?"

"Yes," I said.

"Do you think you can get off here again tomorrow and walk to our house without me?"

"Yeah."

By the following week I had school down pat. I knew to raise my hand to talk or ask a question. I knew I needed teacher's permission to go to the bathroom. I knew to stay in line when my class moved to and from the lunchroom and playground. And I could walk home from my bus stop by myself.

* * *

Mom, Verlon, and I finished our Friday supper without Dad, almost always bad news when we did.

Mom usually started a worry countdown every week on Wednesday and her tension would rise. I would catch the drift, and like a contagious illness passed along, I'd get infected with worry, too. Would Dad come straight home from work or get wild drunk on his way? After five thirty, every second of the clock that passed before Dad arrived home meant he was more likely soused.

With Verlon beside me on the couch, I didn't so much watch TV as look at the screen, since the thought of Dad's lateness interrupted me every other moment.

Mom cleaned up in the kitchen.

Seven thirty, according to my reckoning by the TV program, the crunch of tires on our gravel driveway signaled someone's arrival.

Dad. Had to be. Who else? I didn't want to think Dad would be drunk, but couldn't not think that.

A car door creaked, then slammed shut.

The front door opened, and with one quick glance—I didn't want to attract his attention—I determined Dad was unsteady on his feet, his face reddened, fixed, and serious.

Oh, Jesus.

Without a word, he made a beeline for the kitchen.

Verlon looked at me, his eyes the size of quarters.

Here we go again. Nothing good had ever happened around mean-drunk-Dad.

"Where were you?" Mom said. "We've already finished supper."

"I worked late," Dad said in a gruff voice.

Verlon's lip quivered.

"Shh," I whispered.

"I smell alcohol on your breath," Mom said.

"So what? I work my ass off and I'm a grown man," Dad said.

"Did you stop at a beer joint, again?" Mom said.

"That's none of your goddamn business," Dad replied.

"Cecil, you know we need that money to pay our bills."

"Quit your bitching," he said. "Don't try to tell me what to do."

"We got a late notice on the water bill today. I thought you said you were going to pay that. They'll turn off the water next week if we don't pay them."

"Don't worry about it."

"I can't help it. You know I don't like dealing with late notices and bill collectors," Mom said. "What am I supposed to do?"

I tried to unhear their words by focusing on the TV. Couldn't, no way, no how. Though Mom talked in a reasonable way, Dad's loud, angry words left little to my imagination and I dreaded what he might do.

"What's for supper?" Dad asked.

"I've already put it away. It makes me a nervous wreck when collectors come to the door and threaten to garnish your paycheck."

"Then get my supper and find your own job."

I heard the refrigerator door open, then the scraping of dishes, and a few moments later a plate set on the table.

"This all you got?" Dad asked.

"That's all we had," Mom said.

"Ain't that a bitch."

"We need to go grocery shopping," Mom said. "You need to stop spending money on drinking."

Smack.

"Ow. That hurt, Cecil."

"There's more where that came from, if you don't get off my back."

"Cecil, do we even have enough money to buy groceries for next week?" Mom's voice started to break.

"Don't give me your sob story. We can go grocery shopping tomorrow after I get off work."

Dad worked on Saturdays sometimes, but not always.

Something in the corner of my eye drew my attention.

Mom had hurried into the bedroom and the loud, sharp clanks and scrapes of silverware against a plate and a glass set upon the kitchen table replaced angry words.

When Dad came into the living room, he changed the TV channel without a word, then sat in his chair. I said nothing, all the while staring ahead at the TV. I remained still, sandwiched between what had happened and the anticipation of what might come next, knowing mean-drunk-Dad could explode again any second. Tensed, I didn't want to let anything leak out for him to see, wouldn't dare talk, didn't dare look at him, though I could hear his heavy breathing.

* * *

Mom returned to the kitchen. There was the slosh of water, as she washed Dad's dirty dishes, I guessed, all was mixed with Perry Mason's plea to a judge.

"Overruled," the judge told Perry in no uncertain terms.

Yep, you're overruled, Mom. I didn't want to get overruled, too. And I didn't know what was worse, my fear of their loud fighting or my sadness at their silence afterwards.

"Connard, Verlon, it's time for you to go to bed," Mom said.

My spell broken, I wasted no time, and I made a dash for the bedroom.

After I'd climbed the ladder to my bunk, Mom said good night to Verlon and me. Wide awake, I hoped peace had come to our house, but, though muffled, Mom and Dad's confrontation soon continued in the living room. Relieved and thankful I heard no slaps, I looked to sleep as an escape, though I remained vigilant until I thought their argument over.

* * *

Saturday morning, Mom's wet cheeks silently screamed at me after I'd entered the kitchen for breakfast.

No big surprise. "What's wrong, Mom?" I said.

"Oh, I'm just worried," she said. "I worry we can't pay our bills."

Not news to me. As she laid a warm bowl of oats on the table for me, I noticed a dark, purple spot on her arm, where I guessed Dad had hit her.

If Mom couldn't prevent Dad from hitting her, what could I do?

"I'm thinking about getting a job," she said.

Things might improve, if she did. Maybe, Mom wouldn't worry so much. Maybe, we wouldn't run out of food late in the week and need to eat biscuits and gravy. Not that I didn't like biscuits and gravy. I wanted some variety, though, like meatloaf, spaghetti, or chicken and dumplings. I liked the way Mom cooked those things.

"Go watch TV," Mom said once I'd finished my bowl of oats.

A knot settled in my stomach as I watched TV. Well, tried to watch. Mighty Mouse and Superman protected good people from bad ones. Would Dad come home drunk after work again today? He didn't usually drink on Saturdays, but who knew? Who would protect Mom from Dad? The Lone Ranger and Tonto had a shootout with bad guys, and won. Roy Rogers put a bad guy in jail. How could we stop mean-drunk-Dad? If I tried to stop him, could I be like Heckle and Jeckle and escape getting beaten to a pulp? Why did Dad act that way? Was it because he didn't love Mom or Verlon, or me? Was there a vaccination against drinking like the one I'd gotten at school for polio?

* * *

As I've realized in adulthood, although I'd worried at times I might take after my dad, I'm not a mean drunk. I'm more talkative and social, though I can be quiet too, and I do experience intense anger, with or without alcohol. I've learned that inebriation and abuse are quite different animals and can exist separately.

* * *

"Supper's ready," Mom called.

"Is Dad coming home late again, Mom?" My usual shorthand way of asking if he'd be drunk.

"I hope not, but supper's warm and we should go ahead and eat," she answered.

It wasn't that Mom had cooked an early supper; sometimes we ate a half-hour earlier or later. Tonight's supper was a little on the later side.

"Why does he stop at beer joints?" I asked.

"To cash his paycheck, I think," she said. "That's what he told me, anyway."

25

"Why does he drink?"

"I don't know. He's been doing that for a while now," she said.

"Can you make him stop?"

"I would, if I could, Hon," she replied.

Dad's drinking and their fights were never this bad when we lived with Grampa and Gramma Hogan, that I remembered, though they had argued. Dad's drinking and arguments with Mom, after we'd moved into our new house, had worsened like the turn of weather before a tornado. In retrospect, most likely the proximity of his parents restrained Dad's behavior, though I've wondered if Verlon's birth hadn't added some kindling to the fire in Dad.

But that night, Dad arrived home sober, like a normal dad in my mind, lacking all the bad he's-been-drinking signs I'd learned to recognize. And I breathed a little easier.

*　*　*

Verlon had been born in early July 1953 when we lived in the attic of Grampa and Gramma Hogan's house on Tallulah. Mom and Dad slept in one bed and I slept in a smaller one nearby. Later, when we got our first TV, a black-and-white model, we kept it up there, too.

I don't remember when we'd moved in with Grampa and Gramma Hogan. I could've been three or four.

My memories of that time and prior, like shadows cast by a crescent moon on a partly cloudy night, are elusive and dim. And though I have distinct images of some events prior to living with Grampa and Gramma Hogan, I don't recall specific instances of fighting between Mom and Dad, neither his drinking nor her heartache. Regardless, I have the visceral sense that the discord between Mom and Dad had started early on and I'd been exposed to his volatile temper. And, if for no other reason, Mom's emotions would've leaked out like sweat on a hot day. Perhaps, I witnessed no hand-to-hand fighting, though hard for me to believe, or I'd been shielded somehow. Or I've deeply repressed my earliest traumatic experiences.

I've concluded I'll never recover additional memories of my very early childhood. However, over the years, I'd learned things from Mom which led me to conclude her marriage to Dad hadn't been idyllic from the start. Even as a child I'd understood that the easiest and quickest way to deal with something wrong or bad was to pull away. I'd learned that well enough when I'd touched a hot stove. For years I've wondered how, when, and why their marital problems had started, and if my arrival had worsened their relationship.

* * *

Mom had tried to prepare me for Verlon's birth. She'd explained, "You're going to have a brother or sister."

Always the center of Mom and Dad's attention, at least most of the time, at four-and-a-half, I had no idea what a brother or sister's arrival meant, nor how dramatically my life would change.

The day after Mom had left, her belly big and round, she returned home with a baby and was given the bed in one of the two downstairs bedrooms, Gramma and Grampa's room.

What a commotion. Everybody gathered around Mom and baby. I heard their oohs and aahs as Aunt Linda ushered me in for an introduction.

"Hi, Hon, this is your new brother," Mom said. "We named him Verlon." She held him in her arms and he was wrapped in a small blanket. "I'll need to take care of him for a while, so I'll be down here."

Not upstairs?

Everyone in the house doted on Mom and Verlon. In short order, I'd lost a good part of everybody's attention to him, my brother. I didn't like the idea of sharing Mom or Dad, nor Grampa, Gramma Hogan, and Aunt Linda, not one bit. Nope, didn't want any part of that.

First chance—I couldn't contain myself—I made my exit and stood in the corner created by the staircase in the other downstairs bedroom, Aunt Linda's room. With both bedroom doors open I watched the hoo-ha from across the hallway.

Aunt Linda came to me. "Come back in and be with us," she said.

"I don't want to." I wouldn't budge.

Though everything had not always gone my way, that brother-thing clearly wasn't swinging in my favor.

* * *

Some days later, when Mom returned upstairs with Verlon to sleep, things didn't change much, except I became more aware of his crying. And he still got most of everyone's attention. Not that he'd done anything to me on purpose, I knew, but the bottom line boiled down to this: He'd arrived and I'd lost my special place on the throne of my tiny kingdom. I missed Mom's attention the most.

Before we moved in with Grampa and Gramma Hogan, I'd always liked being at home with Mom, just the two of us together while Dad was away at work. When we lived on Granger Road, some distance from Highland Park, we'd laugh and have fun, take walks, she taught me numbers and reading a clock, and I helped her wash our laundry. The clothes swirled in the washing machine tub, then we'd wring out the water with hand-cranked rollers and hang everything on a backyard clothesline.

There seemed little I could do to reclaim my position as the center of everyone's attention once Verlon had arrived. Well, I considered one thing, but knew murder wasn't a solution, nor a good idea. My thinking confused me. I didn't want to hurt my brother, but then

I did. I would, then I wouldn't, then I would again. So, I worked to keep all that secret, though sometimes it leaked out, anyway. At times, I removed myself to avoid Verlon, but at least Mom put him in a bassinet to sleep, so he and I didn't share the same bed. And she often encouraged me to go play downstairs or outside during the day.

* * *

Over the years I've wondered about the role Dad's anger played in my relationship with Verlon. I have no way of knowing if my murderous rage towards Verlon was heightened or compounded by Dad's anger. Nor do I know if the intensity of the sibling rivalry that developed was of the normal variety, though Verlon and I have been on good terms as adults. But I've concluded, if anything, Dad's role-modeling had heightened our tensions.

* * *

Sent off to occupy myself, I encountered the good, the bad, and the ugly.

Alone in the backyard, I heard a crow call, then something rustled around my head, and I felt a rush of wind and swooshing sounds. Waving my arms, I screamed, "Grammaaaa."

Gramma Hogan burst from the kitchen door. "Shoo. Shoo," she said as she flapped her apron with one arm and waved her other as she ran towards me. "That silly crow. You just let me know if it bothers you again."

"Okay, Gramma." I wasn't going to let that bird stop me from playing outside.

Little could I appreciate, however, that I was learning, at least in some small way, how to face adversities, to do things in spite of my fear, especially when supported by a gramma.

Tobacco Seedlings

May 1955

When we arrived for our next visit to Gramma and Grampa Riggs' farm on Friday evening, Uncle James had finished disking a field near the house with the tractor. He'd formed the loose dirt into straight rows.

As we gathered at the supper table, Mom looked at me with a smile and asked, "Do you remember your Grampa's two mules, John and Beck?"

With a pause and furrowed brow, I tried to remember. Neither helped. "Nope."

She went on, "I remember we were watching your Grampa plow with his mules and you said, 'Grampa has a John and a Beck, but I don't have no John and Beck.'" Then she chuckled.

"I don't remember that."

Uncle James said, "Dad bought the tractor new in 1953, but still used the mules for a while after that."

* * *

Saturday morning as we sat at the breakfast table, Uncle James told me, "We're going to plant tobacco seedlings today. Want to help?"

Seedlings? "Can I wear a T-shirt, Mom?" I said.

"Yes," she answered, "I think it's okay to wear a short-sleeved shirt, but you need to be careful not to sunburn. We'll be out there a while."

I welcomed the warm days of spring, when Mom would give her official approval to wear short-sleeved shirts. "Yay, no more winter," I said. "Spring days are the best."

After breakfast, along with everyone else, except Dad—*Not going to help? What was he up to, that cheat?*—I walked the stone's throw to the new-plowed field. I could almost taste the heavy smells of fresh dirt and spring green in the air. Gramma's flowers, beside the house, displayed splashes of color. Green-bean vines climbed tobacco sticks in Gramma's vegetable garden while tiny yellow flowers on the tomato plants stood out among green leaves. Birds chirped their songs and flew about. Bugs, too many to count, filled the air. Everything and everybody was busy, except Dad.

"Do you know how to plant a seedling?" Uncle James asked.

A total mystery to me. "No," I said, "I've never planted tobacco before."

"Let me show you." He set a box of little plants at the end of one row nearby. "Do it like this," he said and separated one seedling from a clump, careful not to damage the roots.

With a free hand he picked up a short wooden stick, one end sharpened, placed the sharp end at the start of the row, then pushed the stick into the loose soil several inches.

"You want to put the plant almost to the seedling's lowest branch." He placed the seedling in the hole, roots against the bottom. "Now, add some water." From a nearby can he gave the hole a splash of water. "Water around the roots gives them a head start and a better chance to grow."

Who knew when rain would come? Maybe, several weeks would pass before the next soaking.

With his thumbs he pushed dirt firmly around the roots. "The roots need to touch soil, but make sure not to press too hard."

If I hadn't seen him plant that seedling, I could believe it sprouted there on its own.

"Okay, now, you try it," he encouraged.

Scared I might crush the little thing, as Uncle James looked on, I separated one seedling, grabbed the stick, and created a hole. "Like this?"

"Yeah, that's right."

I put the seedling into the hole, roots to the bottom, poured in some water, pressed dirt around the roots, and checked to make sure the little plant stood tall.

"That's good, that's good," Uncle James said. "You keep doing that and I'll start another row."

"Okay." I'd decided where that little seedling would grow; I'd given it a good start in its new home. I liked that I could do something to help Gramma, Grampa, and Uncle James.

The entire field required a repeat of that ritual hundreds of times before Uncle James and Grampa rested nearer the end of the day. Everyone else, tired like me, had gone to the house earlier.

The sun and the rain would decide the little plants' fate.

* * *

At first chance our next visit, I checked on the tobacco plants. Most, several inches taller, appeared healthy, except for a few along the edges of the patch.

Tomato Juice and Lemons

July 1955

We'd visited the country the previous weekend, so probably wouldn't go again for several weeks, and though I hoped everything would be calm at home that Friday evening, I knew all too well what could happen. Odds were, we'd face another episode of mean-drunk-Dad.

Mom's worry countdown, as usual, started mid-week. And so, of course, had mine. And she'd served biscuits and gravy for supper that Thursday, part of the familiar pattern of feast or famine in relation to Dad's drinking.

Home from school Friday afternoon, I asked Mom, "Will Dad come home drunk tonight?"

"I don't know, Sweetheart. Lord only knows," she said.

Although Mom didn't have the answer, I didn't know what scared me more, Dad's behavior or Mom's inability to stop him.

"Mom," I said, fingers crossed as I whistled past an imaginary graveyard—Dad coming home drunk would mean no grocery shopping that night—"can you get me some tomato juice or lemons?" I hoped when asking that question to avoid jinxing us and up-ending some mysterious, delicate balance.

"Yes," she said.

Mom knew those items were my favorite, but she couldn't know the importance of her willingness to provide them, which offered me encouragement that all was not lost. By doing so she demonstrated her love for me and reassured me that our special bond remained unbroken.

If Dad came home straightaway, we'd enjoy a relieved trip to the grocery, since Mom couldn't drive and we only had one car. If he came home late, our house would likely become a war zone, with another drunk-Dad full-on D-day assault on Mom. The weekly grocery shopping would be postponed. The whole weekend would turn to ruin.

* * *

Odd, but Dad never came home drunk in the middle of the week that I remembered. Mom, Verlon, and I took it as a given, would've laid bets, that Dad would drink on Fridays after work, but not through the week. I realized it was a simple matter of money invariably burning a hole in his pocket as soon as he cashed his Friday paychecks.

* * *

I'd occupied myself with my school homework, which hadn't taken more than an hour to complete, then turned on the TV. Lowell Thomas talked about some far-off place. I couldn't escape my house. I couldn't be where Lowell Thomas was, but at least I could dream of it. I wanted adventure. I wanted to go places, observe other people. I wanted answers to my questions. Did other dads drink, too? Were they mean to their families?

Mom had postponed starting supper.

A fork, scraped across an iron skillet, meant Mom had started the final touches for supper.

An unmistakable sound. Had to be gravy.

"Come and eat your supper," Mom called out.

Dad not home, yet. Bad sign.

At the table, I said, "Where's Dad?"

"He should be off work by now," she answered.

Mom, Verlon, and I knew, or had a good guess where he was. Didn't the sky usually get dark before a storm? Though we clung to hope each week, we'd been disappointed more often than not.

"What are you going to do if he comes home drunk?" I said.

"I'll try to talk to him. He knows we need everything he earns to pay our bills," she said.

That didn't encourage me. Her talking to him had never worked.

"What can I do?" I said.

"You shouldn't worry about that," she said.

That didn't encourage me, either.

"Finish your supper and go watch TV."

* * *

Minutes dragged by as Verlon and I, next to one another on the couch, stared at the TV, while Mom cleared the table and cleaned the dishes.

The crunch of gravel under car tires aside our house signaled an arrival. A car door opened and slammed shut. Seconds later, Dad burst through the front door and went straight for the kitchen.

"I've been waiting for you to get home so we could go grocery shopping," Mom said.

"Fix me some supper," Dad growled.

Verlon's face contorted with fear, eyes filling with tears.

"I don't want him to be mean," I whispered.

"Cecil, we need to go grocery shopping," Mom said.

"Don't start on me," Dad said. "What do we have for supper?"

"Biscuits and gravy," Mom said.

"Can't you do any better than that?"

"As long as you spend your paycheck at a beer joint that's all we have," Mom said.

"What are you saying?" he challenged.

"Let me have what money you have left, so I can buy us at least *some* groceries," Mom said.

"Here," Dad said.

"That's not all of it, Cecil, give me the rest," Mom said.

Dad snarled, "I have the right to do what I want with my money!"

"Not when you have a family to support!"

"Do not tell me how to support this family!"

Slap!

"I am the man here! Not you!"

"Ahh! Stop, Cecil."

Slap!

Verlon whimpered.

If Mom couldn't stop Dad, how could I?

Mom hurried from the kitchen and into their bedroom.

Dad followed a few moments later. "I'm getting tired of your shit," he yelled.

Slap!

"Please, Cecil!" Mom cried.

Slap!

Mom entered the living room, Dad hot on her heels.

"When will you learn?!" He slapped her again.

More like a whine, I blurted in a loud voice, "Stop!"

Dad suddenly turned and glared at me. Without a word, he then went to the kitchen. Was he going to get his belt? He'd swatted me before, but then I'd never tried to stand up to him.

With him momentarily gone, Mom rushed us out of the room.

"I think you two should get ready for bed," Mom said.

As Mom was tucking me in, she said quietly, "Thank you, Hon."

No explanation needed.

Out of sight, out of mind? Not really. I listened for any sharp sounds or a raised voice that would mean they'd restarted their argument. Though I only heard their muffled voices, it seemed to take me forever to fall asleep.

* * *

Saturday morning Mom sported bruises on one cheek and her upper arms.

Verlon and I spent the morning watching cartoons and westerns on TV, as questions without answers swirled in my head.

When Dad arrived home sober, we'd gone to the grocery.

Verlon on the left side of the backseat and me on the right, we kept quiet on the ride to and from the grocery. We remained in the car, rough-housed, and cried, while Mom and Dad shopped.

At the table that evening, I avoided talking to Dad. Couldn't figure why he, whom I loved in spite of his behavior, could be so mean to Mom.

Four Generations

September 1955

At seven, I measured time by the meal, by Mom and Dad's fights over his Friday-night benders. I measured time by opportunities to watch TV cartoons on Saturday mornings, and our trips to Gramma and Grampa's farm. I measured it by the seasons and holidays.

"We're going to the country," Mom said. She started to gather the bundle of newspapers that she'd saved since our last trip. "Get what you want to take," she added.

Don't need to tell me twice. Nothing ever wrong with visiting Gramma, Grampa, Uncle James, and the farm.

And I'd just learned to read and spell the word country in school.

Miss Layman, my second-grade teacher, had written a list, then asked a group of us, "Are there any words on the blackboard that you don't know?"

I raised my hand. "Yes," I said and pointed, "that one."

"Where do you go when you visit your grandparents?" she asked me.

"The country," I said.

"That's right," she said with a broad smile.

A tiny light of discovery had turned on in my head, a puzzle piece slipped into place and provided me another connection to Gramma and Grampa's farm, the place of my joy and hope.

We'd always visited on weekends, once or twice a month, and most big holidays. Though not all, nor always at the same time, other aunts and uncles would visit too, bringing my cousins, about a dozen and a half. But who could keep count?

Sometimes, Dad drove on the toll road from Louisville to Elizabethtown, where it ended, then take 31W to Upton. Sometimes, he drove the entire way on 31W. I never knew which route he'd take beforehand. But eager to get there, I always thought he drove about the speed of a farm tractor, or worse, a turtle on wheels.

* * *

"I brought you some newspapers, Dad," Mom told Grampa in a raised voice—even then a little hard of hearing—as she laid the bundle of our old newspapers next to his favorite chair, which he occupied.

Another example of Mom's care and consideration for others.

"Thank you, Bea," he said. Front-page section of one paper opened and raised above eye-level, he entered his zone. Grampa loved reading the papers, and hungry for news, he'd remain behind the paper unless someone called him away. The growing season nearing an end, outdoor activities ebbed and Grampa enjoyed more free time to read.

A black-and-white TV with crumpled aluminum foil on the antenna rabbit ears sat on a small stand near him, though I'd never seen it on.

Grampa whispered as he read, which by the time I heard them from across the room sounded like "Spe, spe, spe. Spe. Spe, spe."

I almost giggled, but didn't want to make fun of Grampa.

"Spe, spe. Spe, spe, spe," he continued.

"Dinner's ready," Mom yelled, her call for our midday meal.

Straightaway for the table, I beat Grampa through the doorway. Dad and Uncle James had already claimed seats.

When Mom and Gramma finished setting bowls and plates of food on the table and settled into chairs, Grampa started grace.

Serious to the core, some people might've considered Grampa a Bible-thumper. He could talk a mule's ear off quoting verses, which he did on a frequent basis. He never claimed he'd written parts of the Bible, but I sometimes wondered if he hadn't. From what Mom had told me, Grampa, as a young man, had heard "the call" to preach, as we Baptists referred to it. And did so for a time in the Hiawatha Missionary Baptist Church in Highland Park, even after he'd moved to the farm. Mom had also told me that some people addressed him as "Reverend Riggs."

But Grampa never gave me a what for, never raised his voice at me nor lectured me, though I understood he held strict notions.

I gave silent thanks that Dad wouldn't drink at Gramma's house. During our visits there, Dad had never said a word about alcohol, or his drinking, nor did he argue with Mom. No mention from Mom either, at least in front of me. So, I took their cue and kept quiet. I figured Grampa would fetch his shotgun and run Dad off, if Dad got out of line. Grampa had proclaimed on several occasions that he didn't abide alcohol. If Dad hid a stash there, which he could've, he'd never gotten busted that I knew.

After my dinner, I stopped at the calendar on the wall near the table. Seemed a new one got hung there at the beginning of each year. I pointed at the bold blue letters at the bottom of the calendar. "Mom, what does that say?"

She turned to look and said, "Upton Hardware and Feedstore."

"What does that say?" I asked and pointed at top of the picture of a country boy.

"Picture of the month."

The barefoot boy, in coveralls and a straw hat, lay against a log next to a fishing pole at the edge of a pond. *About my size and age.* The straw in his mouth, and his hands in his pockets, suggested he had no worries. *His country life better than my city life?* I lived in a neighborhood with barking dogs, where a rock thrown with my eyes closed would likely hit a house or a car. I lived where a fishing pole would catch questions but not fish, and where a gun in the open could lead to a police visit. *Did he ever worry about his dad beating his mom?* Hard to imagine so. *Wished my life could be that peaceful.*

Back in the living room, I claimed my favorite place on the couch and figured the others would take their usual seats.

Grampa limped in with a green-and-yellow square can in his right hand, then placed it on a table next to his chair before he sat down. He grimaced as he rolled up his right pant leg to expose his knee.

Ew. I'd never seen that bright pink, wrinkled, fist-sized scar behind Grampa's knee. I'd never even seen his bare leg. He'd always been dressed in coveralls or Sunday-go-to-meeting pants and rarely wore a short-sleeved shirt.

Grampa opened the can, which I'd seen but hadn't studied, pulled out a large yellow glob with several fingers, and smeared it on his scar. "Ouch. Agh. Ow."

Must hurt.

Grampa didn't often complain about pain, didn't self-indulge, except perhaps in his enjoyment of food and pride in his knowledge of "the Good Book," as he called the Bible.

I looked at Uncle James, who'd joined us in the living room, then pointed to the salve and asked, "What's that?"

"Bag Balm. It's used on cow udders," Uncle James said, "to help prevent infections."

Yuck, putting that on his leg? I then got a strong whiff of something pleasant. "What's that smell?"

"Eucalyptus," Uncle James said.

When Grampa finished, he said, "I think I'll go for a sit on the swing," and limped towards the front porch.

Dad and Uncle James followed.

Grampa halfway down the hallway, Mom came into the room. I asked in my library voice, "When did Grampa get that scar on his leg?"

"When he was a boy, I think," she said.

"How?"

"I've heard different stories and I'm not sure which is true. He got shoved into a fireplace while scuffling or was in a tractor accident."

"Why doesn't he go to a doctor about it?"

"He doesn't believe in seeing doctors."

"How could he put up with that for all these years?" I didn't think I could.

Mom shrugged. She had fewer answers than I'd thought.

As Mom and I started down the hallway towards the front porch, I asked, "When did Grampa learn to read?" Hard to imagine him in school or as a kid.

"Oh, he had to quit after the third grade," she said.

"Why?"

"He had to help on their farm."

School sounded better than work on the farm. I didn't like the idea of work so much, though I never heard Gramma, Grampa, or Uncle James complain. Dad didn't like the idea of work so much either, it seemed. He changed jobs like the months of a calendar.

* * *

An hour had passed, I guessed, and thirsty, I started for the water bucket in the kitchen through the front door. Gramma's singing sounded like a warm blanket on a winter's night as I headed down the hallway.

When I wanted to find Gramma, I'd listen for her words as she sang "Amazing Grace" or "Shall We Gather at the River?" She, like Grampa, a through-and-through Baptist, often sang gospels as she went about her chores and could ready herself for church at a moment's notice.

Didn't occur to me then, but, as an adult, I've concluded Gramma conducted her own personal ongoing church.

I found her on a bench in front of a mirror in the living room, gray hair down below her waist, longest I'd ever seen.

Her back towards me, she said without pause, "Gramma's doing her hair."

I settled onto the edge of the couch.

Divided into three strands, she braided her hair into a ponytail. She then coiled the ponytail into a bun on the crown of her head and attached the coil in place with bobby pins. That's the way I'd always seen it. She laid her brush and comb in a drawer in front of her. "It's time to start supper," she said.

"Oh, yeah," I whispered and continued to the water bucket.

* * *

On my return to the front porch I passed Mom in the hallway on her way to help Gramma fix supper. I noticed Gramma had started singing again. "Why is Gramma's hair so long? Has she ever gotten it cut?" I asked Mom.

"She had it cut once some years ago," Mom said, "but I don't think she believes in cutting her hair. It has something to do with the Bible."

"Oh," I said, like I understood what that meant when I really didn't. I knew the story of Samson and Delilah from church Sunday school, but that story didn't fit.

Gramma didn't believe in anything fancy, never visited a beauty shop that I heard about and no one else touched her hair that I'd seen. She possessed a no-nonsense attitude. Although I only heard a chuckle or laugh now and then, she smiled often. She never raised her voice at anyone or said anything unkind, although occasionally Gramma interrupted Grampa with, "Oh, hush, Frank," when he grumbled about something.

If only Mom could do that to shut Dad up when he was drunk and yelled, or to make him behave. If only I could.

Up first and before dawn, from what Mom had told me, Gramma would build a fire in the living room coal stove during cold weather. Then, she'd start breakfast on the wood stove in the kitchen, or more recently cook on the newer electric stove. And she'd always do so before others in the house got out of their beds. Mom also told me she'd never heard Gramma whine or complain of feeling ill nor seen Gramma lie down in the middle of the day.

Though I believed Gramma arrived by car from Louisville long after the farmhouse had been built, I pictured her riding to the farm on a covered wagon and helping clear a forest of trees. On TV I'd learned about wagon trains of pioneer women headed west. Gramma seemed the closest living person to an American pioneer woman I could imagine. Take her back to the days of Daniel Boone and she would've fit right in.

* * *

Aunt Shirley and Uncle Walt arrived during dinner, so Gramma and Mom interrupted their meal to make room at the table for Uncle Walt.

After we men finished our meal, Gramma, Mom, and Aunt Shirley claimed the table.

I'd gone to the living room for a rest, and when the sounds of dinner cleanup died away, I heard Gramma say, "You two go rest, I'll finish up."

Aunt Shirley, Mom's younger sister, said as they came into the living room, "Let's look at some pictures, Bea."

Though the men had mentioned a rabbit hunt as they moved towards the porch, they hadn't collected their guns, so I decided to look at pictures, too. I heard familiar noises from the kitchen. The refrigerator door opened, then closed, and iron skillets clanged on the wood-burning stove. *Gramma, doing gramma stuff.*

Mom placed Verlon in the resident crib that someone had brought into the living room, his own little jail. At least, I enjoyed some freedom to roam.

Mom rummaged through envelopes, shoe boxes, and albums stuffed full of pictures that someone had gathered in the small cabinet stand near Grampa's chair. Several loose pictures slid out and onto her lap when she opened an album at the front. Each page of the album, intended for six pictures, held many more tucked in at their corners wherever they would fit.

"This is me," she said after picking up the first photo. She turned the photo for me to see.

Snow covered the ground and Mom stood in front of a tree in an overcoat.

"I know that tree," I said. "That's the tree on the side in the front yard. When was that picture taken?"

"I think that was 1946. Your grandparents moved here from Highland Park in 1944," she said and looked at Aunt Shirley. "Is that right?"

"Yeah," Aunt Shirley replied.

Mom went on, "I stayed here with your grandparents until 1947 when I married your daddy. You were born about ten months later."

"What did you do here?"

"I helped with indoor and outside chores, and watched your uncle James."

"What about when you lived in Highland Park?" I said.

"Everybody old enough was expected to do chores when they weren't at school. The girls worked in the house. They tended to the younger ones. They helped cook, wash and iron clothes, and clean the house. The boys worked outside and ran errands."

"Oh," I said and pictured an army of little worker ants, busy in bunches, scattered in and around their house. I whispered the names of my aunts and uncles as I counted them on my fingers. "So, there's ten of you?"

"I have seven brothers and three sisters. Well, Belva died at eight months old when I was seven," Mom answered.

"Here's a picture of her," she said to Aunt Shirley.

"Aw." Aunt Shirley took the photo from Mom. "I never met her, Connard. She died before I was born."

Aunt Shirley's voice had gotten softer; her words slower. I'd noticed Mom's voice did that sometimes, and even Aunt Irene's, but Aunt Shirley always talked that way about somebody dead or sick.

"Why did Gramma and Grampa move here?"

"Your Grampa had to retire from the L&N Railroad yard because he had arthritis in his hands. You've seen the railroad yard from the edge of Highland Park, it was close enough that he walked to work. When your grandparents moved to the farm, those of us still living with them, Clifton, James, Shirley, and me, helped slop the pigs, milk the cows, draw water from the well, and tend the crops, as well as help with housework."

I'd already learned Grampa grew up in the country on a farm not far from Upton. We'd visited that farm a few times, but nobody lived in the house.

Mom passed another photo. "Here's Dad's old car."

"I remember that old thing," Aunt Shirley said and smiled. "He used to let me drive it up and down the road here. He always came along." She giggled. "I guess he was afraid I'd run it off the road by myself. I couldn't figure out how to shift it very good and never did get my license."

Aunt Shirley referred to the narrow, two-lane, paved country road which divided the farm into two unequal parts. The bulk of the farm lay on the side with the house, while two old barns, a pond, and a sinkhole lay on the other side. Everyone on the farm used the road on their way between the house and the two barns or pond. Though not a major road, and a car might drive by every few hours, everyone usually walked along the side.

"I didn't want to drive with him, Shirley," Mom said in a low voice. "He made me too nervous."

Another clue that Mom's relationship with Grampa hadn't always been easy for her.

She picked up another photo. "That's Uncle Hobert," Mom told me. "You never met him."

I noticed leg braces. "Why is he wearing those?"

"He had polio," Mom said. "I don't think he got around very well."

Aunt Shirley said, "When did he die, Bea?"

"I don't know exactly. He was in his late teens, I think, but that was before I was born," Mom said.

Wow. History to me, things that had happened before I was born, even before Mom.

I pictured a neighbor boy about my age, who'd lived next door when I was about four. I'd played with him, until Mom told me that he'd caught polio. After that I didn't see him much and he ended up needing an iron lung.

"Here's Mom and Dad," Mom said when she handed another black-and-white photo to Aunt Shirley.

"I remember that," Aunt Shirley said. "That's one of Dad's birthdays." She passed it to me.

Grampa, white hair at all angles, sat on a kitchen chair in the front yard. Gramma, probably called directly from the kitchen, stood next to him. She rested one hand on his shoulder and wore an apron down to her mid-thighs over her ankle-length dress. Both had slight, closed-lipped smiles. Their old Ford Falcon sat in the driveway behind them and the black walnut tree stood beyond.

"Yep, Grampa and Gramma," I said.

"This one is your Grampa before he married your Gramma." Mom handed the photo to me.

He stood upright, rigid, and serious, with combed dark black hair. "He looks like Uncle James," I said, surprised. "How old was he?"

"About nineteen, I think," Mom said.

"Hmm, what year was it taken?"

"That would've been about 1910," she said. Her voice lowered as she continued, "This one is four generations." She turned the photo over. "Taken in 1952." She pointed. "This is me, your Grampa, my Grampa, and you. I hadn't wanted to wait too long to get a picture of the four of us together, so had brought you for a visit."

Touching the smooth, slippery, black-and-white photo, I studied the four of us.

Mom's shoulder-length, wavy hair and skirt with matching coat reminded me of some Hollywood actress. She often talked about her wish to travel to Hollywood and see movie stars. She wore dark lipstick, I imagined red, her favorite color. Grampa looked formal and serious with his white, wavy, combed hair—unlike the way his hair almost always seemed a stranger to a comb—and Sunday-go-to-meeting clothes with crumpled shirt buttoned to the collar. Great-grampa grinned with a weathered face. Taller than all of us, he towered above me from behind. He wore pants held by suspenders and a shirt buttoned to the collar, too. And the shortest of all, me? I'd have to take Mom's word. An aviator-style cap, fastened under my chin, covered my head and ears, my head slightly tilted to the side and my eyes squinted.

"I don't remember that," I said and started to count with my fingers.

"You couldn't have been older than three and a half," Mom said.

I pictured the paved, winding road to Great-grampa's farm, where it crossed the railroad tracks in Upton, then what seemed endless curves and hills until we'd turn off the pavement onto a rutted dirt road. A short distance later we'd arrive at the pond and big barn close together on the left side and the house on the right. Three wooden steps led up to the front door of the house.

"I remember Great-grampa lying in bed in the living room near the kitchen," I said. *Must've not been that long after this picture was taken.* "And Great-gramma told us she could take care of him easier that way. Everyone would sit on straight-backed wood chairs and a couch, warmed by a fireplace. How long did he stay in that bed?"

"A few months, I think," Mom said. "Isn't that right, Shirley?"

"Yeah, I think so," Aunt Shirley said.

"How do you remember that?" Mom asked me.

"I don't know," I said.

Seemed like most grownups didn't appreciate what I could remember, certainly not Dad. I also remembered Mom had told me that Great-grampa had passed away. She, Gramma, and all my aunts always referred to dead people as "passed away." Weren't they just plain dead, whatever that meant?

Great-grampa's burial came to mind, the first funeral I remembered. We'd walked a short way along a dirt road from the farmhouse. Great-gramma, near the front of the long line, followed the men who carried Great-grampa's coffin. Farther back in the line, Mom held my hand as we walked towards a place I'd never been. Some people cried, everyone else stayed quiet or talked with hushed voices.

"Where're we going?" I asked Mom.

"We're walking to the family cemetery," she whispered. "We're supposed to stay quiet while the preacher talks."

"Okay," I whispered back.

After we'd passed through an open metal gate, Mom and I stopped in the sun near the shade of a tree. The sun felt warm. Others had gathered around the coffin, which rested on straps over an open hole next to a pile of red dirt. Somebody laid a wreath of red roses on the coffin.

Mom looked at me with a finger to her lips.

A man, who'd been in the front of the line near Great-gramma, opened what looked like a Bible and began to talk, using words like eternal rest, heaven, and God, all Bible stuff. Had to be the preacher.

Everyone remained quiet as he spoke, except for the general crying. A bug flew by. Great-gramma wiped her face with a white handkerchief. The green tree leaves waved in a breeze. Many of the women wiped their eyes. Weeds and flowers, chiggers' favorite hiding places, blanketed the area. Mom concentrated on the preacher. A line of ants crossed a patch of bare red dirt.

When the preacher finished, everyone talked softly and began to walk away.

"I'm going to get a couple of roses," Mom said. "I'll press one in our family Bible as a remembrance of your great-grampa. Would you like one?" Mom asked me.

"Yeah," I said. Wasn't sure what I'd do with it, though.

The green tube she'd handed me was filled with water and protected my fingers from the rose thorns inside.

As we'd walked away and left Great-grampa alone, I'd wondered what it was like to be dead.

"Well, that's enough pictures for now," Mom said. "I'll go help Mom with supper."

"I'll help, too," Aunt Shirley said.

Red roses, their sweet smell, soft feel, a part of death and funerals for me. I couldn't remember Dad being there, though. *Where had he been and doing what?*

I thought about Gramma's collection of photos and how they'd changed. In the older ones, taken before Mom was born, people dressed up and looked serious, even mean or angry. In later ones, my aunts and uncles, in everyday clothes, smiled with their teeth showing. In some newer ones, my cousins appeared blurred, too busy to stand still. I figured somebody could study the history of photography and Gramma's family using her photos.

I couldn't put it into words, but I felt in the presence of something important.

Happy Birthday, Almost

September 1955

Saturday morning, Dad had gone to work.

He and Mom had argued last night over money; the shortage of it to pay bills. The cause of the shortage? Everything pointed to Dad's boozing.

"Cecil, did you pay the electricity bill?" Mom had asked him point blank after he'd come through the front door, late once again.

Another Friday battle?

I'd dared not leave the couch, nor even make a sudden movement lest I draw Dad's attention to myself unnecessarily.

"Why do you need to know?" Dad had said.

"You said, you'd pay it. They'll turn off our electricity if we don't get a payment to them by Monday," she said.

How bad would it get?

"I've been busy," he said.

"You didn't, did you?"

"Get out of my face," Dad said, his voice full force.

He hadn't paid another bill.

"Give me the money to pay the bill and I will."

"Who do you think you are?"

Couldn't help it. I'd seen them out of the corner of my eye as they stood face to face on the other side of the living room.

"Just give me some money to pay the bill," Mom said.

Dad pulled something from his pocket. "Here. I don't want to hear any more of your lip," he said. "Now, fix me some supper."

I'd so wanted to put a stop to their argument, instead, forced to stew in my helplessness, I remained glued to the couch until Mom had cued Verlon and me. "Time for bed, you two."

And neither of us had hesitated.

As I ate my Saturday morning breakfast, Mom said, "I've got to go into Highland Park. You'll be okay here by yourself, won't you?"

"Yeah." I liked that she trusted me to take care of myself, though knew I'd miss her presence. "What are you going to do?"

"I need to pay our bill before they shut off the electricity," she said.

*　*　*

A few minutes later, Mom, now in a whirlwind, caught me on the toilet. "I got you a little something for your birthday. You can use it for school."

My pants down, I'd had little time to react, though I recognized the small globe of the earth right away, a likeness of bigger ones I'd seen. I hadn't expected any presents, yet, as my birthday wouldn't be for a few more days.

"Stay here at home," she added. "I'll take Verlon with me."

"Okay, I will." I pretty much always minded what she told me, and never lied to her on purpose. *I could watch my favorite Saturday morning TV programs.*

I examined my early birthday present. *A pencil sharpener. Made sense.* The pencils I used at school needed constant re-sharpening.

Hoped I'd get more presents for my birthday, but money in short supply, knew I'd likely have to settle for ice cream and cake.

A few moments later, I heard Verlon say, "Why do I have to go?"

"Because I said so," Mom replied. "Let's go." Then in a raised voice, she said, "Bye."

"Bye," I called out, then heard the front door shut.

What was Mighty Mouse up to?

I didn't think it was that bad being alone at home, though I missed Mom more that morning. Didn't always miss her that much. Couldn't understand why, just did.

The Lone Ranger and Tonto chased bank robbers, had a shootout, and killed several. Luckily, the Lone Ranger and Tonto came out without a scratch. If only Mom were so lucky when she had a fight with Dad.

Always a troublemaker, Froggy the Gremlin on *Andy's Gang* planted the idea.

Saturday morning shows over, and Mom not home—I'd figured she'd be home by then—*maybe, I could catch frogs.*

I'd only take a few minutes and I didn't think Mom would mind, as long as I didn't go more than shouting distance from our house.

Mom had warned me that handling frogs would give me warts, but I wasn't so sure about that, even though frogs looked like they were covered with warts. In spite of her words, I'd handled a few, knew they wouldn't bite or sting, though they'd pee when picked up. I'd just hold them away from me to prevent getting wet until they were done.

I'd caught a few in our yard. They liked hiding in the weeds in the back of our yard, but we'd heard frogs' loud croaks coming from the open field, where huge trucks, earth movers, and graders had been moving dirt for several weeks.

You'd never catch me going near those big, loud machines, particularly when they were moving. But the few to be seen sat quietly and I saw no one near them.

No problem, as long as I stay in plain sight and yelling distance of our house.

Frogs, large and small, scattered as I approached them, while tadpoles wiggled about in the rut-puddles.

Easy pickings. In short order, I collected a dozen or so in a small bag I'd carried.

* * *

When Mom returned later, she asked me, "Is everything okay?"

"Yeah," I said. "I caught some frogs. Can I have something to put them in? They need water."

"Where did you get frogs?" She didn't seem upset.

"Across the street."

She still didn't seem upset. "You could put them in the wash tub."

I turned the frogs loose in the two-and-a-half-foot metal tub that we put on our covered back porch. I added water with the garden hose, so the frogs could stay wet. Then, I collected a few rocks and grass from our backyard, so they could climb out of the water.

Mom, Verlon, and I watched over my collection a few minutes, before Mom said, "Now, what are you going to do with them?"

Couldn't keep them in Mom's wash tub forever. She used the tub to rinse clothes, usually once a week. "Keep them a few days, then let them go, I guess."

"I'm going to make us some lunch," she said.

* * *

When Dad returned from work and heard about my collection, he said in no uncertain terms, "Don't you dare bring those into the house."

Why would I do that?

That's all he said and walked away, and I felt relieved he hadn't exploded. I'd half-expected he might. I couldn't predict him, so tread around him with caution.

I liked that Mom allowed and supported my ideas, which I considered reasonable. Dad on the other hand. . . .

Mom and Dad argued again, though I didn't think Dad had gotten drunk between work and home, like the night before. I didn't catch the familiar tell-tale whiff when he walked past.

* * *

"Wake up, we're going to church and Sunday school," Mom said.
School on Sunday? "Aw, do I have to?"

"I want you to come with me," she said.

I'd been to Hiawatha Missionary Baptist church in Highland Park before, though couldn't remember my first or last times.

Why today? I figured Mom needed some time away from Dad after two nights of arguing.

Mom escorted me, an easy walking distance from our house. Verlon stayed at home, lucky dog. Dad, too. I'd heard Dad say enough to know he wasn't the church type.

* * *

"Your Grampa used to preach there," Mom said as we rounded the last corner at Tallulah and Crittenden Drive and the church came into sight.

Grampa preached there. I'd seen churches in westerns on TV like that, built of wood, painted white, steeple with a bell, double doors in the front, lots of windows along the side.

* * *

The one large room, empty of usual furniture and lined with wooden benches on each side of a center aisle, overwhelmed me.

Mom chose a spot on a bench about halfway back and midway in from the aisle. We sat behind several other people on the bench in front of us, and not in direct view from the front, inconspicuous like.

The preacher raised and lowered his voice and gestured wildly with his hands as he talked about God, sin, repentance, all things I'd heard about before, like at Great-grampa's funeral. Uneasy, I couldn't reason most of it, reminded of being scared around mean-drunk-Dad. But the preacher stressed that everyone should accept what he said as faith.

How could he be so sure?

* * *

Once the service concluded, some people left and those remaining milled about a few minutes before they started to collect into groups.

"You go downstairs," Mom told me. She escorted me to the basement where I got sorted into a room with other kids near my age.

The group leader in my room had us read passages and talk about turning the other cheek.

When someone attacks you, let them? I didn't get it. I just didn't get it. Easier said than done, seemed to me. *When Dad beats Mom, let him? Encourage him? No way.*

What was in the Bible that those church people liked so much?

* * *

Though we didn't go every Sunday, Mom's attendance trailed off. She insisted I continue, however.

Once Verlon had grown old enough, he accompanied me to Sunday school.

After that, Mom attended only on rare occasions, such as a wedding, a funeral service, or at Christmastime. And she encouraged, more like insisted, Verlon and I sing in the annual Christmas choral presentations. Regardless, we couldn't have dragged Dad inside with a mule team.

I began to suspect that Verlon's and my absence from home provided Mom and Dad privacy for something secret and between them, a no-cost version of their sending us to the movies.

Not until many years later, Mom confided that she'd attempted to be saved at one point, what our church members called "accepting Jesus as savior." Though she'd voluntarily offered to be saved, I surmised she'd found herself pressured to accept, but couldn't overcome her doubts.

I related. I'd volunteered on one occasion during a Thursday prayer meeting, felt pressured to remain there all night, if necessary. In the end, I caved. As a result, I gave Mom credit for holding to her doubt, rather than lying to herself.

I concluded that, at least, a few of the Hiawatha Missionary churchgoers could, and would, press a hard sale, if they saw an opening.

Later, as well, a cousin informed me that Mom had worn shorts when she ran track in high school, though Grampa was adamantly opposed. My cousin said she felt proud that Mom had stood up for herself. At that moment, so did I. Though I never heard Mom and Grampa come to loggerheads over anything, clearly, there had been tension and differences between them.

Tobacco Worms and Suckers?

July 1956

That year's tobacco crop, planted months earlier and taking advantage of the warm, humid summer days, had added leaves and grown taller.

At the supper table, Grampa said to Uncle James, "It's time to worm the tobacco, again."

Again? "Why do you have to do that?" I asked Uncle James.

"Worms eat the tobacco leaves. Quality and weight determine a year's crop yield. Every bite the tobacco worms take decreases our profit, and spraying with pesticides isn't an option, so we remove them by hand."

Sounded sensible to me. *No problem.* I knew about worms, I'd baited plenty of fish hooks.

Saturday morning, everyone available pressed into service, except for a few holdouts. We put on hats to shade our faces and eyes from the sun, and light, cotton, long-sleeved shirts to avoid sunburn.

"Here, wear this hat," Mom told me. "We might be out there for several hours before a break."

No one liked the chore and some hated it, apparently.

"Aren't you going, too, Betty Jo?" I asked. Her mom, Aunt Irene, Mom's oldest sister, prepared to help. Her dad, Uncle Joe, did not. Nor did Dad.

"Huh," Betty Jo said—she was a few years older than me—"I'm not going to touch those ugly things." She wouldn't go near the tobacco patch. Didn't even leave the house.

"Girls," I said under my breath as I went out the back door.

*　*　*

Warfare began.

The tobacco stalks reached well above my head, but I watched Uncle James, Gramma, and Grampa, veterans of past tobacco worm battles, to see how they did it. Quick and calm, they remained in motion. With alternating hands, they grabbed and squeezed green tobacco worms, then flung them to the ground.

Those worms, the color of the tobacco leaves, hid in plain view.

Fishing worms I'd handled, but these things didn't look like worms. "What are they, Uncle James?" I asked.

"They're caterpillars," he said. "They turn into moths."

Bugs? I decided I didn't want to touch those things, either, and I didn't want one to touch me. The horns on their heads and tails, and the dark spots along their bodies, gave me the creeps. Worse, some were bigger than my fingers. Had one mutated, maybe turned carnivorous? I'd recently learned the words mutated and carnivorous on TV. *Would one lose its footing and fall on me, or worse, jump onto me?* But I needed to do my best to help remove them. After all, this was war, man against bug.

There's one. Head down, the worm munched on the edge of the tobacco leaf. I noticed part of the leaf gone. *Hurry up, stop it, it's eating the tobacco leaf.* I crept up, reached out while I kept a steady eye on the hungry pest. *Will it see me, raise up on its hind legs? Will it bite me, sting me, or somehow squirm away?* I closed in on the caterpillar with my thumb and forefinger, just like I watched the others do. The worm hung onto the leaf with its little feet, like it was glued there. I pulled hard to get it off. "Yuck," I whispered.

The worm wiggled at both ends. I squeezed until dark-green insides oozed out. When I felt my thumb and finger touch, I let go. "Ewww." Dropped on the ground, the worm continued to squirm. "Yuck." I waved my hand to shake off green guts.

Wished I didn't have to look for another worm. Hoped I wouldn't find one. Found another one nearby, anyway. I didn't really want to touch that thing. *Why not just knock it off the leaf and step on it? Yeah, much better, less touching and no green gut juice to wipe off.*

My skills, along with my courage, improved with practice. I knocked them off, then stepped on them. Mashed them underfoot, just like that. Wished I could do that with mean-drunk-Dad.

Our day's war ended with Grampa's words, "I think we got them all." We returned to the house, where supper waited, prepared by Gramma, Mom, and Aunt Irene, who'd retreated from the battlefield early.

"How many times do you have to worm?" I asked Uncle James.

"As many times as we need to get rid of them all," he said. "Maybe, two or three times over several weeks."

Would I be here the next time the tobacco got wormed? And where had Dad been all day? Probably lounging on the front porch swing, chain-smoking and blabbing with Uncle Joe. I figured Dad thought he worked enough in the sun during the week, so he wasn't willing to break a sweat on the weekend. I also had a sneaky suspicion he wouldn't squish tobacco worms, though he'd probably never admit it.

* * *

September, I'd almost forgotten about tobacco worms and hated that another school year had started. I liked school, just didn't want to give up the outdoor freedom of summer.

61

"It's time to sucker the plants," Grampa said.

Sucker? I'd never seen anybody sucker a plant.

"Go get your hat," Mom told me. "We'll be out in the sun a while."

Everyone dressed in hats and long-sleeved shirts, and me with my Little League baseball cap, we marched to the tobacco patch.

Right behind Uncle James, I asked, "What does it mean to sucker the tobacco plants, Uncle James?"

"The tobacco plants put energy into the growth of suckers, the beginnings of flowers, where they form their seeds. But the production of suckers takes energy away from leaf growth, so the suckers need to be removed by hand."

"I've never seen a tobacco seed," I said.

"They're tiny black things," he said, "about the size of a chigger."

Unlike caterpillars, I could see that the tobacco suckers didn't hide or wiggle when handled, but they grew well above my reach. The tobacco plants had grown bigger and higher than when I'd helped worm them. A strong smell filled the air, reminded me of Dad's unlit cigarettes, pleasant and unlike cigarette smoke. I watched and wandered about the field while everybody else remained busy.

* * *

Mom and Gramma had left the field early to prepare supper. Bored, I'd deserted, too, and gravitated to a seat at the kitchen table. Verlon occupied a highchair nearby. Who knew when that thing had arrived at Gramma's? I couldn't remember, but I'd bet I'd been in it.

Gramma heated leftovers on her electric stove, placed in the corner and next to the old, iron wood-burning one. Unlike the electric one, the wood stove took forever to heat up but remained hot a long time afterwards. Meanwhile, Mom set cold items from the refrigerator onto the table.

I noticed the calendar on the wall. That same barefoot country boy that I'd seen before wearing coveralls, and with a straw hat, stood inside a store. It looked like the one I'd gone to in Upton with Uncle James to sell cream. The boy still looked peaceful, not likely that his Dad drank and got mean. *What if my life could be like his all of the time, instead of only when at Gramma and Grampa's?*

Several little symbols of the moon, spaced about a week apart, dotted the calendar, each with a different label like new moon and waxing moon.

What did they mean? And if there was a man in the moon, did he use wax? Mom frequently used the term "the man in the moon." Though I could conjure a face when I looked, I couldn't understand how a man could be in it.

* * *

"The suckering is done," Uncle James said, as he and Grampa entered the kitchen. He waited to wash his hands after Grampa.

Dad sat alone in the living room. To avoid him, I'd remained in the kitchen.

A few minutes later, Gramma called out, "James, would you go pick us some tomatoes for supper?"

"Can I go?" I asked when Uncle James came through the doorway from the living room.

"You can help me," he said.

My stomach growled.

Gramma's tomato crop spread out across open ground. Large tomatoes, some light green, others ripe-red, hung on every vine. Others lay on the ground and waited to rot. Those with small dark-rimmed holes meant some worm had moved in. I didn't want to find out what kind of worm, though.

Uncle James reached down and pulled a red tomato off the vine. "Go ahead, pick one."

I loved tomatoes. Couldn't pick a tomato anytime I wanted, because we didn't grow tomatoes at home. We had to buy them at the store.

I studied the vines closest to me, and narrowed my choice to a big tomato, careful to avoid any with worm holes. I pulled my selection with an added twist; the vine held for a moment before it sprang back. The branches and leaves rustled, the remaining tomatoes swayed. Turned between my hands, I checked for the telltale sign of an unwanted occupant. No worm for me, thank you. No holes or rotten spots visible, I rubbed the tomato against my T-shirt to polish it clean.

At first bite, my tomato burst open. Warm juice squirted free, filled my mouth, and ran down my chin and onto my hand. I slurped and wiped. Five, six, seven big bites later I'd worked my way down to the green navel, where it had attached to the vine, then tossed the nub to the ground.

Uncle James plucked a second tomato. "Get another one."

For several more minutes, we absorbed the ripe-red tomato-ness from our second choices, before we collected a half-dozen plump ones, which I carried in the pouch I formed with my T-shirt. Gramma would slice and lay them on a plate. I would eat some of these, too.

"Those were the best tomatoes I'd ever tasted, Uncle James."

Gramma would collect and can tomatoes later in the summer, after most had ripened and the vines begun to wither. Several bushels of tomatoes would get boiled briefly. Their skins would be removed. They'd then be cooked in a large pot on the kitchen stove. After that, they'd be sealed inside glass jars, left to cool, and stored in the root cellar. There, they'd wait their return to the kitchen on a chilly mid-winter's day and remind everyone of warm summer days past, as well as the promise of the coming spring. But, would Gramma or Uncle James encounter that snake in the root cellar?

"Here you are, Gramma," I said as I unloaded the tomatoes on the counter next to where she sliced a cucumber.

"Thank you, Son," she said. "We need some water. James, would you go draw us a bucket?"

"Okay, Mom," he said without hesitation.

"I'll come, too, Uncle James." I hurried to join him.

*   *   *

A full bucket of well-water delivered, everyone in a seat, Grampa started grace from his reserved position at the head of the table. I bowed my head, though peeked, and silently prayed Dad would stop drinking and quit hitting Mom.

What to eat? I settled on several slices of cucumber that Gramma had presented in a bowl of salted water, several slices of tomato, and a fried chicken leg. I knew there'd be some dessert afterwards, but first things first.

Dogwood Tree

Late September 1956

"Mom, look what I got at school," I called out when I returned home. I'd advanced to the third grade.

She entered the living room from the kitchen. "What do you have there?"

My two-foot specimen in a small plastic pot held up for inspection, I beamed, "They let us pick out a tree at school to bring home and plant."

"What kind is it?" she said.

"Dogwood." *Heck, the name alone meant my tree was special.*

The other kids in my class wanted the trees that seemed common to me, like oaks and pines and such, trees you could see anywhere. But when I spied that one and only dogwood, and learned that it would grow pretty blossoms, I chose it. No one I knew had one, nor did I remember ever seeing one.

"Where will you plant it?"

"The front yard?"

"I think that will be alright, but we should ask your daddy," she said.

With Dad's blessing on the location, I chose a spot where it had plenty of room to grow, about halfway between the house and the street, though not directly in front of our door.

As well as at Gramma and Grampa's, I could help at home, too. I considered my tree a good contribution. But the dogwood paled compared to helping Mom prevent Dad from beating her, so I continued to observe him with a keen eye. I hoped I'd helped Mom, but couldn't tell if I had when I told Dad to stop hitting her. Maybe, I could fling myself between them somehow if Mom's life came into question. All too aware that Dad could beat me to smithereens, if he chose, my fear of losing Mom would need to overcome my fear of him.

Dad's drinking episodes didn't occur every Friday—although any one time was one too often—but, though relieved, I was surprised when he came home sober. I still stewed in images, lodged in the forefront of my mind, of his behavior and the terrible sweet smell of his alcohol breath.

But I kept my mouth shut about Mom and Dad's fighting at Grampa and Gramma's. No way I'd talk about that. I didn't want Dad coming after me with his belt.

Double, Double, Toil and Trouble

October 1956

Friday evening, a few weeks later, Dad parked our four-door Ford by the big oak tree, which shaded the better part of Gramma and Grampa's front yard in the summer.

Mom told Dad earlier in the week she wanted to come. But with nothing for sure, I'd kept my fingers crossed that Dad would come home straightaway on Friday, we'd pack the car, and drive to the farm without a problem.

I jumped out of our car once we'd come to a halt and started towards the back door. Before I continued around the house, I stopped to examine the closest rain barrel, the bottom of which was easy to see through the shallow pool of water.

Summer hadn't abandoned us yet, but the air, in the shade beside the house, cooled as I spotted Gramma further along the worn footpath. She stooped next to a blackened cast-iron kettle, about two-gallon size, and added small pieces of wood to a fire under it.

"Hi, Gramma, what're you doing?"

"Hello, Son. Gramma is making lye soap."

Lie soap? Tom Sawyer's mom had threatened to wash his mouth out with soap for using foul words and I supposed a lie was about as bad.

Gramma shoveled white chunks into the kettle.

Sizzle!

"We'll let that heat a while," she said.

"What was that, Gramma?"

"Pork fat scraps."

*   *   *

A swallow of communal bucket water from the dipper went down well. A piece of soap rested next to the washbasin. Gramma's homemade lie soap, no doubt.

Mom and Gramma talked women-stuff at the table a few minutes, Verlon playing on the floor nearby.

Gramma said, "I'm going back out to check on the fat." She looked at me. "Want to watch Gramma?"

"Yeah."

Gramma gave the bubbling fat a good stir, then added a mix of gray and white powder.

Double, double, toil and trouble. But Gramma wasn't a witch.

"What did you put in now, Gramma?"

"Lye and coal ash." She gave the kettle another good stir. "We'll let that boil a little more."

*   *   *

At rest at the kitchen table, Gramma and Mom continued their women-talk.

Mom asked Gramma, "How are you doing, Mom?"

"Oh, I'm doing good. Just getting over a touch of something. A cold, I guess."

I'd imagined Gramma possessed superhuman power, able to avoid sickness and worries that afflicted everyone else, as I never overheard her discuss any personal sickness or unhappiness.

69

A few minutes passed. "Time to check on the soap," Gramma said and rose from her chair. She grabbed one of her large kitchen knives and a section of newspaper that Grampa had finished reading.

I followed.

Using a dishrag to grab the thick wire handle, she lifted the kettle off the fire and set it on the ground. "Once this cools off, we can cut it."

* * *

After another break we returned to the kettle.

Gramma carved the soft, waxy blob into blocks small enough to hold in one hand. "There," she said, the last piece stacked on the newspaper, "that should last a while. Gramma can use them to wash clothes. Would you carry them in for Gramma? I'll douse the fire and put the kettle away."

While Gramma busied herself with cleanup, I hauled the soap into the kitchen.

Soon, she appeared and stored the soap on a shelf under the communal water bucket and washbasin.

* * *

"Would you go draw some water for me?" Gramma asked Uncle James, after she'd noticed the communal water bucket.

I asked, "Can I come?" as Uncle James rose from his chair.

He pumped until the bucket was nearly full and said, "Want to carry it back in?"

I grabbed the handle, this time lifting it off the spout by myself, and swayed the bucket one step at a time towards the house.

"Can you get it in?" Uncle James said as I reached the backdoor step.

"I think so," I said.

He held the door as I stepped up with a grunt.

I put the bucket in its special place on the small table by the door. "That's good," he said.

"Thank you, boys," Gramma said.

I'd helped.

* * *

Saturday morning, Mom called to me, "Get up lazy head." She'd let me sleep in and I liked that.

As I finished my breakfast of milk, egg, bacon, and toast with Gramma's homemade strawberry jam—I loved strawberries— Gramma said, "Gramma's going to gather some eggs for tomorrow's breakfast. Do you want to come?"

"Yeah," I said, though hesitant as I pictured chicken beaks and claws. I'd always approached chickens with caution—that crow on Tallulah must've given me bad ideas about birds—but I figured I'd be safe with Gramma. She wasn't afraid of any chicken, though maybe a little cautious of the roosters. I'd heard she'd been attacked by one and Grampa had wrung its neck. Gramma kept enough chickens to supply the farm with fresh eggs, even some to sell, and for a chicken sacrifice on occasion. "Nobody I know has chickens where we live in Louisville, Gramma, just dogs and cats. We got two rabbits once and built a wooden cage for them, but they chewed their way out the next day and the neighborhood dogs killed them."

"Dogs will do that," she said, as a matter of fact. Without surprise or drama, Gramma had an even-keel, steady way of dealing with things, which reassured me.

When she allowed her feathered flock to roam outside their pen, they scratched for odd bits around the main house, and the tool and water sheds. I remained close as Gramma entered the wire-mesh chicken pen, then the wooden henhouse.

Inside, some hens rested on wood poles at different heights above the floor, which reminded me of the stadium seating where I'd watched Kentucky Colonels Minor League baseball games in Louisville. The rooster and a few hens milled about on the dirt floor while other hens occupied nesting stalls.

Straightaway Gramma proceeded to the nests and shooed off a hen. I watched Gramma with one eye. With the other, I watched the rooster and hens on the ground. They talked their chicken language, something I didn't understand.

"You can help Gramma by gathering some eggs from the nests."

I wasn't so sure about that, but approached a sitting hen. She looked at me.

Buc, buc, buc!

I imagined she said, "Who are you and what are you doing?"

"Just reach in and push her off," Gramma said as she collected another egg.

I looked at the hen's beak. I didn't want her to peck me with that thing. *Going to let me steal her egg?*

"Go ahead, she won't hurt you," Gramma said. She'd already collected another egg.

I reached in, gentle like, to nudge the hen. When she moved, I could see one light-brown egg, nice and warm to my touch, which I placed in Gramma's basket.

Ten eggs collected, Gramma said, "That's enough," and turned to leave.

As a trespasser, scared of an ambush planned in chicken language, I kept a sharp eye and followed in hot pursuit.

Gramma left the chicken coop door and pen gate open.

I quick-stepped, couldn't relax until in the kitchen. *Whew. Would those tricky devils catch me off guard next time?*

* * *

I'd waited as long as I could in hopes the chickens had forgotten me.

"Mom, where's the toilet paper?" I said with a raised voice to make sure Mom heard me. Wouldn't dare leave the house without some.

"Here you are," Mom said as she offered me a small supply.

Though I figured to maintain a safe distance, I saw no chickens. *Still in their coop?* I slunk to the back of the tool shed, the popular toilet site after the old outhouse had been abandoned.

Uncle James had told me, when I'd asked about it, "We stopped using it because it was full."

The rear of the tool shed was a prime hunting ground for Gramma's chickens. They favored that spot when allowed free range in search of seeds and bugs, I guessed. Who knew what all? I'd seen them at times, though thought it gross and never stared. Besides, that was chicken business, not mine. And though their foraging patrols helped clean that area, I took special care where I stepped.

With little privacy, I wouldn't dawdle. What if someone else needed to go? Meanwhile, I studied the old outhouse, a few yards away. Surrounded by high weeds, the gray-weathered boards leaned to one side, as if in a slow-motion fall.

Without warning, quietly, swiftly, and in her ninja way, except those times when she was singing hymns, Gramma appeared on the path some twenty feet away that ran between the chicken coop and tool shed, though not towards me.

Oh, Jesus. Pants down, I couldn't run, couldn't hide.

Aware of my presence, she said, "It's okay, Gramma won't look."

"Okay," I replied and hoped my response sealed the deal, though I kept an eye on her, anyway. I watched her through the leaves of a pear tree between us as she continued on her way.

She didn't change direction. I relaxed a little. I trusted Gramma. Well, maybe not totally, but more than any other person I knew, except Mom. Neither had ever lied to me, tricked me, or made fun of me. On the other hand, I couldn't, wouldn't, trust Dad.

If only Gramma and Grampa had an indoor bathroom with a toilet. . . . *Why didn't they?*

Grampa had a penny-pinching streak, or so I'd been led to believe by Mom. Did Gramma? Did she agree with him or was she unable to talk him into paying for one? Either way, I pointed the finger at Grampa's unwillingness to spend money.

* * *

Several weeks had passed when we visited again.

Mayflies long gone, birds off their nests, weeds grown tall, corn ripened, everything seemed worn out from the summer's heat and humidity.

I accompanied Uncle James that Saturday morning as he gathered tobacco leaves that hung limp onto the ground. He brushed off any dirt and smoothed them with his hands.

"Why are you doing that?" I asked.

"I'm gathering good leaves. They'll mildew if they get wet and lay on the ground. We'll take these to the barn."

* * *

Back in the kitchen, I heard Gramma say to Grampa, "Frank, go kill us a chicken for supper." She'd put a pot of water on the stove to boil.

Clack! Grampa went out the kitchen screen door in search of a plump hen.

No way I wanted to end up in the middle of a chicken sacrifice, but I was curious, so I positioned myself at the living room window, a safe place from which to watch.

The chickens roamed in the side yard, engaged in their daily shopping. Their heads bobbed up and down as they pecked at things on the ground which I couldn't see. Through the windows, I heard what sounded like a casual chicken conversation.

Buc, buc!

I imagined that hen said, "I just found a juicy bug."

Buuuc!

"Where?" another replied.

Buc, buc!

"Under a leaf."

Buc! Buc, buc!

"Okay. Hey, jackpot."

BUC! BUC!

"Heads up, girls, the old man just came out of the house."

I'd witnessed several sacrifices in the past, beheadings to be exact. Positioned over a wood stump in the yard, the victim's head chopped from its body by one swift blow of an ax. Gramma and Grampa had planned out those murders in advance, I figured, since they'd carried their weapon with them. But the wood stump was nowhere to be seen and Grampa approached barehanded. He looked over his choices for several moments before he settled on one hen and moved in. She had a different idea and headed away from him.

Grampa doubled his effort and so did the hen. In a dead run, she flapped her wings. But Grampa outwitted her, cornered her next to the house, and grabbed her.

She screamed.

Grampa held both her feet together with his left hand, turned her upside down, and carried her away from the house. Limp and quiet, her wings hung out from her body. Several loose feathers floated to the ground.

In the middle of the yard, Grampa grabbed his victim's neck with his right hand and spun her several turns until her body, separated from her head, fell to the ground. Then, he pitched her head off to the side.

Not a pretty picture, her blood sprayed in all directions as she flopped about and Grampa stepped back. I figured, as devout Baptist and not a pagan, he wasn't interested in bathing in blood.

Nothing good ever happened around the sight of blood in my estimation. Blood meant injury, or death, from an accident or someone's bad behavior. Plenty of that on TV. And though scary to consider, I was reminded once again that I didn't want Mom to suffer a similar fate at the hands of mean-drunk-Dad. I wanted to prevent that possibility no matter what.

The hen lay still within the minute.

I arrived in the kitchen to see Grampa hand the dead hen to Gramma.

With one hand Gramma held the bird over an empty pan, and with the other poured scalding water over it, then plucked the feathers and gutted the corpse.

I pictured a single, lonely egg left in one of the nests in the coop. *Could a similar fate happen to me?*

* * *

Even though I'd watched her die, when fried and set upon the table, the hen tasted delicious. I must've been hungry and appreciated that she'd given her life to benefit me. I tried not to think about how she'd died, but knew the other chickens had witnessed the sacrifice. I also knew that, if I'd seen them through the living room window, they'd seen me.

What did the other hen's think about the sacrifice? I imagined their chicken conversation.

"Did you see what the old man did to Margaret?"

"How awful. I couldn't bear to watch. I just had to run away."

"And that boy looked through the window and did nothing."

"Hey, he was the one who stole my egg this morning."

Cause to take revenge during my next trip to the chicken coop?

Everyone treated killing animals as a necessary way of life, as a food source, certainly never for sport or pleasure. As a city boy, I had a different take on that. I always felt uneasy about killing an animal that could look me in the eye. I equated the death of one animal pretty much to the death of any other on some level, regardless of the reason.

However, spiders, tobacco worms, ants, and other bugs, like chiggers and ticks, were pests and fair game to be squashed on sight. Without warm red blood, according to what I'd learned in school, I equated them to alien life forms.

* * *

As fall advanced, the air turned colder at night and remained crisper during the day. The last of Gramma's vegetable garden withered. The lower tobacco leaves had turned brown with patches of yellow, while those higher on the stalks only still hinted of green.

When Mom, Dad, Verlon, and I arrived for a visit that Friday evening, I spied Uncle James in the tobacco patch. From one corner, he had worked his way down each row and whacked off each stalk at its base with a machete.

My labor enlisted straightaway, sweat rolled down my forehead as I steadied a five-foot wooden tobacco stick, placed upright in the ground near the stalks to be cut. The thick smell of tobacco mixed with the taste of dust and my salty sweat. Using a metal cone placed on the top end, we skewered eight tobacco stalks onto a stick, spaced evenly apart as we worked. Each stick joined a growing pile on the wagon bed and waited to go to the barn.

Slow work; one stalk, one stick at a time.

My stomach growled. I imagined the whole field would take forever to cut. "Why does Grampa grow so much tobacco?"

Uncle James wiped his brow. "Tobacco is a cash crop for us, so we grow as much as we can. We're allowed one acre."

With all the rows still to be cut, that acre seemed enormous. *One acre?* "How come one acre?"

Uncle James paused. "The state regulates the amount each farmer can grow, based on the size of their farm, in order to prevent an over-supply on the market. That's as much as we're allowed on a sixty-acre farm," he replied.

The farm had always seemed humongous, beyond what I could picture, most of its edges somewhere out there and unknown to me.

"Well, that's enough cutting for today," Uncle James said. "Let's collect all the scraps and take them to the barn, too."

Once in the barn, Uncle James climbed into the rafters and looked down. "I'll hang each stick about two feet from the last. You hand them up to me."

From the flat wagon bed, I passed the tobacco to him, one stick at a time. Though big enough to lift the sticks, I couldn't hold them up for long. Secretly, I wanted Uncle James to grab each one quickly, so I timed my lift when he turned for the next stick. "Why can't we just take the leaves off now?" I asked.

"Every leaf needs air to dry out. We'll give them about two weeks up here."

I noticed that, although the barn's metal roof shielded everything inside from rain, air circulated in and out of the barn through narrow spaces between the wooden boards on the sides.

I couldn't have been more glad when we headed toward the house.

* * *

Several weeks later, I'd almost finished my supper that Friday evening, when Uncle James said, "The tobacco leaves are dry now. Want to help me strip and tie tobacco leaves tomorrow?"

"Yeah, I'll help."

Fresh tobacco smelled wonderful to me, unlike the cigarette smoke I endured at home, in our car, and in the houses of aunts and uncles. Most adults I knew chain-smoked and I couldn't figure out why. I'd learned to detest the smell of cigarette smoke.

* * *

Saturday morning, a light frost covered the ground, and though snug in my warm jacket, my breath froze as Uncle James and I walked to the barn. We skirted the patch of bright-orange pumpkins, which looked like some kid-giant's bag of scattered marbles, left in a hurry when his mom called him to supper.

Though drafty, the barn sheltered us from strong breezes, and the air felt heavy and thick. I blew into my cupped hands and rubbed them. I shifted my weight on my feet, willing to do anything to avoid feeling cold.

With quick work, Uncle James stripped leaves from their stalks, counted out eleven, and tied that bunch together with a twelfth leaf.

"Why are you tying them with a leaf?"

"We can't use anything else. The tobacco companies won't accept them otherwise," Uncle James said.

"When are you going to sell them?"

"We'll take them to auction around Thanksgiving and tobacco company representatives will bid on them according to quality. We don't know how much money we'll get until the auction. It depends on supply and demand. Some years we get more money, some years less."

I thought back. *Squish tobacco worms again next year?*

We'd stripped a bunch of tobacco stalks—I hadn't counted—with what seemed an endless number yet to do. Uncle James paused and said, "That's enough for now. It's about suppertime. I'll finish the rest later."

"Tomorrow?"

"Monday. It won't hurt them to hang a little longer."

Grampa didn't allow work on Sundays. Guided by a god of fire and brimstone, from everything I'd witnessed, Grampa worked hard but never on Sundays. "The Lord's day of rest," he'd said a number of times in my presence. Who was I to question that? So, I did my part, and as I didn't want to encourage a sermon, I steered clear of talk of religion.

"Okay," I said, eager to get back to the warmth of the house.

Dobbs House

December 1956

I'd opened the front door, come straightaway from the bus stop after school, as requested by Mom. "I'm home."

Verlon lay on the couch watching TV.

"Hello," Mom said from the kitchen in a cheery voice. "I found a job at the Dobbs House," she continued as she came into the living room. "Let me show you where it is."

I followed her onto the front porch. She pointed to a building on the right and just beyond the big empty field across from our house. The airport terminal was beyond the field to the left. "There. I can walk from here and be home by the time you get back from school."

"What do they do there?" I said.

"Cater food for the airplanes at the airport," she said.

"What will you do?"

"Help prepare and put the food on the serving trays."

"Does Dad know?" I asked.

"I'll tell him tonight," she said.

"What will he think? I said.

"You leaving Dad?" Verlon asked.

"No, don't worry. I haven't decided to do that," she said.

* * *

Dad didn't seem too happy about Mom's news. At least it wasn't Friday night and he hadn't been drinking that I could tell. Better yet, he didn't explode. Still, he seemed to go into a slow boil.

"It'll help us pay the bills," Mom explained.

"We'll see," he said.

Why wasn't Dad happy about the news? Mom wouldn't need him to take her to work or pick her up, even though she didn't know how to drive. Supper could be on the table as usual when he came home, if he didn't get lost in a beer joint on the way from work. Had he somehow figured out that Mom, Verlon, and I could leave him if Mom earned her own money?

Looking back, I've considered he felt embarrassed and insulted by the idea that his wife would need to work, because he couldn't earn enough on his own. Or, he could've been threatened that she might earn more than him. Worst, he'd felt threatened that she might become too independent and leave him.

Dad, a work nomad, changed jobs often enough that Mom, Verlon, and I grew accustomed to that news. Accustomed, though still surprised. He usually delivered his news in a cavalier fashion, sometimes several weeks afterwards and when Mom had spied his paycheck or stub. On occasion when he hadn't stopped at a beer joint on his way home, he surrendered his paycheck to her.

* * *

At first, Mom seemed happy with her job, but it didn't take long before I heard her talk of it with Beulah, Mom's closest first cousin.

"How's your job, Bea?" Beulah asked her.

Beulah's two sons, Carl William and Gerald, and Vernon and I lay on their living room floor in a semi-circle. We watched *Sea Hunt* on the TV within a few feet of the kitchen, where Mom, Dad,

Beulah, and her husband, Carl, occupied their table. I'd tuned in my hearing radar to their talk during a commercial break.

"I don't know how long I can keep it up, everything is always a constant rush," Mom said. "As soon as we get one order out, we have another. Each order is different. They check every order before it goes out and yell at us if it isn't perfect. I like working with food, though, and I can walk there and back home."

"I wish I could earn some money and I wouldn't mind working with food," Beulah replied, "but without a car, I don't know how I'd get there. I don't think there's any jobs around here that I could walk to. I doubt Carl would drive me anywhere."

I could see a portion of the kitchen table; Carl's back in full view, Beulah's right side towards me, Mom faced me, and Dad sat out of sight.

Carl finished his bottle of Fall City's beer with a swill. "Don't I earn good enough money for you?" He worked as a plumber at the Naval Ordinance Plant, near Highland Park.

"I'm just saying, it would be nice to have my own spending money," Beulah said.

"I can't get Cecil to understand, either," Mom said.

In less time than an eye-blink, Dad followed Mom's comment with, "I'm ready for another one." As if with emphasis, *Clank!*, another empty bottle joined a loose collection on the kitchen counter.

"Grab me another while you're at it, Cecil," Carl said.

By that point Dad and Carl had worked their way through one six pack, prepared to do serious damage to a second.

"You probably wouldn't like working there, Beulah," Mom continued. "Sometimes, they change an order right before it's due out. The other girls show up late or call in sick, which leaves us shorthanded. And then, the supervisor wants us to stay late to cover until that order is ready to go out. The whole thing makes me a nervous wreck."

Commercial break over and Lloyd Bridges in his scuba gear, I tuned out the kitchen talk. Good news. Things were peaceful and I'd take what I could get. Dad wasn't swearing to high heaven and pounding on Mom. But then Dad never did that in front of anybody but Verlon and me.

When *Sea Hunt* signed off, us four boys begged for quarters from our dads so we could buy candy bars at the pharmacy next door. All seemed well with the world for the moment.

* * *

The next Friday night Dad arrived home too late for him to have come directly from his construction job. All doubt that he'd gotten lost in a beer joint was removed, when he came wild-eyed through the front door.

Mom asked him, "Where have you been?"

"None of your goddamn business."

"Dad being mean?" Verlon whispered.

"Yeah," I whispered.

"Did you spend your paycheck in a beer joint again, Cecil?" Mom said.

"What's it to you?" Dad said, voice raised.

I tried to focus on the TV but couldn't.

"What do I have to do, Cecil? You know I got that job at Dobbs House to help us get caught up with our bills. And I don't even like it there!"

"Then quit."

"How will we pay the bills?"

"I earn enough for both of us."

"Not when you spend it on booze!"

"I earn it. I can spend it the way I want!" he said.

"A letter came today from the bank," Mom pleaded. "They've sent us notice. They'll foreclose on us, Cecil, and take the house, if we don't make a payment!"

Everything plunged downhill from there, impossible not to hear every mean thing Dad said. He peppered the house with four-letter words. Mom pleaded for him to change his behavior. They moved into their bedroom.

"Damn you," Dad snorted.

Slap!

"Augh," I said.

Tears welled in Verlon's eyes.

"I'm tired of your shit!" Dad yelled.

We heard Mom scream in pain as she hit a bedroom wall.

"I've told you to get off my back!" Dad snorted.

Another wrenching scream from Mom, as Dad now dragged her into the living room by her hair.

Oh, Jesus.

Verlon whined.

"Stop, Cecil, please!" Mom said.

"Stooop!" I yelled. Maybe, he'd drag me across the floor or beat me into a heap, if he wanted, but I couldn't help myself.

"Don't!" Verlon added.

"Stooop!" I repeated, at the top of my lungs.

But Dad didn't stop until he'd crossed a good part of the living room floor with a firm grasp on Mom's hair, while Mom's arms and legs flailed.

As soon as Dad released his grip, Mom got off the floor. She came to Verlon and me. Grabbed each of us by a hand, and said, "Let's go." No hesitation or question in her voice.

We approached Grampa and Gramma Hogan's open front door, second house down the street, where they'd moved, along with Aunt Linda. Mom called, "Anybody here?"

85

Aunt Linda appeared at the screen door.

"Let us in, Linda, Cecil's out of control," Mom said, out of breath.

"What's wrong?" Aunt Linda said with horror, as she surveyed Mom's bruised face.

"He's been drinking."

The screen door locked behind us, and the four of us watched Dad approach within moments. Aunt Linda and Mom gasped when Dad yanked the screen door open with one jerk. We had no place to hide, no place to run. Dad stood within arm's reach of Mom and Aunt Linda. I stood off to one side, also within Dad's reach. Verlon, on the other side of Mom, held her hand.

"What's wrong with you, Cecil?" Aunt Linda asked. "This is your wife, have you lost your mind?!"

Red-faced, Dad continued to fume and yell. All I could do was stand frozen, hope, and agonize.

I couldn't say how long it took before two policemen arrived.

"We got a call about a domestic disturbance. What's the problem here?" one policeman said.

The neighbors between my house and Gramma's must've called the police. In all the commotion, Mom and Aunt Linda never had the time, and Grampa and Gramma Hogan weren't home.

"My wife and I have a difference of opinion," Dad said.

"Is that so?" the other officer replied, then asked Mom, "Are you okay, Ma'am."

"I'll be alright now, I think," Mom said between breaths. "I just needed to give him a chance to cool off."

Had he? Could Dad ever really cool off?

"Are you going to behave yourself?" the second officer asked Dad.

"Yes," Dad said.

"If we have to come back, we're going to arrest you. Is that clear?" the same policeman said.

86

"Yes," Dad said.

Then, the policemen left. They just left. Got into their squad car and drove away.

Why didn't they put Dad in their car and take him? Why hadn't Mom told them to take him? I wanted them to take him. But at the same time, I didn't. For sure, I didn't want him to drag her across the floor again.

Though Dad had settled down, for all I knew he could erupt again in a second. And what would happen then? How bad would it get before Mom would press charges?

In hindsight, the police had erred on the side of non-involvement in a domestic affair. They'd deferred to Mom, the abused spouse, at a moment when her shock, confusion, and uncertainty reigned. They'd accepted the responses of both parties and avoided an arrest. And, so their business wrapped up with us, they'd moved on to the next domestic crisis, or whatever. But what should be expected of an abused woman, a battered wife, a mother in that situation? Yeah, arrest him? Throw him in jail? Cost us money for bail or fine we didn't have? Or cause him to lose his job if he didn't show for work? Let him stew in a jail cell until he returned home? Except for the immediate police presence, and the talking to that Dad had gotten, no long-term support had been provided to Mom to deal with his wanton drunkenness and rages.

At that point, Mom led Verlon and me home.

Once there, she told Verlon and me, "You two watch TV."

A minute or two later, Dad arrived. Though he remained silent, I could easily see that he fumed.

Verlon and I froze in position on the couch and I listened to the noises of Mom making supper.

The battle had stopped, replaced with a painful silence as loud as any of Dad's four-letter words. When would their conflict start again?

* * *

The next morning, Mom called, "Connard, Verlon, wash up and come for breakfast."

Dad was nowhere to be seen. I figured he'd gone to work, and the house would remain peaceful, at least until he returned.

"Good morning. I cooked some oats," Mom said, as she ladled Verlon and me a bowl each. A large purple bruise covered a portion of her face around her right eye, and another spread over her right upper arm.

Seemed to me that Dad favored hitting Mom on the face and upper arms, but then again, I couldn't see through her clothes.

"Good morning," I said. Wanted to cry out, but didn't. Ate my oats in silence after I'd spread sugar on top.

"Do you think I should leave your daddy?" Mom asked.

What? I didn't know how to answer that. Would that be better than their fighting? I hated their fights, didn't want Dad to hurt Mom. But I didn't want them to divorce, either. I still loved Dad, in spite of my fear and anger. Still, something had to give. "You should leave him." *There, I said it.* After a short pause, I asked, "Why did you marry Dad?"

"I loved him," she said.

Do bruises and upset have to come with love, I wondered? Does marriage mean ongoing arguments over money? From the glimpses I'd seen of other marriages and families, I didn't think so, but. . . . "Does he still love you?"

"I think he does, but I wonder sometimes,'" she said.

"How did you meet?"

"He approached me in the park on Crittenden Drive," Mom explained. "Said he'd seen me there."

She'd perked up a little, left no doubt to me that she'd loved him. And I knew that park, two streets away, within walking distance of our house. I could find my way there and back on my own.

"Why can't Dad be more like Carl?" I asked. "Carl doesn't come home drunk on Friday nights, beat on Beulah, or spend his money in beer joints."

"I don't know. Maybe, your daddy acts that way because Grampa Hogan had a temper and drank when Cecil grew up."

Those comments added pieces to my puzzles about Dad and Grampa Hogan. "Grampa Hogan got angry-drunk?" He was always easygoing around me. "I didn't know that."

"Yeah, your Grampa Hogan had quite a temper. He was in the army during WWI, but received a dishonorable discharge for hitting an officer."

Another piece went into the puzzle. *Dishonorable discharge? Hit an officer in the army? Dad's temper is not unlike Grampa Hogan's.* I concluded some apples don't roll far from their trees. "I'm going to watch TV, Mom," I said, my head filled with questions. Saturday morning cartoons and westerns would provide me something else to think about, at least until Dad got home, when who-knew-what would happen.

* * *

Dad didn't say a word when he came through the front door early afternoon. With a red-flushed face and unsteady gait, he crossed the living room like a hell-bound freight train, straight for the kitchen.

Oh, Jesus. The sight of him jolted me like I'd poked my finger into an electric socket.

I didn't want to talk to him. Didn't want to be near him. Didn't want him to be near Mom. What had Mom, I, or Verlon done to make him so angry?

Unmistakable, the faint whiff of sweet alcohol breath reached me when Dad roared in the kitchen. "Don't you ever embarrass me again in front of my family."

Smack! Slap!

"Ow, Cecil," Mom cried out. "That hurt."

What could I do?

Slap! Slap!

"Stop, hitting me, Cecil," Mom said.

"Just remember," Dad said, "there's more where that came from," and he raised his voice to emphasize his words, "if you ever do that again."

"But, Cecil, I just wanted to give you time to cool off."

"Shut up and fix me something to eat."

Both eyes and one ear on the TV, the other ear tuned toward the kitchen, I expected Dad to continue his assault.

Instead, the sounds of footsteps across the kitchen floor, the refrigerator door, the clanks of dishes, and utensil scrapes filled the silence.

Me? Watching the TV hadn't provided any measure of escape, though I'd wanted to make it so. But what could I do? And Verlon, still beside me on the couch, hadn't moved.

Ornate Bedroom

New Year 1957

Summer gone, then Thanksgiving, I was eight and halfway through the third grade. I considered that the Christmas and New Year's holidays were positioned halfway through the school year, and I liked that. Knew they weren't, but wanted to think of them that way. Seemed to me, winter, my least favorite season of the year, would always drag on forever.

Everybody remained cooped-up indoors at Gramma and Grampa's house, except for necessary trips for canned supplies from the root cellar, water from the pump house, a private something behind the tool shed, or a rabbit or squirrel hunt. Snow drifts hadn't kept us indoors that Saturday, because the ground lay bare. The temperature hadn't kept us in the house, either, as ice in the little puddles of water I'd seen from the living room window melted by mid-afternoon. It was more we preferred to avoid the cold wind and mud.

Worst part for me, Billy wasn't there.

Supper cleanup done, Mom said, "I'm going to play the piano. Anyone want to sing along?" She loved to sing and play Gramma and Grampa's roller piano.

Sounded good to me. I liked when Mom laughed and smiled. During these times, did she forget Dad's treatment of her? Could she? I couldn't.

"I do, Aunt Bea," older cousin Betty Jo said.

Aunt Shirley grinned. "That'll be fun."

"Put on your sweaters," Mom said. "It'll be chilly in there."

While fires kept the kitchen and living rooms heated when everyone was awake, the door to the hallway remained shut. As a result, the front two upstairs bedrooms and two downstairs bedrooms, as well as the hallway, stayed unheated. On many evenings during the winter, Grampa requested Uncle James build a fire in the more frequently used downstairs bedroom, where everyone socialized until bedtime.

Verlon and I tagged along as Mom led the procession down the cold hallway carrying a lit coal-oil lantern.

"I'm coming, too," Aunt Irene, Mom's older sister, said as she shuffled along behind to catch up.

* * *

Mom, on the bench pulled close to the roller piano, tested her fingering with several chords. The rest of us stood behind her or sat on the two padded chairs in the room.

I followed along as best I could. "Put another nickel in, in the nickelodeon, da-da da. . . ."

Paused for a breather between songs, I looked around what I came to call the ornate bedroom. Everything about that room appeared old and formal, and reminded me of a museum. On school trips to every museum I'd always been told, "Don't touch anything, just walk by and look."

Dolls, each in some girlie dress, lined the fireplace mantle, and stared at me, stone-faced, like kids in a church pew controlled by the threat of a rap on the knuckles. *Could they talk like ventriloquist dummies? Would they?*

In one corner a king-sized bed, with a black wooden footboard and matching headboard, waited for someone to climb between the covers. Pictures in ancient looking frames hung on the wall, like others I'd studied around the house which contained pictures of places I'd never been and people I didn't know.

No firewood rested in the large fireplace, nor ashes, if it had ever been used. That room was the lesser used bedroom downstairs as far as I knew. I couldn't remember being in there before. Probably had been, but couldn't remember. Thick curtains covered the windows. Closed, they could block out light during bright summer days. Now, they prevented the pitch-blackness of winter from sucking our meager light away. Large pink flower blossoms on the wallpaper contrasted with a closed, bright glossy-white wooden door, along with three high steps, which led up to the door.

"Let's see if I can remember this." Mom sounded out several chords and began to sing, "Shine on, shine on harvest moon, up in the sky. . . ."

I mouthed the words I knew, ". . . since January, February, June or July." *What's a harvest moon, anyway?*

"Aunt Bea, can you play 'Sentimental Journey?'" Betty Jo said.

I examined the glossy-white door behind me. "Where does that door go, Mom?"

Focused more on Betty Jo's request, she tested several chords, then said, "Oh, it goes upstairs."

Closed for some reason. A secret passage behind that door that goes upstairs?

Mom hit a wrong note. "Oops," she said.

"How did you learn to play, Aunt Bea?" Betty Jo asked.

"I play by ear. I sat down at the keyboard, pecked out a melody, added chords, and played a song until I memorized it. I learned to play the accordion that way, too."

93

Mom had obtained a used accordion, which she'd play at home. Occasionally, she'd take it here and there to play for others, a version of a portable piano.

"Why didn't you take lessons?" Betty Jo said.

"I would've given anything to take lessons, but we didn't have the money when I was growing up."

A ghost haunt the secret passage? One had to. If I were a ghost that's where I'd stay. That, or maybe, in the root cellar.

Mom continued, "I've always loved music. Wanted to be able to sing and dance. I'd love to go to Hollywood to see movie stars and get their autographs. I had a crush on Gene Autry before I met Cecil."

As a child, I understood Mom was enamored with the glamour of Hollywood, and the fame of movie stars and performers. I considered her dream an expression of her wish to escape marital-heartache. Only years later, I came to appreciate that her dream of escape had likely started as a reaction to Grampa's rigid beliefs about sexuality and gender roles.

"Well, you play and sing good, Aunt Bea," Betty Jo said.

"Better than I could do." Aunt Irene chuckled. "I can't play a lick."

I glanced at the door. *That ghost sneak out and grab me?*

* * *

After a number of songs and what seemed a long time, Mom pushed the bench back from the keyboard and rubbed her fingers. "That's enough for now. I don't think I can play another note."

We talked in strained, excited voices and breathed hard from song and laughter.

Rolls of papers atop the black, upright piano drew my attention. "What're those, Mom?"

"Those are the rollers. They play songs."

"Oh, can we listen to a roll?" Betty Jo asked.

"Okay, if I can remember how to do it," Mom said. She set about putting a roll into the piano.

I'd better keep an eye on that glossy-white door.

A few minutes later, Mom said, "I think this is right," and started the piano.

The roller paper began to scroll. The black-and-white piano keys moved up and down, as if played by a ghost. *Could that be the ghost from the secret passage?* I pictured a frantic piano player in a western movie saloon stealing glances of a brawl as his fingers danced across the keyboard.

Problem was, Mom couldn't play her way out of beatings from Dad.

When the song finished Mom said, "Okay, that's enough for now." She closed the lid on the keyboard.

I wouldn't stay in that room by myself, and not to be last out, I moved in front of Mom.

The bedroom silent, I glanced from the hallway to assure myself the glossy-white door remained closed.

* * *

The house overflowed with family, an after-the-fact Christmas gathering, so Gramma pressed every bedroom into use.

"I'll put you in here," Gramma said to Mom as she led us down the hallway to the ornate bedroom.

What?

"You and Cecil can sleep in the bed and we can make a pallet on the floor for Connard and Verlon. I'll go get some things."

With Mom and Dad awake in the room, I didn't concern myself, too much, about what lay behind the glossy-white door.

One doll rested by the pillows on the bed, eyes wide and fixed.

Don't stare at me. Not so tough when you're by yourself, are you?

Mom moved the doll to a table nearby and turned down the bed. Dad climbed in straightaway.

At least that doll lay flat on the table and stared at the ceiling, instead of at me.

Take that.

Through the wall, I heard Gramma getting something from the storage closet under the hallway stairs, where she stored pillows, blankets, sheets, and quilts. Stuffed full, probably, like the last time I'd seen inside it.

Gramma returned with a load of soft things to make a pallet.

I didn't mind sleeping on the floor, my idea of camping indoors, as long as Verlon stayed on his side of our pallet. Angry at him over something—I don't remember what—I complained, wanted to make sure Mom and Gramma knew it. "I think I'm going to throw up," I said.

Gramma brought a dishpan. She and Mom acted like nurses, remained nearby, provided me reassurance. I complained about Verlon, vomited, protested, and vomited some more. When the wave of sickness passed and I'd vented my complaint, I calmed.

"Good night," Gramma said and carried the pan out of the room.

Dad snorted when Mom slipped into bed.

The room otherwise quiet, Verlon lay motionless and breathed heavy on the pallet beside me.

"Stay on your side of the bed," I whispered.

I looked around the room one last time, prepared myself for my fate. *Yep. The glossy-white door still shut.* Once asleep I'd be helpless. Gramma had put us there for good reason, must've known something I didn't. Sleepy and no crybaby, I mouthed, "Okay, okay, if you want me, come get me. I don't care."

The dolls stared at me from the fireplace mantle like a line of accusers. I couldn't tell, but one doll seemed to move. I watched. *Do it again, I dare you. No wait, don't do it.* My head had played a trick, I hoped.

I rolled onto my other side away from the dolls, facing the upright roller piano. *Now, I lay me down to sleep, oh, Jesus, don't let a ghost get me.*

* * *

"Wake up sleepy heads," Mom called.

Sleep wiped from my eyes, I raced Verlon to the breakfast table.

Yay! Another Saturday morning at Gramma and Grampa's house. Down side? No Saturday morning cartoons on TV. Up side? Another Friday-evening argument between Mom and Dad avoided.

"Do you want to go to the general store with me to sell a container of cream?" Uncle James asked me. He'd talked the cows out of a supply of milk before I'd gotten out of bed.

Going with Uncle James might be the most exciting thing I could do all day. "Yeah." I hurried my last bites of toast. Didn't want to miss a chance for adventure. Uncle James made things interesting and fun. He didn't drink, didn't swear, or get mean, unlike Dad and several of Dad's brothers.

"Put on a jacket," Mom said.

Could've guessed she'd say that. "Okay," I said, not willing to risk Mom changing her mind and not letting me go.

Upton, about two miles away and Podunk compared to Louisville, had a general store, a feed store, a pharmacy with a soda fountain, a clothing store, a furniture store, road junction with a blinking-yellow light, and two train-track crossings. Dad always slowed when we drove the main road, 31W, through town on our way to and from Gramma and Grampa's. Mom and Uncle James had told me stories of their experiences in Upton. Mom usually smiled, sometimes laughed, when she did. I'd go along with either of them whenever I could. While on the farm, Upton seemed like Disneyland. And now I'd ride the tractor to go there!

Uncle James lifted the container, placed it onto the tractor near the seat, and climbed up. "Hop on," he said, and held out one hand to help me. "Hang onto the can."

As Uncle James drove, I leaned against one of the fenders beside him. I didn't feel in danger. We weren't breaking any speed records. I fancied an excited dog could keep up. An eye out for dogs and children on the loose, I looked at the familiar houses along the road and saw two people working in their yards. Watched one car traveling the other way. *Whoosh!*

When we passed the graveyard near the stop sign at the junction with 31W, I pictured the people in their graves. Tried not to, but did anyway. Couldn't help doing that ever since I'd searched that cemetery with Mom for somebody's headstone. Couldn't remember who we'd looked for, some relative I'd never met, I think. The worst part? Sunken graves with little sinkholes, which creeped me out.

I knew if those people had died, everyone could, and from everything I'd heard, in particular Grampa's quotes of biblical verses, everyone would. Great-grampa Riggs had. And Mom, my aunts, and Gramma talked all the time about visiting dead people in funeral homes whom they'd known. So, I knew all too well that Mom could end up in a graveyard, too, and though that was the last thing I wanted to think about, I couldn't avoid it. No doubt in my mind, mean-drunk-Dad, with alcohol-angry breath and hard green eyes, could kill Mom, if he had a mind to. Nothing I could do to stop him. Mom could even die by accident. Either way, what would happen to me, if Mom died?

* * *

Uncle James slowed the tractor for a train-track crossing as we passed Hornback's Drugs.

I pointed. "I remember going in there with Mom."

Uncle James turned his head. "Yeah, I've been in there many times."

"The silver-painted walls reminded me of waffles," I said.

"Hang on," Uncle James said. The tractor shook as he eased us over the tracks.

I continued, "Mom and me sat down on stools at the long wooden counter. Fans blew air on us from the ceiling. Coca-Cola signs were on the walls. I ordered a root beer float."

Mom's way of letting me know she loved me, I had no doubt. Whenever I'd done something wrong—I usually knew when I had beforehand—she'd scold me. But we always had fun when we were on the farm, even if she'd punished me. At home, we were mostly quiet and serious. At home, I worked to not rile Dad and I'd bet my Tooth Fairy money that Mom and Verlon did, too.

* * *

"We'll park here," Uncle James said as he pulled the tractor into an open spot in front of the general store.

Mud splattered cars and trucks, their wheels, doors, fenders coated and windshields smeared, sat parked in a graveled area opposite the store from the railroad tracks.

The farmers proud to show off their caked-on dirt?

"That sure was a good ice cream float," I added as an afterthought, fingers crossed.

Wooden steps welcomed customers from the road and the side parking lots onto a covered porch, which ran along the entire storefront.

I strained to help Uncle James carry the container up the steps. "How much cream is this, Uncle James?"

"Five gallons," he said.

Both of us gripped an opposite handle near the top of the can, which felt like two tons about to pull my arms off.

Several men occupied wicker chairs on the porch. A few chairs remained empty. More men stood near the front door. Others came out of the store. Several talked of tobacco prices, others about the weather and mud. But Uncle James and I didn't have time to stop. We had important business inside.

Uncle James held open the screen door and I shuffled my way over the doorstep while I wrestled my part of the weight.

The place smelled of burned coal, bare wood, tobacco smoke, and dirt, not anything like the well-lit stores with mopped linoleum floors where Mom shopped at home.

Inside, the can set next to the counter. Uncle James told the store clerk behind the cash register, "We have some cream to sell."

A potbelly stove claimed the right side of the large room, along with a group of empty wooden chairs. Ceiling fans turned. The wood floors showed wear and smears of mud.

"How much you got?" the clerk said.

Canned goods, along with bags of white flour, lined wooden shelves taller than me.

"Five gallons," Uncle James said.

Jars of sorghum occupied a section of shelf.

"I'll put that on your credit balance."

A revolving stand at the end of one aisle displayed a variety of Burpee flower and vegetable seeds.

"Okay," Uncle James said.

At the back of the store a US Post Office sign hung on the wall of a little room.

"You ready? Let's go," Uncle James said.

"Yeah." I turned to leave.

The clerk lifted the can and started towards the rear of the store.

"Let me show you something," Uncle James said.

I followed him across the street to a spot next to the railroad tracks.

"See that stand?" Uncle James pointed to a tall, silver-painted metal frame between the store and the tracks. "That's where they hang the mailbag for the train pick-up. Want to watch?"

"Yeah." I couldn't say no to that. Sounded more exciting than selling cream. I pictured a train that would slow, or even stop, then a mailman with a dark-brown cap would lean out and grab the bag with one hand. A uniformed mailman looked important to me, like a policeman or a fireman. "Do they have to stop?" I said.

Uncle James grinned. "No, they don't need to do that."

The storekeeper brought a big canvas bag from the store and hung it on the stand.

"The train should be coming soon," Uncle James said.

We didn't wait long before a train appeared from around the sweeping bend to the north, coming from Louisville. Even at that age, I had a good sense of direction.

"Here it comes," I said.

A rumble grew. The train whistled with a long blast. The crossing bells clanged and the crossing lights flashed. The wooden-arm barriers dropped across the road. Everything warned cars and people to stay off the tracks. My heart raced. A few feet to the right and I'd be directly in front of that thing. *Jump the track and run over me?*

As a boy I understood bad things happened. I heard about bad things on TV news all the time. Police arrested criminals, cars crashed into one another, buildings burned, sick people filled hospitals, and dead people filled graveyards.

The train didn't seem to slow at all. The engineer, wearing a gray cap, his right arm propped and head tilted out the window, pulled a cord and the train whistled again. I couldn't tell if he looked at me or not.

"It's big," I said, my words drowned out by the noise. *How could anybody not know that thing was coming?*

Run. Don't run. It didn't feel much different than when mean-drunk-Dad, big, powerful, and noisy, came after Mom. But with Uncle James beside me I stood my ground, *Come hell or high water,* as long as he didn't move.

The ground shook. The engine worked hard, belched black smoke, its heavy weight on the tracks, metal against metal. Loudest thing I'd ever heard.

The engine cleared the crossing.

Whoosh!

My hair whipped about. My shirt and pants flapped.

A hook extended from one train car somewhere in the middle of the long line and snatched the mailbag from the stand. I followed the bag, saw somebody pull it into the train car as it passed by, then I looked back toward the metal stand.

Empty.

The caboose rushed by. The rumble stopped. The wind calmed. The crossing bells went silent, and the gates lifted.

The air smelled of diesel fumes and the red light on the rear of the caboose grew smaller as the train sped away, mailbag rushing south toward Nashville.

Elephants in a Pit

March 1957

As usual, Mom's worry countdown started on Wednesday, her tension worn on her blouse sleeves. And, as usual, no way Verlon and I could avoid front-row seats.

* * *

Friday's supper laid on the table, Dad nowhere in sight, we dreaded what was to come.

"Dad drunk again?" Verlon asked.

"I don't know, Hon," Mom said.

"There got to be something you can do," I said.

"Lord knows, I don't know what," she replied.

"What about Gramma and Grampa Hogan? Can't they do anything?" I said.

"I talked with your Gramma Hogan when we lived with them on Tallulah," Mom said. "She sided with your daddy, made it clear I was the outsider and could leave."

That news cut to my quick. "Why did Gramma Hogan say that?"

"I don't think she's ever cared that much for me," Mom said. "Eat your supper before it gets cold."

That added another piece of the puzzle about my family's history, though created more questions. *How did I fit into that scheme of things? And what about Verlon?* I never considered that Gramma Hogan didn't love me. I'd never had a doubt, but if she didn't like Mom, that tainted my relationship with Gramma, somehow. Unsettled, I didn't want to think less of Gramma Hogan. Wounded by that news, without doubt, a rift opened between me and Gramma Hogan.

Another half-hour passed as the chance grew Dad would arrive home tanked.

* * *

He did. On a mission, he headed straight for the kitchen. Didn't look at Verlon or me, nor say a word.

Just as well. I didn't want to draw his attention or get in his way. *How bad would it get?*

"You're late," Mom said.

"So what?" Dad answered.

"Cecil, I smell alcohol. Where's your paycheck?"

"In my pocket, where else do you think?" Dad snorted.

I didn't believe Dad one bit.

"We got another notice from the bank today," Mom said. "I thought you said you were going to make a payment. They'll foreclose on our mortgage, if we don't."

"I will. Get off my back," Dad said. "Where's my supper?"

"You know I left my job at the Dobbs House," Mom said. "You kept telling me to quit and that made me a nervous wreck."

"You said you hated that job."

"But we need extra money, because you keep wasting your paycheck on drinking."

"I told you to get off my back," Dad said.

Slap!

"Ow!"

"Shut up and get my supper."

"We'll lose the house, if we don't make a payment this month."

Slap!

"Ow, Cecil!"

"Stop hounding me," Dad said.

They grew silent. The sounds of scraping and clanking indicated Mom was fixing him a plate of food.

"Here," she said.

I noticed her go into her bedroom. A while later she told Verlon and me to get ready for bed. She'd been crying.

* * *

Saturday morning, Mom called, "Wake up, you two. Time for breakfast."

Sleep had provided me escape from Mom and Dad's argument, though I couldn't escape my dreams. I awakened with fresh impressions of falling into a deep pit between two raging elephants. I'd attempted to cross the hole on a plank, though I had fallen in. I had no way out, and stuck between the huge, angry animals, I was afraid they'd crush me. Confused by my dream, I didn't mention it.

I studied the black and blue marks on Mom's arms when she gave me breakfast cereal. I could see she'd been crying again and wanted to say something to make her feel better, but didn't know what would help. "Where's Dad?"

"At work," she said.

"Mom, what does foreclose mean?"

"The bank will take our house away, if we don't make a payment," she said.

Huh? "Then what?" I said.

105

"We'll have to move."

"Why?" Verlon said.

"The bank wants their money repaid," she said.

"They can take away our house?" I said.

"Yes," she answered. Tears welled in her eyes. "You know I tried working at the Dobbs House, but I was a nervous wreck between Cecil hounding me about working and the constant rush to get the orders out, so I quit."

"Where would we go?" Verlon said.

"You don't worry about that."

Verlon and I, quiet all morning, watched cartoons, *Heckle and Jeckle* and *Mighty Mouse*, and the westerns, *Roy Rogers* and *The Lone Ranger*. I half-expected the next fight would start when Dad returned from work.

* * *

Another weekend wrecked, a Friday night of terror, followed by a Saturday and Sunday of licked wounds in awkward silence. Now, though, things were worse because we could lose our home.

* * *

Mid-week, Mom told me, "We're going to the country this Friday."

Yay. At least, I hoped so. Maybe, another Friday evening knock-down drag-out between Mom and Dad could be avoided.

Almost Beyond Words

May 1957

I welcomed our Friday evening arrival at Gramma and Grampa's,
another blowout between Mom and Dad prevented. Blossoms on
the small fruit tree across the road from the driveway caught my eye,
reminded me of my dogwood tree.

* * *

The next morning started as one of those cool, cloud-dreary days
that could've passed for almost any other day of the year, except for
a swelter-of-summer day or a sleet-blowing-winter day. Kentucky
weather changed more often than Mom wanted me to change
my underwear, which was pretty often and more than I thought
necessary.

Chores done, Uncle James said, "Let's go fishing."

That's what I liked about Uncle James, he offered up opportunities
for adventure. Dad never offered to go fishing. I wondered if he'd
ever even baited a hook.

Uncle James gathered a ball of twine and some fish hooks, while
Mom asked around, "Who wants to go fishing?"

"Me," I said. Didn't need to ask me twice.

"It'll be fun," Mom said.

"I'll go, Aunt Bea," Betty Jo said.

"I want to go, too," Verlon chimed in.

The five of us walked east, and up the Old Road, as we called it. Uncle James had told me it connected Upton and Munfordville before 31W had been built. And, with few flat places on the farm, you were usually going uphill or downhill, though everywhere a gentle slope.

We turned right near the top of the rise, stepped off the pavement and onto the rutted dirt-rock road towards the two barns and pond. As we passed by several cedar trees, I picked a berry. I loooved the smell of cedar. No cedar tress grew in Highland Park that I knew about.

*　*　*

Betty Jo and Mom watched as Uncle James, Verlon, and I dug for worms with a pitchfork in the soft, wet, smelly dirt next to the barn.

After a few minutes we stared at the squirming handful of skinny things we'd uncovered, which Uncle James held in his hand. "These will do," he said. He dropped them into a can he'd carried from the house. "Hold this while I get us some fishing poles," he said to me.

He disappeared into the barn and a minute later appeared with five wooden tobacco sticks. He tied a piece of string he'd cut to about eight feet to each stick, then a hook to the end of each string.

"These will do," he said. "Everybody gets one."

We spread out as we worked our way down the gentle slope and as close as we dared towards the near edge of the pond.

Tracks from Grampa's cows created an uneven surface of water-filled hoof prints sunk into the mud. Cow pies dotted the bank. I'd learned to identify those even from a distance.

"Try to stay out of the mud," Mom said.

"And the cow poop," I added and giggled.

Dragonflies flitted about in connected pairs while water bugs skimmed the water's surface. Shrubs, thick brush, and small reeds grew along the opposite side of the pond, which almost formed a circle.

Uncle James pointed towards the far-right side, where a thick growth of three-foot cattails poked above the water. "We won't go over there," he said, "it's swampy."

Wouldn't dare. I couldn't see through the first inch of the brown pond water, too muddy for a swim. You'd never catch me in that. Besides, the cows probably pooped and peed in it all the time. Cows didn't seem to have any sense about where they pooped or peed. No matter where, they'd just raise a tail and let 'er rip, unlike us people who went behind the tool shed.

"I don't like touching worms," Betty Jo said. "Uncle James, can you put the worm on the hook for me?"

Bzzzzzzz!

From the telltale sound, I knew a horsefly had landed in my hair. They hung around the barn. I swatted it away with, "Don't bite me." A horsefly bite was worse than a mosquito's.

Not afraid to touch worms, Verlon, Mom, and I baited our own hooks.

Croak! A bullfrog had sounded-off from the safety of the small reeds across the pond.

Quiet for several minutes, Verlon hollered, "I got one!" He acted like he'd landed a whale, instead pulled a little sunfish out of the water. Uncle James helped him remove the busy little sharp-finned-pancake from the hook. Nothing to yell about, it looked pretty though.

Betty Jo screamed, "I got one!" She, too, pulled a small sunfish from the water. She reached to grab the fish, but pulled away when it moved. "Uncle James, will you take it off the hook for me?"

Uncle James to the rescue.

"Thank you, Uncle James," she said, then looked sheepish. "Would you bait the hook for me again?"

"You call that fishing?" I said with my library voice.

Over the next hour we caught five scrawny sunfish and a small catfish, none much bigger than my hand, before we grew bored after they'd stopped biting. Our tiny catch wouldn't provide bragging rights, much less supper. Too bony, not worth the effort to clean them. But they wiggled and jerked on the line to no end when hooked and that excited us. Well, at least Verlon and Betty Jo, who caught the most.

"One puny fish. Isn't fair," I grumbled to myself and kicked a clump of wet dirt. "I can bait a hook better than they can."

We'd taken the few steps back uphill toward the barns when Uncle James asked, "Anybody want a piece of sugar cane?"

"Yeah," the rest of us said and nodded, almost in unison.

"Stop here, I'll cut some," Uncle James said. At that point we stood next to a small stand of tall growth along the fence line near the storage barn.

"I've never had sugar cane," I said.

"We ate it all the time after we moved here," Mom said.

Uncle James selected one stalk with a reddish color at its joints. With his pocketknife he cut the stalk into four-inch sections and discarded the joints. "Here," he said and offered a piece to each of us.

The white pulpy center oozed a milky fluid. "How do you eat it, Uncle James?"

"Chew on it, then swallow the juice, but not the pulp."

My piece squeaked between my teeth as the tough, outer skin of the stalk gave way. *Sweet, but not too much.* "Mm, so that's why they call this sugar cane."

"We used to have molasses made from it," Uncle James said. "We'd cut the stalks like we do tobacco, strip off the leaves, and remove the tips where the seeds grow. A local miller would grind the stalks and distill the juice into molasses, then take half the product as his pay."

Molasses. No, thank you. I'd tasted molasses and sorghum. Didn't like either. Though sweet, they smelled and tasted like weeds, as best I could say. I couldn't understand how anyone, even Gramma and Grampa, liked molasses or sorghum, but they did. Go figure. They loved horehound candy, too, another strange, strong taste I didn't like. *What was horehound made from?*

With each bite, my piece produced less juice and became harder to chew. The stringy stalk suited a cow's teeth and stomach, not mine. *Human cud.* I spit my piece to the ground.

* * *

"You stink like fish," Mom told Verlon and me when we returned to the house. She wet a wash cloth, then ordered us, "Come over here so I can wipe your hands and faces."

Aw.

Held hostage, I missed the chance to go into town with Uncle James, sent straightaway by Grampa.

Back from his errand, Uncle James reported, "I just heard Sam Johnson was killed by a train."

"What? When?" Grampa said.

"An hour or two ago," Uncle James said.

"Aw," Mom said in a hushed tone.

Train? I pictured the train picking up the mail bag, big, loud, powerful beyond my words.

Everyone's attention riveted on Uncle James, we gathered in the living room to hear the story.

"The driver's-side door of his truck wasn't closing properly so he'd tied it shut with a rope," Uncle James explained. "He'd been driving his truck around like that for a while, I guess."

Uncle James didn't explain the way the rope had been tied but I considered that detail unimportant, even as I attempted to picture it.

"He tried to beat an on-coming train across the tracks and his engine stalled. He wasn't able to start his truck again and couldn't get out before the train hit him."

"Law, law," Grampa said as he shook his head. He'd explained he said that instead Lord to avoid a blasphemy.

* * *

Gramma had declined a trip to the scene of the accident with, "I don't need to go see that." She remained in the kitchen when the rest of us left.

Well, all of us except Dad, who swayed on the front porch swing with a lit cigarette. *What was he up to?*

At that time, I never suspected Dad of mischief while at the farm, figured he went into some vegetative state and chain-smoked cigarettes. Never crossed my mind that he might have a hidden bottle of booze strategically cached. He never appeared tipsy, nor had the smell of alcohol on his breath. Though I knew Dad to be sneaky, and I imagined he contemplated a drink now and then, he would've had great difficultly avoiding detection.

* * *

Grampa, Mom, Uncle James, Verlon, and I lined the sidewalk across the road from the wreckage. No train, no policemen, no ambulance nor tow-truck in sight, each of us conducted our versions of silent investigations. Or funerals.

"The train had been traveling north towards Louisville," Uncle James said. I felt relieved when he added, "They've already removed Mr. Johnson's body."

"Aw," Mom said in her low voice. A moment later, she repeated herself.

Hushed by the scene, although I didn't want to see Mr. Johnson's mangled truck, I couldn't help but look. From a distance I stared at the distorted pickup's remains, still where it had come to rest, I guessed, pushed down the tracks some distance from the crossing before the train shoved it aside.

I didn't know what to think. I'd seen and heard about accidents on TV and radio but hadn't been at them. But that wreck had occurred right in front of where I stood, just across the road. I could look at the whole scene and in broad daylight, which made it worse somehow.

I imagined the screech of train brakes after a terror-stricken engineer applied them. I imagined Mr. Johnson attempting to escape his truck in a panic. I imagined the violent sounds of metal crunched, torn, and twisted, glass shattered, the squeal of tires shredded off their wheels. I imagined the truck tumbling as the train forced it down the track. I wondered about Mr. Johnson's last thoughts. Didn't want to, but did anyway.

Then, I imagined me, crushed in a pick-up truck by a train.

I worked to blot those images out of my mind, as best I could. But like every other bad thing, I couldn't.

In hindsight, my ability to empathize, honed in the crucible of danger, must've stemmed from my concern for Mom when she faced Dad's wrath. I'd gained an acute appreciation for the potential of harm, not only for Mom but for myself. As well, I'd learned my farm sanctuary wasn't a perfect haven.

No Way to Make Friends

May 1957

Santa Claus had brought me a bike the previous Christmas. I'd passed the eight-and-a-half-year mark and suspected an adult conspiracy surrounded Old Saint Nick. We didn't have a chimney at my house and I'd concluded Mom and Dad had gotten that bicycle for me. The tell-tale winks and nods by TV weather forecasters no longer convinced me of the whereabouts of Santa's sleigh. And to visit all those homes and eat all those snacks? No way.

First chance, I'd said, "Can I take it outside?"

"Yes, but be careful," Mom said.

"I don't know how to ride it," I said.

"Hold onto the fence," Dad said.

Did he know how to ride a bike? Ever own one? I doubted that. I'd never seen him ride a bike, or talk of doing so. And everything I knew about his childhood pointed to a hard life of poverty, Dad one of ten kids. Gramma and Grampa Hogan didn't own their own farm and he'd been a carpenter. Talk of hand-me-downs shared between Dad and his siblings, left me to imagine no desserts at supper, no trips to the movies, and few, if any, Christmas toys and birthday presents.

Most of the time Dad left me to myself and I alternated between fear of or anger at him. I treated him like a snake in Gramma Riggs' root cellar, not sure if or when he'd bite me.

A jacket kept me warm enough in the cool air, while our driveway fence served as a good brace until I learned how to balance myself.

Lickety-split, I started to explore our street in both directions with Mom's permission.

* * *

I'd grown proficient on my bike by the first warm spring Saturday.

Encouraged to venture to the nearby basement mom-and-pop store for ice cream, I'd managed to bum some allowance from Mom.

On my way home, I spied a gathering of kids, about ten boys and girls near my age, in an empty lot. With an interest to expand my circle of friends, I rode part way across the open field before I laid my bike on its side.

"Hi," I said and pointed. "I live over there."

"What do you want?" the biggest boy said.

Their leader, no doubt, the oldest of them, maybe a little older than me.

"I wanted to come over and play."

"Let's see if he wants to join us," another boy said.

"You'll need to do what we say," the oldest said. "You'll need to play captive, if you want to join us."

What did he mean? Hesitant, I said, "Okay."

Their leader singled out another boy and pointed. "Take him over there and hold him."

What was that guy up to? I walked the few feet to the top of a dirt mound.

I stood facing the loose grouping of kids while my captor held my arms from behind.

"We're going to see how brave you are," their leader said.

He picked up a dirt clod and threw it in my direction.

The other kids followed suit.

Most clods missed me, some by several feet. Others landed at my feet. But after several hit me, I decided that had been enough.

"Let me go," I told my captor. If that hadn't proved I was brave enough, I didn't want these kids as friends anyway.

"Not yet," their leader said.

The guy holding me didn't loosen his grip while the others continued their target practice.

"Stop," I said and worked to dodge clods, though I couldn't keep up against the hail of projectiles.

One kid, a runt, threw something, which grazed my head. A sharp pain followed. *What hit me?* "That's enough!" I said and struggled to free myself. A warm trickle ran down my face.

"Let him go," the biggest kid said.

With a glance I spied an exposed nail in a small piece of wood near my feet. Dirt clods were bad enough, but no way a nail had been part of the deal. Loose from my captor's grip, I touched my face and discovered blood on my fingers.

On a beeline for the half-pint who'd thrown the wood, I didn't care who I'd need to fight. He backed away as I rushed toward him, until against the nearby building, he could go no farther.

"You hit me with a piece of wood with a nail in it, you coward!" I yelled.

He wailed and shielded himself from me as I pummeled him.

Some of the kids screamed and yelled to egg on the fight, while others scattered, though none attempted to stop me.

Exhausted, I backed away and watched the kid run to a nearby house.

I pushed my bike across the empty field to the street pavement and rode home, mostly a short downhill coast.

Not my friends. No way, no how.

* * *

116

"My God, what happened to you?" Mom asked when I entered the house. "Cecil, come look at this," she called out.

As Dad entered the room, I said, "Oh, I got hit by a piece of wood."

The dried blood on my face, my badge of courage, surely suggested a more threatening wound. My pain had diminished to an ache, though I grew more unsettled by Mom and Dad's reactions.

"Who did that?" Dad demanded.

"Some kids from the next street," I said.

Mom started to wipe my face with a wet cloth, but Dad interrupted her. "Leave it," he said. "I'm taking him to find out who did this." He grabbed a sharp knife from a kitchen drawer and tucked it into his back pants pocket. "Come on," he told me. "We'll put a stop to this."

I'd dealt with the situation as best I could, and considered it a done deal, but I wasn't past dishing a little more revenge.

"Where do they live?" Dad asked, as he drove us to the next street in a hot minute.

I pointed the way, then said as we drew near, "He went into that house."

As far as I could tell Dad hadn't been drinking that day and I didn't want to see him in a full-blown fight, but Dad wasn't hiding his anger and I was in no position to tell him what to do. At the same time though, I liked that he was standing up for me and considered that a sign that he loved me.

In hindsight, I realize Dad's poor conflict resolution role-modeling set a bad example, which I unwittingly absorbed. His MO? Let your anger build, then come on like gangbusters.

* * *

After several loud raps on the door, an older white-haired man answered.

That kid's grampa?

117

"Take a good look at what your son did," Dad said. "Hit my son with a piece of wood. Have your son come to the front door."

I noticed Dad's face had turned red and his breathing become heavy. *He could pull that knife any second.*

With the look of alarm, the older man said, "I'm sorry that your son got hurt. There's no need to have him come to the door."

"I don't want this to happen again," Dad said. "What are you going to do about it?"

"I'll talk with him about what he did."

"You do that," Dad replied.

Though Dad appeared and sounded calmer, if only a little, I eyed the knife in his pocket. Not that I could've done anything, if he'd pulled it.

"I'm sorry. I'll see to it that the boy knows not to do that again."

"Make sure of that," Dad replied. After several moments of staring, Dad turned and said to me, "Let's go."

* * *

Back in the car, he asked me, "What were you thinking?"

"I only wanted to make friends and play," I said in a half-whine, afraid Dad would lower the boom on me.

"I don't want you to go over there again," he said.

"I won't." *Not my friends. No way, no how.* You couldn't have dragged me over there again using a mule.

I never saw Dad get physical with anyone, other than with Mom, who always got the short end. I'd heard a fight he'd had with one of his brothers in our front yard after work one Friday, though. I knew Dad had a short fuse and could blow any moment once riled, with drink only making it worse.

* * *

A few days later, the middle of the following school week, I'd completed my homework before supper, and so after we'd eaten, Mom told me I could watch TV. I didn't love homework, but didn't mind it that much. At worst, homework served as nothing more than a nuisance.

I lay stretched on the couch, belly down, propped up on my elbows, minding my business, when Dad arrived home and came straight to me.

"Con*ard*," he said, with an "ard" sound as in aardvark, rather than the usual way he and Mom had always pronounced it with an "erd" sound as in shepherd.

"Don't," I said, "I'm watching TV."

"Con*ard*, Con*ard*, Con*ard*," he repeated.

"Stop. Why are you doing this?" I looked at him, noticed his fixed stare and strange grin. *Been drinking?*

"Con*ard*, Con*ard*, Con*ard*," he repeated.

"Dooon't," I said, "you're making me want to cry."

He continued his taunt, "Con*ard*, Con*ard*, Con*ard*."

"Stoooop. Why are you being mean?" I figured he loved me, pretty sure, particularly after his going to bat for me the previous weekend. But this left me puzzled.

After he relented, I decided I wouldn't let him do that to me again.

* * *

First thing the next morning while getting ready for school, and Dad gone off to work, I said to Mom, "Why is Dad so mean? I don't like him that way."

"Hon, I don't know why he gets the way he does," she said. "I do my best to get him to stop drinking, but don't know what I can do. Maybe, his anger has something to do with being in the navy during

World War Two. He woke up from nightmares for a long time after he came home."

Nightmares from hand-to-hand combat like I saw on TV? Bloody, primal, desperate eye-to-eye encounters that lead to a death. Or Marines ripped apart on Pacific Island beaches by machine guns? Must have been bad, whatever it was, but, though I visualized the worst for a moment, I couldn't bear to dwell on it.

"Oh, and we're going to the country this Friday," Mom added.

"Yay," I said to Mom, then under my breath, I whispered, "Please, please," in case that might help seal the deal.

While in Vietnam years later, I gained a greater appreciation of Dad's WWII experience. Though I never faced direct combat, living 24/7 for twelve months under the threat of harm or death, not to be announced beforehand, created constant stress, which couldn't be dismissed.

Calling me to her desk in front of the class, my fourth-grade teacher said, "You've misspelled your name," loud enough that everyone heard.

I knew full well why she thought I had.

As her accusing finger pointed to my homework, I stuck to my truth. "No, I didn't." *With two N's, that's how my name should be spelled. Harder to mispronounce.*

She tapped the paper with her finger where I'd written my name and repeated herself.

Having come that far, I didn't waver. "No, I didn't," I said and shook my head. I wondered if she'd direct me to the principal's office, but she said nothing else and sent me back to my seat.

I didn't tell her that I'd changed the spelling of my name the night before because of Dad's taunts.

I don't remember telling Mom that I'd changed the spelling of my name, but she would've seen my homework at some point. Regardless, I never told Dad, didn't want him to know. In my defiance, I'd created a safe space for myself and intended not to allow him to invade it. Years later, to finalize my decision, I sent a letter of request to the Kentucky Department of Records when I neared my eighteenth birthday. When a copy of my original birth certificate returned, a second handwritten "n" had been inserted into my first name.

Yeah. I'd achieved another small victory against mean-drunk-Dad's tyranny, though I was amazed at the handwritten change on what I considered such an essential document of record.

* * *

I worked to forget Dad's displays of rage and treatment of Mom, though fighting a losing battle. I wanted to push all the hurt and sadness out of my mind, while Mom worried openly. Too much, she said many times, which only forced me to rehash events all the more. Okay to let my guard down on the farm, but at home? I wanted not to be fearful of Dad, but what could I do? Maybe, Mom would need my help at a critical moment. Maybe, I could say something, do something, anything, to make a difference, all the difference. Propelled into a state of vigilance, I honed my radar, listened to every sound, and watched every motion for clues of what Dad might do next.

* * *

Several weeks passed as Mom and Dad continued to argue over the bills, then Mom called Verlon and me together one evening before Dad returned home from work. "I have something to tell you," she started. "Your daddy and I have decided to declare bankruptcy."

Bankruptcy? Didn't sound good to me. "What's going to happen?" I asked.

"We have to give up things like our furniture and TV, but get to keep our clothes," she said.

"Are they going to take my bike?" I said.

"No, you get to keep your personal things, but we're going to lose the house," she added.

That was the closest thing to being thrown into the streets I could imagine.

"Where will we live?" Verlon said.

"You don't worry about that," Mom said. "We're going to the country this weekend for Thanksgiving," she added with emphasis.

Dad's fault. All Dad's fault.

To me, following the news of bankruptcy, a trip to the country was a bowl of ice cream after a plateful of canned spinach.

Feeding Riggs' Army

November 1957

Wednesday, after work, Dad drove us to the country.

I sat behind him in the car. That way I didn't have to look at his face, and he couldn't see me except through the rearview mirror.

With high hopes, I asked Mom, "Is Billy coming?" as Dad eased our car up to the oak tree in front of Gramma and Grampa's house.

"I think so," she replied.

Goody. I couldn't wait.

Grampa's garage sometimes housed his tractor or car, but his Ford Falcon occupied the driveway under the bare branches of the walnut tree, and his tractor, nowhere to be seen, must have been in, or near, the barn.

"What're those barrels for, Mom?" I asked her as we got out of our car. I'd been meaning to ask about those two rusty-red-brown barrels for some time.

"Your gramma washes herself and her hair with that water," Mom said.

I'd never seen Gramma wash her face or hair, nor wear make-up or lipstick. She took care of herself with no fuss. "Why does she use that water?"

"Because it's soft."

Drawn to the nearest one, I discovered that barrel almost empty. I'd watched rainwater pour off the front porch roof into those uncovered barrels during spring rains. And I'd noticed they'd fill before summer and run dry during winter. *Soft water?* That water looked no different than what we pumped into the communal bucket from the water shed, but I accepted Gramma considered that rain-barrel water special somehow. I promised myself not to spit into the barrels.

Much later I learned that Gramma's rainwater wasn't soft, though much more so than the mineral laden water filtered through Kentucky limestone bedrock.

On the curved, dirt footpath and about thirty feet ahead of Mom, Dad, and Verlon, I couldn't make out their conversation. But I was on a beeline to the back door. Strangers, and those not familiar, approached the main entrance of the house at the front, where their knocks might go unheard in colder weather. Family and friends used the front door in summer and the back door in winter, though not consistently. Gramma and Grampa kept their bed in the living room where they spent most of their time. Closer to the back door than the front one, they could respond to visitors at the kitchen door quicker. And with a back-door approach, they could avoid the chilly hallway in winter.

* * *

I expected Uncle Tunney and Aunt Betty to come through the back door any minute, Billy in tow. Billy was the oldest of their four kids, which included Bobby, Patsy, and Deborah.

And as more family arrived, like an ant-gather swelling over a picnic sandwich, the house filled with grownup gossip and sounds of kid-play, a familiar and soothing background of noise to me and far cry from my house last Friday night.

I anticipated glorious fun with Billy. Though play with Billy held first place on my to-do list, I'd developed flexibility and an adventurous attitude toward farm visits. So, if he didn't show, though disappointed, I'd make do with back-up activities. No end to the things I could do. Maybe, I'd play with other cousins or Verlon. I could accompany Uncle James on an errand. I might help Gramma with a chore. Perhaps, I'd listen to grownup stories and pick up more tidbits about Dad's past. The possibilities seemed endless. At the very least I could entertain myself; I'd had four and a half years to perfect my methods before Verlon had arrived. And honed those skills after Mom's encouragements to play outside.

When Uncle Tunney and Aunt Betty did arrive, Billy and I joined forces.

* * *

The next morning after breakfast, a partly sunny day, cool, but not chilly, Dad and several uncles left for a rabbit hunt.

Billy didn't like rabbit hunts, though I didn't know why, so I stayed at the house with him. Besides, I wasn't keen on Dad right then anyway.

While our moms worked on our Thanksgiving feast, we kids played inside the house, until Billy said to me, "Let's go outside."

"Okay." But I asked Mom for permission, anyway.

As always, she answered, "Put your sweater on."

"Aw, do I have to?"

"I don't want you to catch a cold," she said.

Instead of rabbits, Billy and I hunted for treasures in the little dirt trench beneath the porch-roof overhang out front. Then, both of us focused on the effort, we jostled one of Gramma's rain barrels to one side in search of a fresh discovery.

"Don't spit in it," I told Billy.

"Why not?" he said.

"Because Gramma washes with it," I told him.

We looked for anything of interest that might be under the barrel, before we moved it back. Then, we played stay-away from Verlon and Bobby. The more they tried to get to us and the more we kept them at a distance, the better.

*   *   *

Early afternoon, Aunt Betty opened the front door and called out, "Dinner's ready. You kids come in and get your plates."

Didn't need to tell us twice. Hungry kids swarmed the kitchen.

Our large family gatherings required a shift-approach. Even when Gramma instructed the men to add leaves, as she called them, to make the kitchen table larger, no more than a dozen grownups could be seated at once, even when squeezed in. And with the family expanding, cousins appearing like weeds in the fields, I couldn't keep track of everyone.

The older boys joined the men at the big table or a small foldout set up nearby, likewise for the older girls when the women took their turn. The youngest kids, who needed watching, got assigned to the foldout table within sight of their mothers, if big enough to feed themselves. The littlest kids were fed on their moms' laps or while in the highchair. The kids in-between, like me, trusted to be on our own, were directed to go find a place to eat, usually in the living room or out on the porch, depending upon the weather.

Mom handed me a plate. "Get what you want and go outside," she said.

I looked over my choices, glad to serve myself. Mom allowed me to decide, once again, after my recent scare.

Several months ago, she'd told me, "Something is wrong, you're too skinny. I'm worried about you."

I hadn't felt skinny. "I'm just not hungry," I said.

Mom, suspecting a tape worm, as she'd put it, administered a teaspoon of sugar doused with turpentine, per recommendation from Dr. Gramma.

A few days later, she said, "I'm taking you to a doctor. I guess it wasn't a tape worm."

Ugh. "I don't want to go to a doctor." Didn't prevent Mom taking me anyway.

The doctor told Mom something about iron deficiency and suggested, "Give him Geritol."

My open mind about that concoction closed after my first tablespoon.

"How long do I have to take this?" I asked Mom.

"Until you start eating enough and gain some weight."

Some? What did that meant, exactly? I dreaded daily doses. Would as soon eat dirt. Decided to make an effort.

Seemed to take forever, but when the bottle emptied, I asked Mom, "Do I have to take more?"

"Just eat and I won't buy another one," she said.

No argument from me.

Even then I'd suspected my lack of appetite stemmed from my stark-raving fear of Dad.

I looked over the table. So much to choose from, so little room on my plate, and no way to keep things separate. No way I wanted cranberry sauce next to the turkey. Not a bad spot, but the juice had a way of running all over the plate when I wasn't looking. But, no time to dillydally. The men would arrive soon and I didn't want to get caught in the traffic jam nor give Mom the idea I needed more Geritol.

Mom fussed with Verlon. "Well, what do you want then?"

I gave my plate a last second check. *Everything in its right place and under control.*

"No, you can't have dessert until you finish that," Aunt Betty told Billy.

"Go outside and eat," Aunt Shirley said to her oldest daughter, Brenda, one of my younger cousins.

Mom and Gramma summoned the men to the table by name as I started down the hallway and out of hearing range of the kitchen.

"Frank, James, come to dinner," Gramma called.

"Cecil, Tunney, Walt, Joe," Mom called.

The front door propped open by one of Gramma's cast-metal irons, the screen door offered me no resistance.

Clack!

Situation surveyed, I claimed my favorite spot on the edge of the porch. Not my overall favorite place on the front porch, which was the swing, but my second. I knew the swing, hung on springs, would bounce around and excite my peas and cranberry sauce, and I couldn't have that.

At the edge of the porch, I sought elbow room, where Billy could sit next to me and I could eat in peace. The whole time I remained careful to keep my plate level. I didn't want the peas to make a break for it and roll over to the cranberry sauce. I didn't want the gravy and cranberry sauce to get wild ideas and sneak around the turkey to meet up.

Billy pulled up beside me.

I inventoried his plate. "Don't like peas?"

"Nope, never will."

Wish I could be that picky. From what I knew, Uncle Tunney didn't drink and get angry like Dad, though he seemed to hover around Aunt Betty at times. And I never heard that Aunt Betty resorted to biscuits and gravy on a regular basis. Mom fixed biscuits and gravy for us many weeks when, after one of Dad's Friday-evening binges, few other items remained in the pantry. We ate biscuits with gravy until I thought they would come out of my ears. Biscuits and gravy for breakfast, biscuits and gravy for dinner, except on those days I got lunch at school, and biscuits and gravy for supper.

"I like almost everything," I told Billy and tried to send that message to Mom using my thoughts.

Billy pulled a hard look at my plate.

"I just don't like sweet and salty together," I said.

My plate cleaned pronto, I returned for seconds of turkey, dressing, and gravy. The men, busy with their meals, discussed men-things, while several of the women hovered about in the kitchen.

"Can I have seconds?" I asked Mom. *That should impress her.*

"I'll get some for you. Give me your plate." She leaned toward the table beside Dad. "Cecil, put a little turkey, dressing, and gravy on that."

Dad put small portions of each on my plate, while I kept an eye out to make sure he didn't add cranberry sauce. I wanted to prevent the danger of a cranberry-gravy collision at all costs.

I relaxed when he told Mom, "Here."

"Come back for more later, if you want," she said.

Ah, maybe Mom had gotten my drift and I'd escaped Geritol.

In the hallway, I passed Billy and Verlon on their way to the kitchen.

"Going for more?" I asked.

"Turkey for me," Verlon said.

Billy answered, "I'm getting dessert."

My pace of eating slowed. *Pumpkin pie? Ice cream? Cake?* But before I'd finished my seconds and started for dessert, the men, done with their meals, arrived on the front porch in ones and twos. They smoked cigarettes and talked about men-things, like cars, work, and the weatherman getting the forecast wrong. *Pumpkin pie! That's the ticket.*

The table belonged to the women now. Aunt Roselee, who'd married Uncle Clifton, the next older brother to Uncle James, fed Tony, my newest cousin, placed beside her in the resident highchair.

The women chatted about women-things, like which of their children had done what, and who'd been sick or passed away. I didn't hear mention of their favorite soap-opera or color of lipstick. Word between them on other occasions had led me to understand Gramma didn't want to hear of such things discussed in her house.

I stopped next to Mom. "Can I have some pumpkin pie with whipped cream?"

"Yes, you can," she said, sounding like she felt pleased.

I hurried back to the front porch.

Billy took a bite of his cake with ice cream as I reclaimed my spot beside him, then noticed me examining his plate. "I wanted cake and ice cream," he said, with a look like what he'd picked was better.

What was he going on about? "I like pumpkin pie," I said.

I ate my way across the orange-brown sweet piece of heaven before the white blob of whipped cream melted to nothing.

In no hurry, I'd listened to the men talk before I returned my dirty plate and fork to the kitchen. There the women, done with their meal and in no rush, chatted as they cleared the table and washed the dishes.

How did they cook all that food?

Toenails and Blackheads

December 1957

I was knee deep in the fourth grade. We'd moved into a rental house on Woodlawn, the next street from Harding and closer to the Dobbs House. Same neighborhood where that gang of my captors must've lived.

Ready for Christmas, our tree up and decorated, Dad grabbed a bag of store-bought walnuts and claimed his favorite chair before he discovered his mistake.

"Where's the nutcracker?" he asked. Hardly missing a beat, he added, "Connard, go find it and bring it to me."

"Aw," I mumbled with a crinkled face. I hated doing Dad's personal errands, but that's how he operated. And in no position to refuse, I caved every time. Didn't want him after me with his two-inch-wide leather belt.

* * *

Only a few days before, I'd sat on a chamber pot in the kitchen. Our rental house had no indoor toilet, and aside from needing to use the pot, I thought I'd be safely away from another heated argument.

After another Friday evening bender, Dad raged at Mom in the next room, where they argued over money. What else? One way or another, most of their fights involved money.

"And another thing," Dad yelled, "never go to my parents' house again to complain about me!"

Slap! Slap!

"Stop, Cecil, that hurt."

What brought that on? That had been months ago. How long could Dad harbor a grudge, anyway?

"Do you know how humiliating it was to have the cops come?!"

Slap!

"I didn't know what else to do, Cecil! I told you that."

"You do what I tell you to do, understand?"

Slap!

"Yes, Cecil, I understand."

What could I do to stop Dad? Something needed to be done.

Without warning he'd rushed into the kitchen, picked up a supper plate from the table, looked at me as he threw the plate against the wall, then stormed away without a word.

I got a whiff of his sweet-booze-breath and felt ill.

I'd cringed, as the dish missed me by an arm's length and shattered into a spray. *Had he considered throwing it at me? What had I done?* I'd wanted to cry, but didn't.

* * *

Nutcracker found and delivered, Dad said, "Clean my toenails."

Oh, God. His recent rage display still fresh in my mind, I dared not say I didn't want to be within arm's reach of him. He'd requested—more like ordered—I remove blackheads from the back of his neck before. *Now, touch his feet? As bad as searching someone's hair for cooties.* I whined, "Do I have to?"

"Yes, you have to," he said.

Cleaning my own toenails was bad enough. I'd put that off as long as I could, usually until Mom had noticed and ordered me to do it.

As I slaved away, he said, "I picked up some foot rot in the jungle during World War Two. It got under my toenails."

Ewww! I pictured him knee deep in mud, mosquitoes, and leeches everywhere, and his feet covered with fuzzy growth, like green bread mold or tiny mushrooms. *Could I catch it?*

When I'd finished to his satisfaction, he pulled the car keys from his pocket. "Go out and get my pack of cigarettes from the car."

Why me?

* * *

At first glance, I saw no cigarettes in the glove compartment. *In the trunk? Probably not.* But since I had his keys, I decided to look anyway.

Ahh. Though no cigarettes, I found a boxed train set, and with that discovery Santa Claus died. I'd confirmed my suspicions of the grand adult conspiracy to sucker kids into behaving, though at the same time I thrilled over a train set.

I closed the trunk lid with a minimum of noise, then rummaged again through the glove compartment.

Pack of cigarettes found and delivered, and smart enough to avoid a confession, I kept my discovery to myself.

* * *

I couldn't wait to escape the house and play outside. When I could, I avoided the other neighborhood kids. *Not my friends. No way, no how.*

133

As it turned out, Aunt Linda had a nephew by marriage, Larry, who lived next door. Once we'd met, Larry and I fell in together, much like Billy and I. We painted our faces, stuck feathers in our hair, and played Indians every chance.

Seemed we hadn't lived on Woodlawn long, before we moved, yet again. We relocated to a rental across the railroad tracks, closer to the center of Highland Park, and near a furniture factory called Shyrick's.

The part of moving I hated most was losing another friend, Larry, and I still hadn't gotten over losing my dogwood tree.

My nightmares grew stronger, more vivid. The one of angry elephants in a pit repeated frequently and flying-escape dreams started.

Ashamed of them, I kept my deepest thoughts to myself. I tried to avoid my inner turmoil by building models of cars, army tanks, artillery pieces, ships, and airplanes, which Mom bought for me. But as hard as I tried, things would still leak out.

I'd found a discarded handbag and put a kitten in it, added some water. Then, for fun, I played toss, until I discovered I was being watched. *Busted.* Our landlady, who lived in the connected duplex, had spied me through her kitchen window. Petrified that she'd tell Mom and Dad, I acted nice to the kitten a few minutes, then released it.

Looking back, I know my anger had intensified to an unhealthy level, yet as a boy with Dad's role-modeling, I had no clue how to express it.

Shadow Dance

February 1958

Although we were at the farm, I hated the gloom of winter-gray skies and chilly winds. Dustings of light snow, which melted under bright sun and turned bare ground to mud, didn't lift my moods either. We'd suffered a long stretch of cold. Kentucky weather felt less predictable than a rabbit when flushed from hiding and running a zigzag escape pattern. Who knew when we'd see the return of short-sleeved-shirt warm days?

But one good thing: Mom, Dad, Verlon, and I had Gramma, Grampa, and Uncle James all to ourselves.

Cooped up in the house, Gramma and Mom cleared the table after breakfast and the men sought the warmth of the potbelly stove in the living room.

I spied a little book that Grampa kept on a small wooden stand near the kitchen table. Curious—at nine, I'd learned to read well enough—I picked it up, a *Farmer's Almanac*, and thumbed through the pages.

The little book suggested best times to plant and harvest, and provided weather forecasts. ". . . the last frost for the season would be late April. . . ."

How could they know the weather months ahead? Must be some superstition, hocus-pocus, or just plain guessing. Even Grampa, Uncle

James, and Dad complained that weathermen couldn't get their weather forecasts right most of the time. Seemed nobody could tell the future. I couldn't. For sure, I couldn't predict when Dad would come home drunk. Wouldn't take my weekly allowance money to the bank based on that almanac. No way, no how.

But I did find the explanations for new and waxing moons. Turned out, the man in the moon not only didn't use wax, he didn't exist.

*　*　*

Before supper, pitch-black outside, Grampa asked, "James, would you build a fire in the front room?"

Grampa meant the most often used bedroom in the front of the house.

Heat from the coal stove in the living room encouraged me to remain in my favorite spot on the couch nearby.

When he returned a few minutes later, Uncle James announced, "It'll be warmed up by the time we're done with supper."

Yay, an inside campfire!

*　*　*

After supper, our migration to the front room began. Dad and Uncle James led the way, while Verlon and I hurried behind. With a limp, Grampa brought up the rear of us men. Mom and Gramma remained in the kitchen to clean up.

Favorite chair claimed, Dad asked, "Think the weather will be any good for a rabbit hunt tomorrow, James?"

"Well, Cecil, the weather report said it might snow several inches tonight but if it's clear in the morning that shouldn't be a problem."

"Let's see how it looks in the morning, then," Dad said.

A group of wooden chairs, arranged in a semi-circle, faced the fireplace where several pieces of wood burned. The electric ceiling light and two electric lamps remained off, as well as a coal-oil lamp left on a chest of drawers. The light provided by the fire—all we needed once our eyes adjusted—made the room cozy. A supply of wood, carried in by Uncle James earlier in the day, lay in a low stack off to one side of the fireplace.

Two large beds, one on each side of the fireplace, dominated the high-ceilinged room.

I moved my chair closer to the fire and extended my hands even closer. I pictured a gentle, rolling, white-covered landscape and imagined icicles from roof edges. Unlike everything outside, shrouded in blackness and blasted by sharp-stinging wind, I felt protected.

Mom and Gramma chatted as they came down the hall. They continued without pause when they entered the room and took seats.

"I think I'll bake a cobbler tomorrow," Gramma said.

Got my vote. "I like peach cobbler, but I like blackberry cobbler more," I said. *Hint, hint.*

"I brought some cake mix," Mom said. "Thought I would bake a cake, but if you're going to do a cobbler, the cake can wait. Maybe, you can show me how to make the cobbler crust from scratch."

Their chairs squeaked as they settled in and shifted their weight.

"Yes, I can," Gramma said. "The crust is easy, Bea. You just roll in some lard, butter, milk with flour, but I'll show you."

Yum. I could hardly wait. "I looove cobblers." Not to leave it to chance, I added, "Can you do a blackberry one, Gramma?"

"Yes, I can make you a blackberry cobbler," she said with a grin.

That Gramma would do that made me feel special. She didn't always bake blackberry cobblers, but her willingness to do that meant that I was loved, like Mom's efforts to buy lemons or tomato juice for me.

Pop! Crack! Sizzle! The fire added to the conversations of familiar, soothing voices. I'd learned in school that people passed knowledge by word of mouth before they'd invented written language.

A gust of wind pushed against the windows.

My imagination danced with our shadows on the ceiling and walls. I pictured people gathered around fires in woods, in caves, and tee pees. I imagined they sang, joked, talked about the next day's weather, and discussed hunting plans. I guessed they watched the flames and kids studied their shadows dancing behind them.

I couldn't imagine a better place to be right then, peaceful, pleasant, welcoming. Couldn't have been any more different than what it was like at home.

"It's getting a little warm," Grampa said. The wooden legs of his chair screeched as he pushed back from the fireplace a couple of feet.

The heat toasted my hands and face. I moved my chair back, too.

Everyone could join the conversation, whenever they wanted.

"A Jehovah's Witness came to the other door," Grampa started. "Well, I set him straight."

Grampa could discuss others' wayward beliefs with them any time of the day without prior notice.

He continued, "Gave him a what for, I did."

I imagined some dumbfounded guy at the front door, at a loss and machine-gunned with Grampa's biblical passages, cited chapter and verse, until he'd withered.

"Does anybody want some hot chocolate?" Mom asked.

"I do," I said, no hesitation.

"Me, too," Verlon said.

"No, not for me," Grampa said.

Mom looked at Dad. She emphasized the two syllables in his name, "Ce-cil?" She often used that technique on me to express annoyance or get my attention. Worked like a bullhorn and I hated it.

Dad shook his head. "No, I'm good."

Mom turned to Uncle James.

"I'd like some, Bea," he replied.

"Time for another one," Dad said and tossed a fresh piece of wood on the fire.

Embers danced in the fireplace. Smaller ones disappeared up the chimney; larger ones fell back into the fire. Some, spat out by the fire in an arc, landed on the concrete pad in front of the fireplace. One, on a bold escape plan, made it all the way to the wood floor, where, when it didn't die within a breath or two, Uncle James' well-placed foot crushed it.

"I'll go make some, then," Mom said.

A spate of glowing embers on the concrete faded away in star-light twinkles.

"I'll help you," Gramma said, before Mom could get to the bedroom door. Tough and thin, Gramma's stamina seemed endless, even though she'd given birth to eleven children.

"Oh, you don't need to, Mom."

I heard them chatting on their way down the hallway.

"Well, I don't think he'll be coming back anytime soon," Grampa continued. "And I told him to tell the rest of those Witnesses not to bother me and waste my time with their nonsense."

And that was the end of that!

After a few moments of silence, my mind on hot chocolate, Uncle James said, "How's work going, Cecil?"

That was Dad's cue. "All right, I guess." He chuckled. "John, a real greenhorn, started work last week and was supposed to help me build an outhouse. Never done a lick of carpentry in his life. Couldn't drive a nail. Didn't know how to read a tape measure. So, I said to him, 'Go get me a right-handed screwdriver from that toolbox over there.'"

That got my interest. I'd never seen a right-handed screwdriver. When Dad told stories, I'd listen for every scrap of information

I could get. He talked about work mostly with a few war stories scattered in, like the seeds of a watermelon.

Dad chuckled again. "Ten minutes later John came back with a screwdriver. I told him, 'Take that back, that's a left-handed screwdriver.'"

Dad paused.

I heard Mom and Gramma in the hallway and pictured cogwheels turning in Dad's head.

As the bedroom door opened, Mom asked, "Okay, who's ready for hot chocolate?"

In order to claim dibs, I said, "Me," without hesitation.

"Me, too," Verlon said.

Dad continued, "After another ten minutes, he came back and said, 'I can't find one.' So, I told him, 'Well, somebody must have taken it. Bring one to work tomorrow.'"

Dad and Uncle James chuckled.

Grampa shook his head. "Law."

Mom, Gramma, Verlon, and I remained quiet. *What did we know about the finer points of carpentry?* I sipped my hot chocolate.

"Well, you know how that went?" Dad continued. "The next day John came to work and, in all seriousness, told me, 'I couldn't find a right-handed screwdriver, Cecil.'"

Dad and Uncle James chuckled and Grampa shook his head.

Something's up.

"'Well, you'll just have to learn to use that one with your left hand,' I told him," Dad said.

Dad and Uncle James laughed even louder.

Yep. Dad was pulling a fast one.

It would be a few years later, when I'd spent time with Dad on his construction projects and after he'd started working independently, that I finally got the joke.

"Well, I think I'll head off to sleep," Grampa said.

"I've already made up the bed," Gramma told Grampa before he could get clear of his chair.

A round of good-nights followed. Creaks from the wood floor announced Grampa's heavy steps and slow progress out of the room.

"Let's make up your beds," Gramma said to Mom.

After they'd sorted out a blanket and quilt on the bed for Verlon and me, and did the same on the other bed for Mom and Dad, Gramma announced, "It's time for me to go to bed. Good night, everybody."

Another chorus of good-nights followed.

Then, ninja-Gramma turned her attention elsewhere and moved out of the room with a whisper of noise.

Uncle James stoked the embers and threw the last of the wood onto the fire. Tiny red-hot sparks swirled, and disappeared up the chimney.

Wasn't long until the crackles and pops faded away, and the conversation settled on talk about the fire and the glow of embers. Then that talk faded, too, as the burnt wood crumbled into ash and the light dimmed. Somehow, I felt connected to all the people, past and present, who'd ever gathered around a fire.

"Well, I guess I'll turn in," Uncle James said.

Dad took a deep breath and sighed. "Yeah, me too. We'll see about that rabbit hunt in the morning."

"Time to get into bed," Mom told Verlon and me.

"Aw," I moaned. I wasn't sleepy. I wanted to hear more. But after a short pause, I knew that the stories had ended for the night, so I hurried to remove my shoes, shirt, and pants, and I jumped into bed. Verlon had already claimed the side closest to the wall.

"Brrrrrrr." I squirmed and kicked under the cold covers.

Verlon squirmed beside me.

"Stay on your side of the bed," I said.

"You stay on your side," he replied.

Up to my chin, the thick, heavy covers and quilt weighed me down so I could barely move, but warmed me like a good coat and somehow made me feel safe. I knew in the morning I'd have to leave the warmth of the bed for a cold room, then realized there had been no mention of the radio or TV all evening. At home, I would've watched TV until bedtime, once I'd completed my schoolwork.

* * *

Dreams of places and people I didn't recognize, doing and saying confusing things, faded away as I woke to scratch an itch. I'd been flying, too, which made no sense. I knew I couldn't fly, though wished I could whenever Dad and Mom argued.

The next morning, Mom opened the bedroom door. "Get up lazy heads, breakfast is ready." As she closed the door behind her, she looked back at us, smiled, and said, "It snowed last night."

I worked up the nerve to face the cold. Jumped out of bed and put on my clothes as I glanced through the window. "Brrrrrrr." The ground was covered in white and I thought about a rabbit hunt in the snow. "Beat you to the kitchen," I told Verlon.

"Uh-uh," he said.

We raced to hot breakfast at the kitchen table.

How cold was it outside?

No Place Like a Home

August 1958

B etween the fourth and fifth grades, I was nine and wallowing in the school-free glorious days of summer when Mom delivered the news to Verlon and me. "We're going to move in with your aunt, Aileen. We may stay with her for a while."

Semi-nomadic, that's what we were. "Moving again?" I said. I didn't mind leaving that house, mostly. I hadn't planted a tree there, like the dogwood on Harding.

"Why are we moving again?" Verlon asked.

I could've answered that. Money. More precisely the lack of it. Dad's fault, all Dad's fault.

* * *

I didn't mind living with Aunt Aileen and Uncle Tyke. I liked them. Aunt Aileen was my favorite of Dad's three sisters and they had an indoor toilet!

We hadn't lived with Aunt Aileen that long when Mom went for a week's rest in the hospital. Seemed that lasted forever.

I didn't quite understand the idea of a rest in a hospital. Sick people went to hospitals, but Mom hadn't seemed sick. What was I missing?

I don't recall Verlon being at Aunt Aileen's at that time. Maybe, other relatives looked after him.

I didn't know my way around Aunt Aileen's neighborhood, didn't want to learn, instead I remained inside. Why bother? Our stay was to be temporary, though I didn't know for how long. In Mom's absence I was quiet and withdrawn. I listened for what seemed hours to Aunt Aileen's 45rpm record collection, and felt comforted by her presence.

"Honeycomb, won't you be my baby, oh, Honeycomb be my own. . . ."

I understood even then that I searched for close connections, connections without doubts and conflict, connections with people who were calm, understanding, and peaceful. Aunt Aileen was one such person and I loved her for that. Not until much, much later did I realize that the barrier I'd erected to shield myself from Dad had trapped me within.

When Mom returned, her visit to the hospital didn't get much air time. Hush, hush.

But without doubt Dad either drank less, or hid it well, and Mom and Dad didn't fight at Aunt Aileen's.

* * *

On school mornings, Dad dropped me at James Russell Lowell Elementary, where I started the fifth grade, just days before I turned ten. Our talk sparse, I didn't have much to say to Dad and he didn't have much to say to me, instead we listened to the radio on the way.

As winter settled in and the temperature fell, exhaust clouds and frost on car windows reflected my gloom, the low point to which I considered my family had descended. I blamed Dad. His fault, all his fault. Fact was, Dad drank, couldn't keep money in his pants, and we suffered.

As I've thought about it over the years, I've developed a suspicion Dad hadn't kept his private parts in his pants, either. I wasn't dumb; even as a kid I picked up ideas watching TV.

* * *

Midway through the fifth grade, Mom pulled Verlon and me aside. "We're going to move into our own house." She sounded excited.

Again? "Where?" I said.

"Fairdale."

"Where's that?" Verlon said.

"Not far from the airport," Mom said.

I'd never heard of that place. "When?"

"This coming weekend," Mom said.

A mixed blessing. It's not that I thought that we'd live with Aunt Aileen forever, but this was a last-minute deal. At least, I could ride my bike and roam freely, I hoped. But each move meant learning a different place and different people. I dreaded starting over in school and making friends.

I postponed telling my teacher I'd be leaving. Just couldn't work up the courage. I considered my leaving a bad reflection upon me and anyway I liked her. After lunch that Friday, my last day, I'd stalled as long as I could, thought I would bust, until I blurted the news. Not angry, more surprised and concerned for me, she shifted into high gear. I watched her rush to complete notes on a report card and papers for me to take. I wished I didn't have to leave and felt bad that I hadn't told her sooner.

Chamber pot in tow, we moved into a rental house in Fairdale, one with no indoor bathroom, no toilet, no tub, no shower. Instead, an outhouse stood about thirty yards from the back door and adjacent to a two-floor garage.

The two-floor garage, which had a phone, would've been a better place to live than the house, except it lacked insulation. I liked the idea of an upstairs.

A church occupied the property on one side of our house, with a partial intervening fenced-residence where its preacher lived. Behind that house, an open area provided easy access between our yard and the church property.

Two houses occupied the lot, one in the front and one in the back, on the other side of our house.

* * *

Straightaway, without a bathroom, tub, or shower, Mom resorted to giving Verlon and me sponge baths in the kitchen sink.

I didn't want Mom to see me naked. Forced to sit on the countertop with my feet in the sink filled with water, I loathed my sponge baths like a cat.

* * *

Our first Sunday there, about mid-morning, Dad told me, "Go empty the chamber pot in the outhouse." No ifs, ands, or buts.

Verlon and I'd taken turns with that chore the first week and I'd dreaded every trip.

I peeked out the back door. *Oh, God.* People milled outside the church buildings. Getting fresh air between services, I figured. With nothing to hide behind, no way I could avoid being seen.

"Do I have to do it right now?" I whined.

"Yes, you have to do it right now," Dad said.

In broad daylight? In front of all those people? Why now? Why me? Why didn't we have a bathroom with a toilet? Your fault Dad, all your fault. He'd drunk us out of house and home. We'd lost nearly everything when we'd left our house on Harding.

"Can't I wait a little while?" I said.

"No, I want you to take it now," Dad said. He sounded angrier.

What was with him? Near tears, I took a firm grip of the wire handle, as well as a lungful of air, and, with a heave, swung the back door open and started across that thirty yards of no-man's land.

Ashamed, though I couldn't, wouldn't say it, questions swirled in my brain. Ashamed of the chamber pot, which everyone could easily identify? For sure. Ashamed that anyone would immediately know what filled it? Absolutely. Ashamed for my sense of poverty because we lived in a house with no bathroom and needed a pot? Definitely. Ashamed that some of the kids in my class and school might recognize me and blab around? Totally.

Don't look at them. Keep moving. Walk as fast as you can. Be quiet, avoid big gestures. I swung my free arm to counterbalance the weight of the near-full pot as I hurried with short steps. All the while I hoped to avoid a total spill from a mishap or a slosh from a bump against my leg, either of which would surely draw stares.

Once I'd reached the outhouse, I didn't know what was worse, the smell inside the outhouse or the chamber pot when dumped. I did my best to hold my breath, but that didn't prevent me from gagging.

After that first Sunday I worked to time my trips when I didn't see people outside the church.

My shame, our poverty, caused by Dad's drinking. Dad's fault, all Dad's fault.

* * *

Didn't take long for me to meet Freddie after we'd moved in. He lived right across the street from Fairdale Elementary where I'd joined a fifth-grade class mid-year. I had a straight shot from my house alongside the church, then down a gentle-sloping field to Freddie's back door, not more than two football fields.

We hung out together, exploring nearby woods, taking bike trips farther and farther from home, though I paid attention to Mom's orders about when to return, usually by suppertime.

Dad

"Cecil" Woodrow Hogan, US Navy

1941, 17 or 18 yo.

Mom

Beatrice "Bea" Roberta (Riggs) Hogan

Circa 1942, 17 or 18 yo.

"Four Generations" - Mom, Grampa, Great-grampa, and I pose for what is likely the only existing photo of the four of us together.

Beatrice "Bea" Roberta (Riggs) Hogan
James "Frank" Riggs
"Thomas" Barnett Riggs
"Connard" Hogan, 3 yo?

Circa 1950?

Brother "Verlon," Dad and I pose in a happier moment for perhaps the only photo of just the three of us together.

"Verlon" Hogan
"Cecil" Woodrow Hogan
"Connard" Hogan

Circa late 1954

"Uncle James" holds cousin "Timmy," their oldest son, and "Aunt Brenda"
stands alongside, while the pump house (left), the chicken coop (center),
and the tool shed (right) occupy the background.

"James" Russell Riggs
Timothy Riggs
"Brenda" Sue (Bennett) Riggs

Circa 1966

Gramma and Grampa pose with the big house (left),
tool shed (center), and garage (right) in the background.

"Ada" Pearl (Priddy) Riggs
James "Frank" Riggs

Circa 1970

The main farmhouse, aka "big house," approached from
Upton on the Old Road.

Circa 1960?

"Uncle James" and "Aunt Brenda" pose during a visit with my parents.

"James" Russell Riggs
"Brenda" Sue (Bennett) Riggs

Circa 1990

*Mom and Dad pose in one of their latter photos together prior to Dad's
diagnosis of lung cancer at an unknown location.*

Beatrice "Bea" (Roberta) Hogan
"Cecil" Woodrow Hogan

Circa 1990

Gramma provides a gentle smile in one of her last portraits.

"Ada" Pearl (Priddy) Riggs

1992

Misadventures

March 1959

B illy started it.
 "Let's go in there," he whispered and turned the knob on the hallway door to the ornate bedroom.

Easter signaled a large family gathering at the farm, always fun and involved a basket of chocolate, I hoped, along with egg hunts and play with cousin Billy.

Midday on that sunny Saturday beforehand, family members had scattered within the house and across the farm. Most of the women congregated in the kitchen. Several men had gone on a rabbit hunt while others talked on the front porch. Kids played together in their own selective groupings. Billy and I took advantage of a rare opportunity to spend quality time together without the nuisance of Verlon and Bobby.

Two ten-year-old boys in the room would surely scare away any ghost behind the glossy-white door, and the dolls, waiting to come to life, wouldn't dare say a peep.

"Alright, but be quiet," I said as we crept in. With no noises from behind us in the hallway, I eased the door shut.

First thing Billy said was, "Hey, look, a telephone."

An old phone, resting on the floor near the door, leaned against the wall.

Like phones I'd seen on TV and in old movies, I listened through its ear part, cranked the handle, and imagined I heard a gentle female voice say, "Operator." And, you know, in the way that sounds like you're pinching your nose. "Connect me to Upton 2345, please." I giggled.

"Let me take a turn," Billy said.

I handed the ear-thingy to him.

He held it to his ear a moment. "Let's take it apart," he whispered and laid the telephone flat on the floor.

"We might get into trouble, Billy."

He paid no attention.

I couldn't help myself. Had to join in.

Mute, we sat side by side. A piece from here and part from there, the phone lay helpless in the presence of twenty busy-boy fingers.

* * *

Midway through our work, Billy lost interest.

"I'm tired of it," he said.

But I was all in. "Let me do it," I told him.

Billy moved to the side, looked on, like some supervisor-boss. I moved to take his spot on the floor, the phone between my legs. Phone parts spread across the floor like a jigsaw puzzle, I felt proud of myself.

I'd almost completed my work, when the bedroom door opened and Uncle Clifton looked at both of us. "We've been looking all over for you two." He turned and called out to the rest of the world, "Here they are." He turned back toward us and said, "What are you doing?"

"Nothing," Billy said.

"We're taking the phone apart," I said. I knew we couldn't lie our way out of it and I didn't want to get my mouth washed out with Gramma's lie soap.

The adults stopped at the door as they arrived on the scene. Each repeated a similar question or observed the obvious before coming in to hover over Billy, me, and the phone parts on the floor.

Grampa arrived last. "Law, law," he said as he shook his head and surveyed the situation.

No one asked me the obvious question; can you put it back together? I figured they thought I was too dumb. The phone didn't have that many parts and I'd taken it apart. Most of it, anyway. Figured I could put the phone back together. Felt pretty sure I could. Thought I might be able to. Was willing to try.

Unfortunately for Gramma and Grampa, as well as their telephone, no one else knew how to reassemble it, so they assumed I couldn't either, but at ten, who was I to question their beliefs? I'd heard several aunts, uncles, even Mom once, say, "Kids are too young to understand." *Understand what?* I always thought, knew, that I understood more than they gave me credit.

Otherwise quiet, I watched Grampa gather up phone parts as Mom lifted me by an arm. "What were you thinking?" she said as she led me out of the room.

Billy got similar treatment.

I didn't answer Mom, hoped she wouldn't tell Dad, who hadn't appeared on the scene. I didn't dare say a word, which I figured would only get me deeper into trouble. I feared the wrath of God and understood Grampa knew how to deliver wrath. Grampa wouldn't hit me, he'd deliver a biblical tongue-lashing, but Dad might use his belt or hand.

While Mom dragged me down the hallway, I waited for the bomb to drop. *What punishment was in store for me?*

"I've got something for you to do," Mom said. "We have a bunch of eggs to color."

Color Easter eggs? Mom was shielding me. Relief!

* * *

The next morning, Easter Sunday, Mom's words roused Verlon and me. "Time for breakfast, sleepy heads."

I'd fallen asleep worried the phone surgery would be the end of me, and hoped I'd redeemed myself by coloring boiled eggs. Hoped I'd get a basket left by the Easter Bunny near my bed, much like gifts left by Santa Claus under a tree, or coins left by the Tooth Fairy under my pillow. Had always gotten one as far back as I could remember.

Phew! My worst fears laid to rest. An Easter basket occupied a nightstand near me, filled with chocolate in various shapes. Verlon had one, too.

Hot diggity. Chocolate eggs, a chocolate bunny, small yellow marshmallow chickens, what we sometimes called Peeps, and an assortment of jelly beans all lay mixed in a layer of stringy green plastic grass.

I noticed Verlon looking my way. "Keep your hands off mine," I said.

"Don't touch mine, either," he replied.

"They're both the same," Mom said. "You don't have to squabble."

That eased my mind, a little. I pictured last year's Easter activities. Eggs, eggs, eggs, a multitude of them, which seemed endless, all boiled and colored. Everyone got the opportunity to hide eggs, hunt eggs, toss eggs, eat eggs. We'd hunted inside and outside the house in groups of kids only, different age groups of kids, adults only, and everyone together. Later, once we'd tired of hunting, everyone congregated on the front lawn to toss eggs or run relay races carrying eggs with spoons. Best of all, one of the men—they took turns—ponied up loose change from their pockets as cash prizes.

Cold, hard cash. Talk about motivation. Even Gramma and Grampa loved to win cash.

Along the way we'd dropped eggs or stepped on them by mistake and squashed some flat. Eggs with cracked shells were considered out of commission, and as our breakfast wore off, we'd welcome them as handy snacks. By day's end, boiled eggs had come out of our ears and eggshells had littered the yard in little scattered piles. But all that would come again later today.

Ooh. One little chocolate egg squished between my teeth.

Mom hadn't left the room and spying this, hustled me off to the kitchen table with, "You need to eat a proper breakfast."

After my breakfast of milk, two fried eggs from Gramma's chickens, bacon, probably from one of Grampa's pigs, and toast with Gramma's homemade blackberry jam, I started off to inventory my Easter basket loot.

Mom must've read my mind. "Save some for later," she said before I cleared the kitchen doorway.

Having liberated several pieces of chocolate from my basket, the outdoors called. I realized the potential of that which was going to waste. For now, as the women cleaned up in the kitchen and collected their wits, and the men hunted or talked in the living room, we kids could play free of parental presence.

I'd grown more familiar with those cousins I spent time around, ones nearer my age, even more so the boys. I never had a problem finding one cousin that shared an interest, within reason, though Billy remained my go-to when available. Beyond that, a gap in interests increased with age differences. At about five years the divide acted like some natural boundary. Cousins grouped together like clumps of weeds sprouted across a new-plowed field. With those whom I played, we engaged in what I considered fun, never anything sinful, except for the phone surgery me and Billy had performed.

Eager to enjoy Billy's company and live free, I sought him out. "Let's go outside and play," I suggested.

Billy needed no encouragement, nor would my other cousins.

He leaned toward me. "Yeah, let's go outside," he whispered, like he was planning a jail break.

But the word got out and a throng of restless boys and girls, confined inside the house overnight and through breakfast, swarmed. We gathered strength until we burst through the front door in search of fresh air and freedom from parents.

The morning sun warmed my face. Scattered cotton-ball clouds floated above. A small fruit tree waited across the road from the driveway.

"Let's climb it," Billy said.

Reminded of my dogwood tree on Harding, I broke into a run to stake our claim. *I missed my tree. Dad's fault, all Dad's fault.*

Mom, Gramma, and my aunts had drummed into me to look both ways before I crossed the road. Hardly breaking stride, I listened for the telltale sounds of a straining engine and whine of tires on the rough asphalt. *A car coming?* I looked both ways as I reached the near edge. With plenty of practice observing mean-drunk-Dad, I'd grown antenna. I'd gotten good at noticing details.

As younger cousins followed, they screamed like an ice-cream man had arrived. Too busy with their ideas of fun, I worried some wouldn't bother to check the road.

Tiny white blooms covered the tree's branches and green sprouts of leaves emerged everywhere. Several branches grew low to the ground.

Billy, close behind me, caught up as I reached the tree. "What did you get for Easter?"

I grabbed a branch about head high. "I got chocolate, some jelly beans, and little chickens," I said as I put my foot onto the tree's lowest branch.

Billy looked puzzled. "Little chickens?"

"Yeah, you know, those yellow marshmallow thingies." I pulled myself up and sat on the branch, big enough for me to lay back on, if I kept one foot against the trunk.

"Oh, me, too," Billy said.

Bobby and Verlon moved closer to the tree. "Let us climb up, too," Verlon said.

"Oh, all right," I said. Giving Billy an eye roll, I held onto a smaller branch higher up for balance and scooted out on my branch. "Don't come out on the branch, you'll break it," I told Verlon.

Other cousins gathered around the tree like Gramma's chickens foraging across the backyard. Billy, Bobby, Verlon, and I hung in the branches, like modern-day monkeys without tails.

The familiar sounds of an approaching vehicle grew louder. Any car's approach always seemed sudden, heard from beyond the gentle rises in both directions of the road.

"Stay out of the road," I said. I'd almost been hit crossing Crittenden Drive near home with Mom.

She had led the way. After she'd checked traffic that was sitting at a nearby stoplight, she yelled, "Go!" and made a dash across the street. I'd wondered was that safe? After a moment of hesitation, I followed. Meanwhile, the traffic light changed. When I'd gotten midway across the four-lane street, the oncoming cars slowed within a few feet of me and blared their horns. Seems Mom's timing hadn't been that good and my delay hadn't done me any favors.

* * *

I realized the fruit tree offered no safety from a car, but didn't want to give up my spot. Younger cousins whooped and hollered, none of us more than ten feet from the pavement and with only a shallow ditch between us and the road. Not huge like a train, but as powerful to us kids, nothing could prevent that car from veering off the road. It could run into the tree or graze it. It could wipe us all out and continue across the field as far as I could throw a baseball before it stopped.

The whine of tires and engine strain increased.

I saw the car top the rise from the east, heading towards Upton at forty to fifty miles an hour. The gears shifted, the throttle opened, the horn blared. That reminded me of facing down that train with Uncle James.

I crossed my fingers. No one else seemed to take notice. "Stay out of the road," I yelled. Would this car veer off the road, seek us out like in some episode of *Twilight Zone*? Only one driver in the car, I didn't study him after first glance, instead kept my eye on the car's front wheels.

Two seconds, three seconds. *Whoosh!*

Years later, I realized that my skills of vigilance, developed around Dad, served as a double-edged sword during my stint in Vietnam. A constant scan for potential threats generated heightened stress. Yet, it restrained me from a more haphazard, careless attitude that could've gotten me killed.

A moment later, I looked at Billy, loosened my grip on the tree, and felt a brush of air.

Maybe, playing in that tree hadn't been such a good idea. I didn't always make the best decisions, but if I could face down a train and a car, maybe someday I could face down mean-drunk-Dad.

Come to think of it, none of Gramma's chickens were in sight. I'd never seen them in the front yard or across the road. If you asked me, why the chicken crossed the road, I'd have told you it sure wasn't one of Gramma's. Her chickens weren't that stupid.

The front door opened. "Come back inside the house so we can start hiding eggs," Aunt Betty yelled.

Billy and I abandoned our claims of conquest.

Another car coming? Nope.

"Let me see what you got in your basket," Billy said, not satisfied with my previous answer.

"If you let me see what you got in yours," I said, not satisfied with his.

* * *

Billy and I compared baskets.

Assured we'd probably received the same amount of chocolate booty, I returned my basket to its hideout, then liberated another piece before I headed to the living room.

"Okay," cousin Betty Jo said. "You're all gonna stay in here until the eggs are hidden and we can start the hunt."

Younger cousin Brenda stomped her foot. "Hurry up."

Wasn't long before someone shouted the signal from the front yard, relayed down the hallway, "Okay, we're ready."

Betty Jo helped shepherd the waist-to-chest-high crowd of egg hunter-gatherers down the hallway to the front door.

I fancied we were prepared for our equivalent of the great Oklahoma Land Rush. I'd recently learned about that in school.

"Okay," Betty Jo warned, "be careful going out the front door." She held the door open while the crazed mob rushed through and fanned out across the yard.

"I found one, I found one," one of my younger girl cousins said. I glanced over. She proudly held it up for her onlooking mother to see.

The older ones of us, like me, stayed busy. We scooped up eggs as fast as we could spot them.

Aha, there's one. I closed in on it.

"It's mine. I saw it first," Verlon said.

I grinned. "I got to it first."

"Uh-uh," he protested.

"Uh-huh," I said, off in search of my next find.

I won some prizes. I lost some prizes. I mean to say, I felt entitled to win all the time and felt cheated when I didn't. And I always listened for a car anywhere in the front yard. I didn't want to end up possum-road-kill that I'd see here and there.

* * *

Not long after Easter, news of Uncle Dave's murder circulated.

Mom, Uncle James, and my other aunts and uncles called him Uncle Dave, and so to avoid confusion I did too, though he was my great-uncle, Grampa's brother, and Carl William and Gerald's grampa.

The first detail I recall must've been immediately following Uncle Dave's funeral service. Family members gathered at his farm house, located about twenty miles out of Upton. I couldn't help but think of Great-grampa Riggs who'd lived, and was buried, less than a mile farther down the road.

Carl William, Gerald, Verlon, and I decided to escape the adults in the house, and out of curiosity or compulsion, went to investigate the scene of the crime.

Thirty yards from the house, we stopped at the pipe-tube cattle gate that separated Uncle Dave's property from his neighbor's and provided his neighbor access to the public road. I guessed they'd argued over easement rights.

"This is where Grampa Dave died," Carl William said.

That's where Uncle Dave died? No signs of what had occurred.

Based on what I'd heard, I imagined the exchange between Uncle Dave and his neighbor had turned pointed and oppositional. Tensions rose, and to demonstrate his resolve, the neighbor raised his rifle as a threat, which didn't deter Uncle Dave. Then, as the neighbor's anger boiled over, he'd pulled the trigger. To accentuate his point, he shot Uncle Dave five more times.

After an unplanned moment of silence, the four of us milled around a few minutes, then gravitated towards the house.

"Grampa's clock stopped when he died," Carl William said.

"I don't believe that," I said. *Bunkum. Carl William's got his facts wrong.*

Carl William insisted, "It's true."

Once back in the house, I studied the grandfather clock. *No, couldn't have stopped.*

In hindsight I can believe that, without attention, the clock had simply run down.

I didn't know what to make of Uncle Dave's death. I knew about gun violence. I'd seen plenty examples on the TV news, though it involved people I'd never met. I didn't know Uncle Dave well, but as family, his death imposed upon me the fact that life on Gramma and Grampa's farm couldn't shield me from the world, in spite of my wishes otherwise.

How close would tragedy come on the farm?

Another Hospital Rest

July 1959

Another school grade completed, my fifth, I looked towards the sixth grade in the coming fall, though in no hurry. I had other places to go and other things to do. Freddie and I stayed busy with jaunts through nearby woods and biked our way up and down this road and that.

I'd returned home after my day's adventure with Freddie. Dad and Verlon weren't there. Dad was at work, likely, but Verlon's whereabouts at that moment? Perhaps, God only knew, but I'd bet Mom had an idea.

She caught me off guard. "I'm going back to the hospital for another rest."

"How long?" I said.

"The doctor says about a week," she said.

"Where am I going to stay?"

"You can go stay with your Gramma, Grampa, and Uncle James," she said, "if you want."

Sounded good to me. "When?"

"We'll go down this Friday," she said.

Done deal. Besides, I wanted an escape from Dad after his last confrontation with Mom. I'd watched and listened, ready to throw myself between them if Mom appeared in danger. At one point when

Dad came my direction, I'd wondered if he'd pound me. Instead, he rushed by and said in a gruff voice, "I hope you never get married," emphasis on never.

Crystal clear, he wasn't happy married to Mom, but why? Seemed to me he was the one making the marriage miserable. If he'd stop drinking like a fish, things would improve.

The next morning Mom's right eye and arms had developed large purple bruises. I could tell she'd been crying, too.

Udderly Simple?

July 1959

We arrived at the farm that Friday evening.

Our visit began and progressed like most others, activities relaxed and simple. We engaged in country routines, to which Gramma, Grampa, and Uncle James were accustomed. The difference for me? I knew I wouldn't return home on Sunday with Mom, Dad, and Verlon.

* * *

Late Sunday afternoon at the supper table, I already felt homesick anticipating the coming week without Mom, Dad, and Verlon. "We'd better be getting back," Dad had said to Mom earlier.

"It's time for me to start supper," Gramma had said. "Do you want to eat before you go? I can fix something up real quick."

"No, Mom. Thanks," Mom said.

I didn't know what to think or say. Didn't want to cry. *What was Mom not telling me?* I could only guess that she'd told Gramma about her planned rest at the hospital. No reason she wouldn't have, but, on the other hand, they hadn't talked about it in front of me. Not even a mention. Regardless, I wasn't about to bring it up; I'd just as soon stir up a wasp nest.

Now, if I had to bet, I'd lay money that Mom would've cited her nervousness as the reason for her hospital stay. I imagined she'd left out the part about Dad's drinking as the contributing factor. But little did I know, even then, that her stay would be at a psychiatric facility.

At the front door, beside Gramma, I gave a last wave as Dad, Verlon, then Mom shut their car doors. *Slam, slam! Slam!* I turned away, then I heard Dad start the engine. On the couch I heard the crunch of gravel as tires backed down the driveway. A blanket of sadness covered me. Gears shifted and our '55 Ford sedan pulled away.

I'd remained on the couch until Gramma called me. "Come wash up for supper."

I pictured the houses along the Old Road towards Upton and the flashing-yellow light in the middle of town that I guessed they'd already passed.

The sight and smell helped, but even though I loved Gramma's homemade cornbread, the cedar trees and reddish dirt along the downhill of 31W just north out of Upton passed by in the movie in my head. I guessed Mom, Dad, and Verlon were beyond that point, too.

After Grampa said grace, he asked Uncle James, "Did you remember to close the barn door?"

"I believe I did," Uncle James said, "but I'll check it directly."

A good helping of navy beans on my plate, I crumbled a wedge of warm cornbread on top and sprinkled on a little salt and pepper. "Mm, beans and cornbread," I said.

Where two-lane 31W curved a little left and lost sight of Upton, oncoming traffic passed by. *Swish! Swish! Swish!* And our car swayed with the tug of wind as each passed.

Grampa crumbled cornbread into a glass of cold milk, something I'd never seen before.

The milk was fresh for sure; I'd watched Uncle James milk their one cow earlier in the day. I pictured Verlon sitting on the left side in the backseat of our car, his usual place.

Grampa spooned out mouthfuls of soggy cornbread until only a small amount of milk remained in his glass. He put down his spoon, turned up the glass, and emptied it. "Ah, that's good," he said and wiped his mouth.

Who'd thought of that? Finished with my cornbread and beans, I asked, "Can I try it?"

"Sure," Grampa said with a hand gesture.

"Yes." Gramma nodded with a smile.

My first taste, less than a spoonful. Sweet cold milk with cornbread. That experience, like the use of fire, now shared with me. For unknown generations past, since cows were milked and cornbread baked, someone had combined them. Now that knowledge had passed to me.

"That's ready, ain't it?" Uncle James said. Other people might say, that's neat, or, that's cool, but Uncle James favored, that's ready.

"It's good," I said. Though much better, it reminded me when Dad had pushed me to try his favorite kind of milk.

Dad had removed a quart-size carton from the refrigerator and a lumpy liquid splashed into his glass as he poured. *Plop, plop! Plop, plop, plop!* He must've noticed the expression on my face. "It's good. Try some," he said.

Chunky milk seemed wrong. I would've sworn lumps meant the milk had spoiled.

Dad tipped his glass and took a long drink. *Gulp, gulp!* "Ahh. Go ahead."

"How does it taste?"

"You'll like it."

I looked at the label, BUTTERMILK it read. I brought the carton to my nose. "Ooh." My face scrunched. "It smells like it's gone bad."

"It's supposed to smell that way. Try just a little."

With a small amount in a glass, I held my breath, hoped it tasted better than it smelled, and turned the glass up for a sip.

A sour, salty taste had flooded my mouth and I'd swallowed without chewing. Maybe I could learn to like buttermilk, in small doses.

"I'll go check on the barn door," Uncle James said.

"Want anything else to eat?" Gramma asked me.

"No, Gramma, I'm going to the barn, too."

Uncle James and I walked up the Old Road. Mom, Dad, and Verlon must've been somewhere on the far side of E-town. That's what we called Elizabethtown.

The barn door shut, Uncle James and I looked inside to check on their cow, anyway. I didn't know if anyone had named Grampa's cow. Uncle James hadn't, but she needed a name and looked like an Ole Betsy to me. She glanced around as we entered the barn, turned back to face the wall, and chewed her cud without breaking rhythm. I wondered if she had one thought in her brain. Wondered if she ever had any thoughts.

We left Ole Betsy alone in the barn and strolled to the pond. Circles grew on the water's surface where dragonflies touched the water, which reflected the pale-red and orange clouds overhead.

"Quiet this time of day," Uncle James said.

From the distance, *Whip-poor-will, whip-poor-will!*

"Yeah. Quiet." Mom, Dad, and Verlon were getting out of the car at home. Maybe, it had been an hour and a half since they'd left. That's about how long it took Dad to drive the sixty miles to Fairdale.

Did Ole Betsy ever get lonely? Did chewing her cud make things easier for her?

***

After breakfast the next morning Uncle James grabbed the milk bucket, looked at me, and said, "I'm going to milk the cow. Come with me."

"How often do you have to milk the cow?" I asked, as we walked towards the barn.

"At least once a day, sometimes twice."

"Why do you do that?"

"She'll go dry if we don't."

I tried to imagine milking a cow every day. Couldn't. "Isn't that hard to milk her every day? I mean, at least I get off school on the weekends and summers."

"Oh, it's not so bad with one cow. When we had six cows, the milk chore took a while."

No mistake, a strong smell of cow poop escaped as Uncle James lifted the wooden arm and opened one of the two big barn doors.

Ole Betsy remained stationary and chewed her cud. *Milking the highlight of her day?*

Uncle James stroked and petted her side and said, "How you doing old girl? Ready for your milking?" The bucket below her udder, he moved a short stool from next to the wall, then sat down beside her. "Don't stand behind her," Uncle James warned, "she might kick you or step on your foot."

Well away from her right hind leg, I stood near Uncle James' left shoulder. Ole Betsy swished her tail several times. Flies scattered and formed a loose group that circled around her backside before they resettled.

Uncle James grabbed a teat with each hand. Alternating, he squeezed and pulled. Each time a thin stream of milk splashed into the pail.

Shh, shh, shh!

"You just have to squeeze firmly," Uncle James said. He opened and closed his hands to demonstrate.

I watched the milk level rise ever so little with each squirt. *Would take forever. Almost forever. May as well be forever.*

When Ole Betsy raised her tail, Uncle James grabbed the bucket, stood up, and pulled the bucket away.

Gush! Ole Betsy let her rip. She had no shame. No shame.

"Wouldn't do for that to get into the milk," Uncle James said.

No argument from me.

Her pee splashed, some in my direction. I edged farther away. The yellow stream and puddle on the ground steamed. A strong smell of cow pee, like mine only stronger, mixed with the cool air.

When she finished, Uncle James repositioned the bucket.

"You try it," he said.

My left foot mere inches from her right hind hoof, Ole Betsy, big and heavy, could step on me before I knew it. *She'll let me pull her boobs?*

I gripped one. *Warm.* I'd never handled a boob before. Figured Mom had let me touch hers when I was a baby, but I couldn't remember that, if she had. "Now what?" I asked, giving a pull with no result.

Ole Betsy swished her tail. *Moo!* Telling me, "Hey, kid, take it easy?"

"You have to squeeze harder," Uncle James said.

Another pull produced a dribble.

Would take forever. "I don't think I can do this very well," I said. Didn't want Ole Betsy mad at me. "You'd better do it, Uncle James."

"Okay. It's a matter of practice. I've had years of practice." Uncle James pointed a stream of milk at me, as if aiming a hose.

I barely avoided the shot to my face.

He grinned.

* * *

Uncle James topped off the pail. "Okay, we're done for now. You can carry it to the house." The stool against the wall, Uncle James patted Ole Betsy on her flank.

Outside the barn, I watched Uncle James close the barn door, while Ole Betsy faced the wall, contented to chew and swish her tail.

"Chewing her cud," I said.

"Yeah, cows will stand around and chew their cud for hours when there's nothing for them to eat. You know, I've heard a cow will die, if they lose their cud."

From boredom? "Really? Have you ever seen any die from that? What is a cud, anyway?"

"Oh, I guess, they might die. I've never seen a cud, but think it's a ball of tough weeds or straw they regurgitate from their stomach."

"Bleah. I'm glad I don't have to chew cud."

A second bucket, almost full of water, sat a few steps from the barn.

"Let me show you something," Uncle James said. He retrieved something from the barn, then dropped it into the bucket. "That's a horse hair. Leave it there a while and it will come to life."

I didn't know whether he was joking or not. I'd heard in school that spontaneous generation wasn't possible.

We stared a few moments at the hair, which floated on the water's surface.

Didn't appear to move.

Several times I checked Uncle James' face for a grin, though didn't see one. *No, can't be true.*

Halfway to the house and carrying the bucket by alternating between hands every few steps, I said, "I don't think I can make it."

Uncle James took over.

Back in the kitchen, Gramma poured the milk into some jars and a pitcher, and placed them in the refrigerator.

* * *

My week's stay, a few months of weekend visits rolled into one. Farm life dragged and left me bored in the evenings without TV, while my homesickness worsened.

Shock Treatment

Late July 1959

At the end of the week, Mom, Dad, and Verlon had returned and spent the weekend.

When we'd piled into our Ford to go home that Sunday afternoon, I knew I'd miss the calm of Gramma and Grampa's lives. I'd miss the way Uncle James acted like how I thought Dad should.

On the ride home, Mom, visibly more relaxed, explained, "It's funny; I just can't remember some things." And when we entered our house through the back door at the kitchen, Mom pointed and said, "I don't remember getting our new refrigerator."

So, a week of rest in the hospital meant not remembering things like the new refrigerator? "Why did you need to go, Mom?" I said.

"They gave me shock treatments to help me deal with my nervous breakdown," she said.

Her nervous breakdown no doubt a result of Dad's drinking and our lack of money. Neither a big secret to Verlon and me. "What do shock treatments do?" I said.

"They help me forget things, so I don't worry so much," she said.

Though that had answered only part of my question, I didn't need an electrician to explain to me what shock meant. I'd gotten shocked a few times.

Dad said nothing in response to Mom's comments. He kept hush-hush, didn't apologize. He'd never apologized for anything.

But, I knew what had caused Mom's nervous breakdown.

Mom's memory returned a little at a time.

And without shock treatments, I forgot about that horse hair in the bucket. Never learned if that hair came to life, though I had my doubts.

Only years later, did I learn that a fungus or a mold growing on a horse hair can make the hair wiggle in water as if alive.

* * *

Mom grew less dependent upon Dad, once she got involved in activities outside of the home with Verlon and me. Must've been following some advice recommended during her hospital rest. She spent less time waiting for Dad to bring home another case of raging-bull on Fridays. She attended PTA meetings when the new school year started and volunteered to be Verlon's first-grade homeroom mother.

Mom had wanted to attend PTA meetings when I went to Prestonia Elementary. She couldn't attend though, because we had one car and Dad refused to drive her. Dad had allowed her to practice driving our car up and down our driveway on Harding, until she backed into the fence. Then Dad blew up and kept the keys in his pocket. Even though Mom had finally gotten her license before we moved to Fairdale, we could afford only one car and Dad maintained control of it.

Mom introduced me to Little League baseball. The field was adjacent to the Community Center, which was located behind the elementary school. And she supported Verlon with tap dancing lessons at the center, too.

She'd learned to skate in Highland Park as a young girl and now purchased a new pair of skates, one each for Verlon and me. Using our garage as a private roller rink, we honed our skills in contained circles to music on the radio.

* * *

We'd heard scratching and rustling in our living room couch for several weeks.

"There must be a rat living in it," Mom had said.

I could only guess what a rat might do. *Bite my butt?*

With Dad at work, Mom said, "Let's get that thing out of the couch. I'm afraid one of us will get bitten. How can we get rid of it?"

"I know," I said, "I could shoot it with my BB gun."

"Okay, but we need to make sure it can't get away," Mom said. "Let's put newspaper on the floor, and make sure it can't get out through a hole or a doorway."

We cleared away furniture and positioned the couch in the middle of the room. To set our trap, we scattered newspaper across the vinyl living-room flooring, overlapped some along the base of the walls, and ensured we'd blocked the doorways.

BB gun nearby, I said, "Okay, I'm ready." We banged on the couch. We tilted and shook it, while we yelled, "Come out of there."

As if to accommodate us, a rat emerged in a full-out run.

We all flinched.

"Watch out, don't let it jump on you," Mom yelled.

Frantic claws scratched at the paper and the vinyl flooring, our quarry's traction limited, as it moved back and forth along the wall baseboard searching for an avenue of escape.

"Look, it can't run," I said. Maybe, we'd set a good trap.

"Cut it off," Mom shouted.

"Corner it," Verlon yelled.

My first shot didn't slow it down.

"Did you hit it?" Mom asked.

"I think so," I said and spotted a weakness in our plan. "Don't let it get under the paper."

On the hunt, nothing would stop us, though the rat evaded us as best it could.

I took another shot, then another.

Didn't seem to be working, but I kept reloading. We held the advantage for the moment. I had a load of BBs, enough that their weight alone would slow that animal to a crawl. But if nothing else, maybe it would die of fright or exhaustion.

I took another shot.

When the rat stopping moving, I took two more shots for good measure.

No obvious wounds nor spewing blood. "I think we killed it," I said. Must've taken a dozen shots. I knew my aim couldn't have been that bad at point blank range. *That was one tough rat or my BB gun was weak.*

Our teamwork had paid off. *Maybe we could apply that to deal with Dad?*

"Would you throw that thing in the outhouse?" Mom asked me.

"Yeah," I said, not embarrassed to dump a dead rat, a righteous kill, and different than a chamber pot.

*   *   *

Another Friday evening, Dad not in sight.

"I think I know where your daddy is," Mom said.

How could she know? Someone give her a report? Had Dad let something slip? Or Mom spot our car somewhere? Regardless, I guessed Dad had made a habit of visiting the same drinking hole once too often.

"Come on, we're going to get him," she added.

Headed for a showdown? Clearly something had shifted. I dreaded what might happen but Dad needed to be straightened out, somehow.

We walked along Fairdale Road, past the high school as we approached the tavern at the corner of National Turnpike about a mile from our house.

I spotted our Ford sedan in the gravel parking lot next to the building and said, "That's our car."

When we neared the open front door, we saw Dad on a stool at the bar busy talking to some woman who sat next to him. He didn't notice us, though.

"Go in and tell your daddy I want him to come home," Mom said.

What? "Why me?" I said.

"Huh, I'm not going into a beer joint," she said.

Aw, jeez. "Okay," I grumbled.

No idea how Dad would react, I approached him from his blind side and stopped next to him. I paused a moment, took a breath, and with as steady a voice as I could manage, blurted, "Mom wants you to come home now." The louder, the better, and I didn't care who heard me.

Dad turned. Said nothing. Stared.

Afraid he'd backhand me, I stood my ground a few moments within easy reach and maintained eye contact before I beat a retreat.

Mom, Verlon, and I headed towards home.

I wondered what was in store when Dad returned home.

"Let's go skating. You two get your roller skates ready when we get home," Mom said.

No argument from me. I expected things to go sideways when we saw Dad again.

Back in our house, I'd grabbed my skates and planned to position myself within sight of Mom, who lingered in the kitchen, when our car pulled into the driveway.

Dad, face flushed, steamed when he came through the kitchen door. "Don't ever go sending our boy in to shame me at a bar again!"

"But Cecil—"

Slap!

"I don't want to hear it!"

"Give me some money for groceries, Cecil," Mom said.

"You need to mind your own damn business."

Dad getting ready to bash Mom?

"Just give me some money for groceries," Mom said.

Dad fumed, but he pulled cash from his pocket and surrendered part of it.

Mom backed away and said to Verlon and me, "Come on, let's go."

Not fit to be around, maybe Dad would get the message if we left him at home alone.

"Where are you going?" Dad asked.

"Skating," Mom said.

Mom, Verlon, and I had long since anticipated Dad's drinking on Friday evenings, but his change of jobs was another unpredictable aspect. Don't like a job? Quit. Don't like the boss' attitude? Quit. Dad kept most everything to himself when sober, other than short mumbles and gripes. I couldn't determine what motivated his attitude toward work, though I suspected he hated being told what to do.

In hindsight, Dad's frequent job changes, with many of his employers doing construction jobs scattered around the county, provided him ample opportunity to scope out watering holes far and wide. Dad probably didn't consider the possibility that he'd get confronted, even when close to home.

* * *

The next Friday evening, Mom, Verlon, and I had finished supper.

Watching TV with Verlon, I noticed our car roll past the window and expected what would come next.

When Dad came through the back door, it began.

"I see you've been drinking again," Mom said.

"Stop trying to tell me what to do," Dad snarled. "I'm free, white, and over twenty-one."

"Here we go again," I said to Verlon.

He whispered back, "What can we do?"

"Cecil, things have to change." Mom said in a firm voice, firmer than I'd heard before.

"It's better if I handle the money," Mom said. "It burns a hole in your pocket."

"What makes you think I'm going to give you the money?" Dad replied.

Slap!

"Ow! Stop!"

I whispered to Verlon, "We talked about this. If both of us stand together maybe Dad will listen."

Though steeped in our own fear from the repeated doses of Dad's drunken episodes, we'd grown bolder. We'd had it up to our eyeballs. We'd dared to think about how we could work together to curb his behavior. If we couldn't stop his drinking, at least maybe we could stop his physical abuse of Mom.

"Okay," Verlon said and nodded.

I braced myself, determination my shield. Though almost as tall as Dad, I remained a bean-pole and he outweighed me by eighty to a hundred pounds, lean and muscular from his manual labor jobs. He'd periodically showed off his biceps, too. His way to remind me he could beat me to a pulp? And the sight of his fixed green-eyed stare, flushed-red face, nostrils flared, and heavy breathing, accompanied

185

by that pungent sweet alcohol breath, created an aura far from that of a loving father.

Slap!

"Let's go," I said. My pact with Verlon sealed, I gave him a nod. Side by side we approached to within several arm lengths of Dad.

"You need to stop hitting Mom, or you'll have to fight us, too," I said.

Dad looked shocked. He glared at me, then Verlon, and said, "Be careful, don't get too big for your britches."

"We don't want you hitting Mom," I said.

Dad looked at Mom. "Here, take the damn money," he told her. Once she'd grabbed the cash, he went into the living room.

* * *

Didn't take long before another Friday evening arrived, without a plan to visit Gramma and Grampa's. As predicted, Dad had grown another wild hair, blown part of his paycheck on booze, then arrived home plastered and in a nasty mood.

Definitely, we were on a bad run.

When Mom asked about his paycheck, he exploded. "None of your damn business."

"Ready?" I whispered to Verlon and nodded towards Dad.

Verlon nodded in return.

On our feet, we faced Dad like we had before. "Don't hit Mom. You'll have to fight us, too," I said in a loud voice.

"Yeah," Verlon said.

Dad stared at us, angry, but grew quiet and settled down.

No doubt in my mind that he understood we meant business. Although it was too early to know if his calm would last, I considered we'd won another small victory.

"Let's go skating," Mom said to Verlon and me.

"Okay," I said.

Dad could come home whenever or not. He could eat a cold supper or not. He could spend time at home without us, until closing time at the rink at ten p.m. That seemed fitting. Though I loved him, what else was there to do? He didn't show consideration for us, when he drank, why should we for him?

Out of the house in a shot, roller skates in hand, we hurried on foot to the Community Center about half a mile away.

Thereafter, on Friday evenings, except when we visited the country, trips to the roller skate rink at the Community Center served as entertainment, socialization, and exercise for Mom, Verlon, and me. As well, we enjoyed our collective escape from Dad's arrival home in a drunken state. Mom served food and drinks from the concession stand. She didn't get paid, as far as I remember, but enjoyed the interaction and kept busy while Verlon and I skated.

* * *

McNeely Lake provided an ideal spot for Sunday BBQ picnics.

I don't remember the first time we went there for a weekend picnic with Beulah and Carl. Though I do know our trips started sometime after we'd moved to Fairdale. Before our move to Fairdale, we'd gone to Iroquois Park. I liked McNeely better.

Mom and Beulah socialized, while Dad and Carl drank beer and attended to hot dogs and hamburgers on the charcoal grill. Carl William, Gerald, Verlon, and I had completed explorations of the nearest portion of the lake and returned to eat.

Our radio, plugged into an outlet with Dad's extension cord, played country music, which echoed under the covered pavilion and spread across the lake.

When the radio station played one of Patsy Cline's popular songs, Mom sang along.

Patsy's words, particularly the last line, "I'm crazy for loving you," seemed to sum it all up.

I'd heard Mom sing along to the lyrics of "Crazy" many times before, and couldn't help but think those words reflected her disappointment and entrapment in her turbulent relationship with Dad. Though Mom's sing-along provided invitations for discussion, no one commented, not even Dad, which made her isolation seem more stark to me.

But, at least, Dad wouldn't get wild-drunk and wail on Mom at the lake.

Watermelon Heaven

August 1959

Late in the summer, we'd arrived at the farm on another early Friday evening.

I'd settled into my usual spot on the couch, when Uncle James joined us men in the living room after he'd completed a chore.

Grampa gave him a few minutes rest, then said, "James, will you go pick us a big, ripe melon for later?"

"Okay, Dad," he said.

Tomatoes vied with blackberry cobbler as my favorite food, though watermelon made the list. We'd never grown watermelons at home, nor any fruits or vegetables.

"Can I go, too?" I said.

Although I knew the location of the melon patch, beyond a corner of the tobacco plants, and a short walk from the kitchen door, I followed Uncle James. The sun, though low in the sky, heated my bare neck and arms and the air smelled thick, heavy, and green.

The seeds, planted in the spring, had grown into vines with fat fruit. Green-striped watermelons of all sizes clung to the vines, which spread across the ground like spider webs. They crowded each other in the patch in numbers Gramma, Grampa, and Uncle James couldn't eat. Every year, Grampa planted more than needed to produce a huge crop. His way of thinking? A bounty was good, even

189

when some fruit would rot on the vine. So, Gramma and Grampa plied visitors with the overload.

Bent over a fat melon, Uncle James said, "Listen to the sound it makes. Do it like this." He tapped with his middle finger. *Thump, thump, thump!*

"How about this one?" I said.

One ear towards the melon, Uncle James checked. *Thump, thump!* "This one doesn't sound ready." He performed the test on a different one. "This one sounds good," he said. With a kitchen knife he'd brought along, he cut a small triangle in the melon, and pried out the wedge with the knife.

The dark-red insides appeared juicy and a sharp contrast to the white inner part of the rind.

The wedge was reinserted. "We'll take this one back to the house," he said. After a breath, he added, "Let's eat one here. Pick out a little one."

The possibilities studied, I tapped. "Is this ripe?"

"Well, let's try it."

With a tug and twist I separated the smooth, waxy ball from its mother vine.

Parted in half with a quick cut through the middle by Uncle James, he allowed one piece to drop to the ground. The other piece sliced into equal parts, he offered one to me.

I knew how to eat watermelon. I swallowed the soft, little white seeds whole. I'd always avoided the hard, black ones in bigger melons, which I'd seen everyone spit out. That juice which didn't drip, wet my lips and chin. The juice I couldn't vacuum into my mouth fell to the ground, all part of the ritual. "Mm, good," I said. *Slurp!* "Warm. I've never eaten warm watermelon before."

"That's ready, ain't it?" Uncle James said.

Mouth wiped with my hand, I pitched my spoils onto the ground.

Uncle James handed me the large melon. "You can carry it."

I cradled our choice in both arms, mindful not to let it fall and crack open.

* * *

In his usual whisper, Grampa said grace. "Bless us and the food we are about to eat. . . ."

Mom and Gramma helped us men settle into our supper meal, before they served themselves. Hands reached and passed bowls. Portions of hot and cold food got spooned onto plates. Requests dominated our talk. Can I have? Will you pass?

Clank! Scrape! Scrape!

"What do you want to drink?" Mom asked me.

"An orange soft drink," I said.

Jars of jelly, mustard, and ketchup occupied the center of the table. Deep-red beets occupied a bowl next to a store-bought jar of pickles. Aside that, another bowl of fresh-sliced cucumbers soaked in salted water. Slices of store-bought white bread lay spread on a plate, alongside pieces of cornbread.

Suck! Slurp! Grampa had attacked a pickled pig's foot he'd pulled from a jar.

I loved the sour taste of pickled pig's feet, but wasn't in the mood for fat and gristle. I wanted meat. "Can I have a chicken leg?"

Once the plate of flour-battered, pan-fried poultry was passed to me, I chose the leg with the brownest crust.

"Can you make me a little chicken leg?" Verlon asked Mom.

"Yes," she said. His plate passed back to Mom, she removed a wing, broke it at the joint, and handed the meaty part to Verlon. "There you go, a little chicken leg."

Mom offered me the bowl of green beans. "Would you like some?"

They appeared shriveled. "No, I'd like some corn on the cob, canned tomatoes, and cornbread." I'd smelled Gramma's fresh cornbread. Everything on the table fair game, no one pressured me about what or how much I ate. At that point I felt out of danger that Mom would make me take more Geritol.

Within minutes Grampa had reduced his pig's foot to bare bones, gristle and all. Then, he sucked on the bones until he'd extracted all their flavor, before he looked over the plate of chicken. "I'll have the neck and gizzard."

A meat kind of guy, you'd never catch me eating gristle, if I could help it. On occasion when I ate pig's feet and gizzards, I left the chewiest parts.

"Those have always been your favorite parts, Dad," Mom said.

"I don't know why other people don't like them," he said, without breaking his search of the table. Grampa faced no competition over those chicken parts, though he did over legs and wings. He never left anything on his plate of what he'd chosen, except fossilized bones.

* * *

Once Grampa, Dad, and Uncle James had left the table, Mom and Gramma started their clean up. Plates and silverware clanked as Mom pushed scraps off the dirty plates into the slop bucket. Bones were separated and thrown into the trash. Water sloshed as Gramma scrubbed dishes.

Mom asked Gramma, "Do you want to save these green beans, Mom? There's not many left."

"No. I've had those out several days, Bea. Throw them in the slop bucket."

"What about the corn bread? There's only two pieces left."

"Wrap those up in foil."

"Should we keep the leftover corn?" Mom said, referring to the pile of loose kernels.

Gramma had cut those kernels off a few cobs with a butcher knife before she'd fried them in a skillet.

"No, let's give that to the pigs. Those are several days old, too," Gramma said.

Well, that explains that. Several must be Gramma's magic number.

"James, would you go slop the pigs?" she called out and poured the dishwater into the slop bucket as he came into the kitchen.

Mom and Gramma chatted away as I followed Uncle James out the back door.

* * *

The wooden trough, about my height in length, had been placed near the walnut tree on the other side of the wire fence from the driveway. Easier of slopping the pigs that way. Free to roam the large fenced-in field, the pigs had created a wallow nearby and under the shade of the tree.

Their little corner of hog heaven.

The majority of pigs lazed some distance away, content in their world of pig thoughts, until Uncle James encouraged them. "Sooie, pig, pig. Sooie."

Grampa's pigs weren't stupid; they knew what Uncle James meant. Heads bobbed. Ears flopped.

Grunt! Grunt!

Talk to each other like we did around the table? I wondered.

"About time, I'm starved," I figured the closest said in pig language.

Grunt! Grunt! Grunt!

"Move over. Let me get to the trough," another said.

They didn't have hands to pass food, so, for them, first come was first served.

Grunt! Grunt!

"Stop pushing."

I looked at the slop, then the pigs. *Better you than me.* I'd never liked the idea of my food getting jumbled together on my plate. Sure, some things went good together, like turkey and gravy. Like mashed potatoes and gravy. Certainly, cornbread and beans. But I didn't like those mushed together. I wanted to taste them separately and know what I was chewing. That was, most food anyway. Cornbread with milk was a different story. That was something to live for.

Grunt!

"Tastes like chicken."

Come to think of it, I wasn't that different from Grampa's pigs. Call me to eat and I'd come running, but keep my gravy and cranberry sauce apart, thank you.

* * *

Mom and Gramma continued to chat as Uncle James and I dropped off the slop bucket on our way to the front porch.

Grampa occupied his chair in the living room.

"Coming to the porch, Dad?" Uncle James asked Grampa.

"In a minute," Grampa said, as he rubbed his leg.

After meals and during the hot summer months, the front porch offered elbow room and an opportunity of relief with a cool breeze.

The sun shone directly onto the porch, though without that midday heat.

Dad puffed on a cigarette as the swing creaked from his slow sway. Uncle James sat in one of the two metal porch chairs. Those silver-gray chairs, hand-painted at least once, bounced like the swing and reminded me of rocking chairs. That's how I used them, anyway. Verlon sat on the porch edge, so I claimed a spot next to him.

I dangled my legs and nudged pebbles with the toes of my shoes in the shallow trench where rainwater always fell in sheets from the front of the porch roof.

Grampa limped across the porch, then sat on the swing next to Dad.

Dad, Uncle James, and Grampa talked men-things, though I wasn't paying attention. I studied the trench, not sure what I might find, maybe a pretty piece of smoothed glass, a cat-eye marble, a jack, or a bent nail.

A short while later and the sun touching the horizon, Mom and Gramma, done with supper cleanup, carried wooden chairs from the kitchen. Soon after, Grampa said, "James, why don't you bring out the watermelon?"

"Okay, Dad." Uncle James disappeared into the house.

Gramma followed him without hesitation.

When they returned a few minutes later, Uncle James carried the melon and Gramma had a butcher knife, a tea towel, and newspaper.

"That chicken sure tasted good, Adee," Grampa said as he cut the melon into long wedges. He always called Gramma that, using a long "E" sound, though I didn't think he did that to belittle Gramma, unlike what Dad had done to me.

Grampa passed out length-wise slices of the rich-red melon to everyone, each piece peppered with black seeds.

My first big bite squeaked between my teeth, and almost more than I could chew, squirted juice out the corners of my mouth.

"There's nothing like cold watermelon," Grampa said.

"You're right about that, Mr. Riggs," Dad said.

"Mmm-mmm, this is sweet," Mom added.

Right there, on the front porch, the general slurp-fest in full swing, we'd died and gone to watermelon heaven.

Pthu! Somebody had launched a seed into the yard.

I wondered what those hard black seeds would do to my insides. "Can I eat the seeds?"

"You can, if you want to," Gramma answered. "They won't hurt you."

I didn't want to swallow a seed whole, so bit down on one. *Pthu!* "I'd rather not."

"Do you think it's about time to worm the tobacco again, Dad?" Uncle James asked.

"No, James, I think maybe we can go another week. I didn't see any today when I looked and Mr. Cruz said yesterday that he hasn't seen any on his plants since he wormed two weeks ago."

Grampa's neighbor, Mr. Cruz lived over the hill to the east. I'd heard talk of him but hadn't met him.

"Maybe, it's because of the weather," Uncle James said.

"Bea," Gramma said, "I finished a quilt I want you to have."

Gramma, always working on a quilt as far as I could remember, would finish one, then start another.

"Oh, I'd like that," Mom replied.

Pthu! "Look how far mine went," Verlon said.

"I can spit one farther," I said. *Pthu!* Shaded by the big oak, the front yard had grown dark, though the open field across the road, and its far side sinkhole, remained well-lit.

Mom yelled, "I just saw a mosquito."

"No, it didn't go farther," Verlon replied.

"Yes, it did," I said.

"Uh-uh."

"I just heard one," Grampa announced. "There's plenty watermelon here for seconds," he added.

"When you're done, put your rinds on the newspaper," Gramma said.

Smack!

I looked around to see that Dad had slapped his neck, which signaled the start of an attack.

On alert, I expected a bite, dreaded the itch.

Mosquitoes come to socialize? They threatened to run us indoors, but we refused to retreat. The high humidity, along with the warmer temperature in the house, made that all but unbearable.

Pthu! "See that one?" I asked Verlon. I heard the familiar buzz of a mosquito and waved my hand. "Get away." I looked at Verlon. "Farther than yours," I said.

"No, it wasn't," Verlon said.

"Uh-huh."

"Uh-uh."

My rind on the pile, I said, "Watermelon bones," and picked up a second piece of melon.

"Adee, bring out some rags," Grampa said in a loud voice.

Verlon spat another seed and pointed. "Mine went all the way out there."

Gramma disappeared into the house.

With my best body language, I spat another seed. *Pthu!* "Mine went farther."

Gramma returned with scraps of clothing, towels, or bedding from her endless supply. Meanwhile, Uncle James had fetched several empty coffee cans from the garage.

Grampa put the rags in the cans and set them afire. "Now, we'll let them smolder," he said.

Uncle James spread the cans across the yard near us. "That usually gets rid of the mosquitoes."

Our watermelon fest continued, interrupted only by smoke.

Cough! I waved my hand to clear the air. Didn't help. The smell of burned cloth wasn't that bad, though. Different, kind of good.

A breeze pushed the thick smoke away.

Pthu! "That's the record," Verlon said.

Couldn't have seen that seed land. I couldn't. Too dark. "Uh-uh."

"Uh-huh."

Uncle James gathered the melon leftovers and carried them towards the pig trough.

"No, it wasn't," Verlon said as I followed Uncle James.

"Yes, it was," I replied with a glance back.

Uncle James leaned over the fence and dumped the rinds into the trough. "Sooie, pig. Sooie," he called.

Grampa's pigs answered as they raced towards us.

Grunt, grunt, grunt!

Now, no doubt, the pigs had gone to watermelon heaven, too.

"Was not," Verlon said when I returned to my place on the porch edge.

"Was, too."

* * *

Everything had grown harder to see. Easy to make out Grampa's white hair and matching long-sleeved shirt. Dad's lit cigarette was a dead give-away. Verlon, not hard to see, sat next to me at arm's reach. Mom, Gramma, and Uncle James? Their voices gave them away.

We sat for a while and I listened as Grampa mentioned eating watermelon as a boy. Then, everybody agreed homegrown melon tasted better than store-bought. I did, too, though didn't say.

The pigs had gone quiet and goosebumps had raised on my arms.

"The house has probably cooled off enough by now," Gramma said.

"Time for bed," Mom said. "Let's go in."

* * *

Verlon and I undressed and climbed into one of Gramma's big comfy beds in the front room. Mom tucked us in under a sheet and gave us a kiss.

"Uh-huh," I said.

"Uh-uh," Verlon replied.

"Go to sleep, you two," Mom said.

* * *

Right after breakfast, Saturday morning, I asked Mom for some toilet paper.

Before Mom could respond, Gramma said, "You'll find some in the new outhouse. Just head toward the back of the hen house."

So, I did, and there it was. Outhouse and toilet paper. Behind the chicken coop, built since my last visit, as if by magic.

Not perfect by any means. The seat, too high for me, and the hole too far back from the front edge, I had no choice but to dangle my legs. Gusts of wind blew through the door and between the wood planks on the sides. Worse, the toilet was open below and behind the seat, and blasts of air blew up through the hole. At least, most of the bad smell got blown away. But better than a squat behind the tool shed, the outhouse provided privacy and a place to keep a dry supply of toilet paper.

Oh, sure, Grampa had replaced the old outhouse, but didn't install a tub, sink, medicine cabinet, or toilet in the house. And I never pushed for an answer to my question as to why Gramma and Grampa hadn't done that. I accepted the situation as a foregone conclusion and it remained a mystery to me.

* * *

Back in the kitchen, Mom said, "We're going blackberry picking. Want to go?"

Blackberries? Couldn't pass that up. "Yeah," I said.

Verlon was in, too.

"You'll have to put on long-sleeved shirts and wear hats," Mom said.

Gramma, dressed in a long dress and knee-length white apron, as usual, carried a large aluminum pan the size of a hand basin. The rest of us carried gloves and quart-sized cans as we walked up the road, then past the barn.

Ole Betsy probably in there alone, facing a wall and chewing her cud in silence.

Tall weeds covered the big open field. A blackberry patch had managed to grow along and out from the fence line, which ran aside the Old Road. Clearly, that ground had been spared from plowing. Like two-legged grasshoppers, we fanned out. Ripe berries, many a shiny darkest-of-blue-purple, grew in small bunches among briars deep enough to prevent our picking every one, even if Gramma wanted that many.

"Where do I start, Mom?" I said.

Gramma, already busy, replied, "It doesn't matter. Just start anywhere."

I reached into the brambles a foot or two, thorns tugged at my shirt and pants. "Ouch."

"Be careful," Mom said.

I stood in place, pulled berries within easiest reach. *One berry, two berries, three. . . .*

They hit the bottom of my empty metal can. *Clunk! Clunk, clunk!* Many others hung inches out of reach, so I backed away from the vine. Thorns tore at my gloves, shirt, pants. *Don't want me to go?*

The clunk sounds stopped when blackberries covered the can's silver bottom.

Thirty-two, thirty-three, one for you, one for me.

I continued to pick. "Mine is full," I said in a loud voice. Though I'd exaggerated a little, I carried my can to Gramma.

She emptied my berries into the pan she carried, which contained many times over what I'd picked. "That's good," she said. "Just pick a few more. We're almost done."

"Okay, but I'm getting tired," I said. Brer Rabbit came to mind. *Oh, please, don't throw me into the briar patch. If you threw me in, maybe I'd have to eat my way out.* I started picking again. *One for you.* I dropped it into the can, *Clunk!* Then, I picked another. *One for me.* I put it into my mouth.

A few berries later, Gramma said, "Okay. I think we can stop now. I'll can these."

I noticed she had a full pan.

The berries left behind would shrivel and get picked over by the birds. Seemed a big waste.

* * *

Late afternoon, Gramma, out of breath, burst into the living room. She grabbed several towels from a drawer as she said, "There's a fire, get some towels and come quick." Then she rushed out of the room.

"Let's all go!" Mom said.

Any fire was serious, who knew what might burn and Gramma and Grampa would lose?

Where was Dad and Uncle James? I hadn't seen either of them in a while. *On a hunting trip?*

Mom, Verlon, and I followed Gramma as she hurried up the road, then turned towards the two barns and pond.

I smelled smoke before I saw the fire, but at the crest of the ridge near the barns and pond, I understood Gramma's rush.

Grampa beat burning weeds near a neighbor's house at the lower end of the field with what appeared to be a burlap sack. The intense sunlight, unhampered by clouds, camouflaged the flames, though the blackened area, about the size of a football field, identified the fire's edge. Scattered wisps of white smoke rose from the field.

Yay, the blackberry bushes along the fence line were okay.

I figured, the Upton Volunteer Fire Department would be of little help. The phone in the house had been dismantled—my bad—and no one could be spared to drive to town. Besides, the volunteer firefighters' response would've probably taken too long, anyway.

Mom soaked my towel with a quick dunk in the pond.

As we ran to join the effort, Mom said, "Pick any place."

We spread out along the line of foot-high flames—that which smoldered could wait—then pounded burning brush as fast as we could. We smothered a small section, then moved to the adjacent flames. With sun above and flames below, I imagined I'd crawled into the glowing-red potbelly stove. With each blow, soot and dust filled the air, along with smoke and sparks.

Cough! I pounded a few moments before withdrawing to catch my breath.

I alternated. In, to battle the flames, then, out, to catch a breath. In, out, in, out. . . . *How long could I keep it up?*

Wet from sweat, my skin collected a layer of dirt and ash. A wisp of wind provided brief relief. A cool, clean drink from the dipper came to mind. A jump into the brown-water pond seemed good, a swim in my neighborhood community pool back home even better.

The outcome not certain, I focused on my chosen section of field.

Slowly, we beat the fire line out, then turned our attention to the blackened areas still smoldering.

I never discovered how that fire had started. Held captive in the kitchen while Mom cleaned me up, I could barely hear Grampa talking to Gramma in the living room. I half-expected getting grief over my part in the phone surgery.

A Family Tragedy

September 1959

T uesday, a warm summer-dog-day afternoon following school, I dropped off my school supplies and told Mom, "I'm going to go play with Freddie."

"Just be back for supper," she said.

I'd turned eleven the week before and Mom allowed me the freedom to pursue boyhood activities after school.

* * *

Near suppertime, as Mom expected, I'd almost crossed our yard to the house, when Mom burst from the back door. Dad hadn't come home from work, since our driveway was empty. Verlon was somewhere. I didn't know where, and hadn't cared while I'd been with Freddie. I wasn't my brother's babysitter.

"Tunney's in the hospital," Mom wailed, "and Betty is dead," her face wet with tears. "What are we going to do? What are we going to do?"

Jeez Louise. "What happened?" I asked Mom.

But she couldn't answer, just sobbed.

I pictured Uncle Tunney's male-pattern baldness, a tuft of hair growing above his forehead. I pictured Aunt Betty wearing dark-red lipstick. First thing I could think of, "We should go to the hospital," I said. We could do nothing for Uncle Tunney, even at the hospital. *And Aunt Betty was dead?*

Mom often visited her brothers and sisters, some more than others, aside from seeing them at Gramma and Grampa's. Verlon and I usually accompanied her and most every time I liked our visits.

I recalled two visits with Uncle Tunney and Aunt Betty.

One time, I'd stayed overnight during a weekend and played with Billy, Bobby, and their two sisters. Everything seemed okay at their house. Uncle Tunney and Aunt Betty hadn't argued, and Uncle Tunney hadn't drank. Both had smiled and joked, seemed to enjoy my visit as much as I did.

Another time, we'd visited one afternoon and Billy played on their living room floor with a toy truck.

"Don't touch it," he said when I attempted to join him.

What's with Billy?

Begrudgingly, he complied when Uncle Tunney told him to share. But, other than Billy's behavior, everything seemed okay at Uncle Tunney and Aunt Betty's that time, too.

In hindsight, something ominous had been brewing, which I didn't detect, nor could know. Maybe, that's what had been eating Billy when he'd been gruff about his toy truck. Hell, I'd had a hard time reading between the lines regarding Mom and Dad and I was around them more than I was around anyone else.

* * *

I wanted to soothe Mom, relieve her pain, but didn't know how. I hoped my presence helped.

After Dad arrived home from work, we rushed to Aunt Shirley's house in Highland Park.

As family members gathered and shared their mix of confusion and sadness, they asked questions and added details. Over several hours, newer pieces in the what-had-happened jigsaw puzzle filled in gaps to everyone's understanding.

Uncle Tunney and Aunt Betty had separated several months ago. In tears at times, he'd talked about his difficulty with their separation and wish to reconcile with Aunt Betty.

"Let's see if it's on the news," someone said and turned on Aunt Shirley's black-and-white TV.

A few minutes later, those of us in the living room called to the others in the kitchen, "It's on the news. It's on the news."

The news reporter interviewed female co-workers, who'd left work with Aunt Betty. The camera showed the exit gate to the street from the Dobbs House, where they worked.

Mom had come that way when she'd worked there, too.

The camera panned around to show Uncle Tunney's car.

One of the witnesses said, "He came up as we passed through the gate and pleaded to talk to her, but she told him she didn't want to talk. She'd told us about her separation from him."

The reporter moved to another witness.

"He insisted on talking with her, but after she refused, he pulled out a gun. We were all frightened. Then, he pointed it at her and fired several shots."

A gun obtained from where, when, how?

That same witness sobbed as she pointed and said, "She fell over there."

The camera focused on the spot where Aunt Betty had fallen, a ditch by a fence in front of someone's yard. ". . . where," the newsman reported, "she died immediately from a gunshot wound to the head."

That's where she died. That's where Aunt Betty died.

Another witness said, "Then he put the gun to his temple and shot himself."

"Aw," Mom said as her voice cracked and she wiped tears.

Aw, Uncle Tunney, Aunt Betty.

The reporter went on to say that Uncle Tunney had been transported to General Hospital.

How could Uncle Tunney have done that? Must've thought he had no other choice. Why hadn't he talked more? I would've talked with him. I would've.

Though barely eleven, I would've done my best, as little as that might've been.

I'd never seen all of my aunts and uncles, along with Gramma and Grampa, upset as much at the same time. I wanted to cry, but didn't. It was all I could do to avoid bursting like an over-filled water balloon. For sure, I didn't want my friends to learn about what Uncle Tunney had done, which I considered the worst thing that had ever happened to my family and me. I knew that event would change my world, would alter my relationship with Billy, though I didn't know how.

Billy's family life hadn't been all that good, I concluded, much worse than I'd known or would've guessed. *Maybe, my family life with Mom and Dad wasn't totally bad. At least Dad hadn't killed Mom or himself, yet. But could Dad be pushed to do the same thing? Could I?*

* * *

For the longest time, I'd suspected Mom hadn't talked about her marital problems with Gramma and Grampa. But years later, she provided me an important puzzle piece when she shared a tidbit she'd heard from Aunt Shirley.

"Shirley told me that she'd talked with your grandparents about her separation from Walt, and they'd told her, 'You made your bed, now sleep in it.'"

I was surprised, though I shouldn't have been. I knew Gramma and Grampa adhered to a strict religious code. No reason their code didn't include all church marriage vows. "Till death do us part," and "What God has joined, let no man put asunder," I'd heard preachers say at weddings.

That information served as a key and back-filled several of the puzzles I'd work to complete. With it, I'd gained a fresh perspective about each of Uncle Tunney's, Aunt Shirley's, and even Mom's marital struggles.

* * *

Everyone gathered in the hospital's waiting room. Gramma and Grampa left periodically for updates on Uncle Tunney's condition, which they passed along.

Nothing to be done, except wait.

I hadn't seen Billy that day, nor was he at the hospital. "Where's Billy, Bobby, and their sisters?" I asked Mom.

"They're with their other grandparents," she said.

Uncle Tunney lingered until the early hours of the morning, when his suffering ended.

Another wave of sadness swept over us.

God. I loved Uncle Tunney. He was always kind and caring around me.

Several days later, Mom told me that Billy, Bobby, and their sisters had gone to live with Aunt Betty's parents, who lived on a farm in a place so far away I couldn't imagine going there. I'd never been to that part of Kentucky. Had never heard of it. Didn't know where it was. Mom also told me Gramma and Grampa had decided not to contest that arrangement.

I had no reason to think that those grandparents would bring Billy for visits to Gramma and Grampa's farm. Why would they? I fully believed they'd avoid anything and everything related to

Uncle Tunney, of which I was a part. So, I doubted I'd have another opportunity to revel in visits with Billy on the farm again, or anywhere else.

Uncle Tunney had shot Aunt Betty several times with a gun, once in the head, and killed her. Then, he put that gun to his temple, pulled the trigger, and killed himself. I'd not only lost Uncle Tunney and Aunt Betty, I couldn't escape the idea that I'd lost Billy, too.

Lucky Rabbit's Foot?

November 1959

We arrived in the country in time that Friday for Dad to talk Uncle James into a rabbit hunt before dark.

My options considered, I decided to accompany Dad and Uncle James. Verlon stayed in the house. I didn't know what we'd rustle up, but I wanted to spend time with Uncle James. I knew in my heart Billy wouldn't show up. I wondered and worried about him, but I couldn't dwell on him. Just couldn't. Maybe, I'd have an adventure or, always on the lookout, get a better idea of what made Dad tick, if he shared something with Uncle James.

We'd walked past the tobacco field and prepared to cross a fence, when Uncle James said, "How's work going, Cecil?"

"Oh, I just started a roofing job this last week," Dad said. "Would rather not be on a roof, but need the work."

Another new job? Not wanting to be on a roof? All ears at that point, I wondered, what else would Dad say?

Dad continued, "You ever been on a roof, James?"

"No, I haven't, Cecil."

"Probably, hotter than hell in the summer, but not that bad this time of year."

"Yeah, I imagine," Uncle James said.

I imagined, too, at least, the hotter than hell part.

Uncle James went on, "I don't particularly like climbing in barn rafters to hang tobacco sticks."

I wouldn't, either. Handing the sticks up to Uncle James had been enough for me.

"Anyway, I damn near fell off at one point," Dad said. "Reminded me of when I'd joined the navy and been stationed to Tule Lake in northern California for training."

What brought on telling us that?

"I was riding in the passenger seat of a two-and-a-half-ton truck on a supply detail," Dad started. "The fool driver drove like a bat out of hell on a one-lane gravel road winding through mountains. I didn't know what to expect. A few times I thought we were going off the side of the mountain. Scared the living shit out of me. I've been afraid of heights ever since."

Afraid of heights? And still climbed onto a roof?

There was much about Dad that he wouldn't say.

Years later, I'd gradually accepted that I would've gotten a more complete understanding of a pitch-dark cave using a match, than I did in trying to plumb the depths of Dad.

* * *

We'd strolled a half-hour across Grampa's fields, before Uncle James and I stopped at the backdoor landing. Dad had already disappeared into the house.

"Ever clean a rabbit?" Uncle James asked me.

"No, I've never done that," I said. *Give it a bath?* I examined the two rabbits Dad and Uncle James had shot but that I'd carried. Dad didn't allow me to handle a gun, so I'd served as their gopher—go for this, go for that, carry the rabbits.

"I'll show you," he said and opened the kitchen door. "Lay them down and I'll be right back."

Warm enough while we hunted, I noticed the cold air as I waited on the marble rock. Every breath formed a cloud that disappeared into the air. *Going to take long?*

Uncle James returned with a butcher knife and some newspaper.

The sight of any knife scared me, since the first time I'd cut my thumb trying to whittle. I pictured the one sticking from Dad's back pants pocket. But, butcher knives were a whole different ball game. Their mention alone made me shiver.

Uncle James spread the paper on the rock and selected one rabbit. "You cut through the skin at the knees on the hind legs." He tugged and sliced, until he worked the skin away from both hind legs from the knees to the butt, then he cut around the tail.

I studied the dark leg muscles. *I might be eating one of those for supper.*

"Now, you pull off the skin," he said. "Hold onto the back feet."

I gripped as hard as I could while Uncle James yanked and pulled the hide forward up to the neck and front legs with one continuous motion.

"That was easy," I said, "and there wasn't any blood."

"No. Hold it up a little higher," he said. "Now, you remove the front feet and head." He severed the front legs at the elbows, followed by the head at the neck, and at places bare of skin.

The fur, front feet, and head fell to the ground—*Plop!*—and lay in a heap.

With a cut along the belly from the butt to the ribs, he said, "Be careful not to puncture the entrails."

A wisp of vapor, along with the smell of mowed grass, rose in the air as warm rabbit innards bulged.

I couldn't avoid watching, even though I didn't like the sight of guts.

With gentle pulls Uncle James pulled out the insides, which remained connected. He severed that mass with several clean cuts and pitched it onto the discarded parts pile.

"Now, you cut off the hind legs." After that, he laid the skinned rabbit on clean newspaper, away from the unwanted parts and other rabbit.

Never saw Dad clean a rabbit. Did he even know how?

When we finished the second one, Uncle James asked, "Want a rabbit's foot for luck?"

Hmm, not so lucky for the rabbit. Wouldn't help Billy one bit, either, but maybe my own luck would improve. Dad quit drinking or stop hitting Mom? Wouldn't hold my breath, but what was the harm? "Yeah, I'll take one."

* * *

When Uncle James and I delivered the skinned rabbits, Gramma said, "I'll fry those up for supper. You two get cleaned up."

Pronto, Gramma sliced the rabbits into pieces, covered them with flour, and fried them in a heated skillet.

Dad or Uncle James must've given her a heads-up.

With everybody called to supper and seated, Grampa delivered grace from his reserved position before we dug in.

I looooved rabbit and must've been hungry, because the rabbit leg I grabbed tasted wonderful. *Too bad those rabbits had to die.*

* * *

The men—Grampa, Dad, and Uncle James—held a general retreat to the living room after supper.

Verlon and I had started to join them, when I heard Gramma say, "We'll need more water to wash the dishes."

Mom followed that with, "Hon, would you go draw a bucket of water?"

I didn't need to look, knew she meant me. Somewhat put upon, I said, "Okay," in a half-grumbling, half-resigned way. I'd grown strong enough to master the chore of drawing a bucket of water, but not strong enough to challenge mean-drunk-Dad alone.

"Put your jacket on," Mom said.

Sheesh. "Okay," I said. "Don't take my place on the couch," I told Verlon.

As I drew a full bucket, I wondered what I was missing in the living room and so hurried. *Verlon better not have taken my spot.*

* * *

Grampa occupied his usual chair, the one I'd always known him to use. Must've established dibs in every room of the house long before I arrived on the scene.

During cold days, we'd all gather in the living room heated by a coal-fired potbelly stove. Grampa, Uncle James, and Dad would talk of rabbit hunts, weather, and jobs. Gramma and Mom would talk of plans for the next meal, who was sick, and who they'd visited recently at a funeral home. Though not as exciting as TV, our country form of entertainment kept me interested. I didn't want to be by myself, or in a cold room. I figured Mom would tie me down with a rope, if I attempted to be off by myself.

Dad was talking about his work with Uncle James. He said something about getting laid off from a job, the one prior to his roofing one.

Laid off? He hadn't quit that one, too?

Grampa jumped in, "James, would you give me a shave and haircut?"

"Sure, Dad," Uncle James said without pause. "Where's your razor?"

Grampa gestured. "I think it's in that drawer there."

Dad didn't let on about his job changes around Mom. His job changes had become nail-biters for her. Besides, he'd made it abundantly clear that his work was none of her business. But since he changed jobs frequently anyway, he somehow had a knack for scrounging work.

Uncle James began his ritual, which reminded me of cleaning Dad's toenails. Nothing yucky about shaving somebody's face, and, as well, a far cry from squeezing blackheads.

Uncle James put a towel over Grampa's shoulders, whisked soapy, warm water in a cup with a shaving brush until he'd worked up a white lather. "I'll stoke the fire," he said.

Cold air brushed my back. *Winter sneaking through the windows.* I leaned towards the stove.

Uncle James opened the hinged stove door, tossed in several pieces of shiny-black coal from the bucket on the floor nearby, and stirred everything with a poker. Gramma had started that fire early in the morning, I'd bet, before she cooked breakfast and I'd gotten out of bed. After that, Uncle James had tended the stove.

Instant heat.

"Uncle James, why do you only burn coal in that stove?" I asked.

"Coal doesn't cost that much. They deliver it and it's easy to put into the stove. We only use wood in the fireplace and kitchen stove."

"Chopping wood must be hard work," I said. "I've never chopped wood." Didn't want to. Glad I didn't have to.

"It takes a bit of work," Uncle James said.

Verlon, returning from the kitchen, sat on the couch.

"Move over," I told him, "you almost sat on me." I leaned into him as I gave a nudge with my arm.

"No, I didn't," he replied.

"Did, too."

Verlon moved a few inches away from me, enough to get separation.

"And stay over there," I said with a stern look.

Uncle James applied lather to Grampa's face and neck, and put a clean double-edged blade in the razor.

I heard the scrape against whiskers as Uncle James pulled the razor across Grampa's face. "Ew," I whispered, soft enough that no one heard me. *Doesn't that hurt?*

Grampa didn't flinch or complain. He gave no sign of pain and no blood appeared.

A haircut with comb and scissors followed.

Grampa's shave and haircut from Uncle James left me feeling bad about hating to clean Dad's toenails. But then I remembered my anger at Dad, and my fear.

Uncle James checked the stove. "Some of the ashes need to be removed." He jerked the grate handle at the bottom of the stove back and forth. *Clank, clank, clank!*

Chunks of dark cinders and fine white ash fell onto the flat metal pan underneath.

Uncle James emptied the coal bucket into the stove and re-stoked the fire. "I'll take out the ashes and re-fill the bucket."

With another rush of heat, a reassuring contrast to the cold outside, I chose to watch through a breath-fogged window.

Uncle James emptied the bucket onto one of the two little mounds next to the footpath. Then, he scooped up fist-sized chunks from the two-foot-high coal pile. His white-cloud breath hung in the air a moment before it disappeared. I felt glad to be toasty warm.

* * *

"Brrrrrr, it's chilly out there." Uncle James placed the coal bucket near the stove.

A slight cool breeze washed over me. "What do you do with the ashes, Uncle James?"

"Your Gramma uses them to fertilize her flowers and make soap."

Oh, so, that's what Gramma had used to make lie soap. And why she'd done it there.

Uncle James stoked the stove again.

Glowing red, the stove drove Dad farther away. I pushed back into the couch as far as I could and wondered if that stove could melt.

* * *

The next morning, Uncle James said, "I'm taking a pig to the slaughterhouse. Come with me and keep me company."

I wasn't sure what to expect, but wanted some excitement beyond listening to Grampa read newspapers. Worse, maybe he would launch into a sermon with a barrage of biblical citations.

I could do without a Grampa-sermon. "Okay, I'll go. I've never been there."

"Put on your coat," Mom said.

She hadn't needed to tell me.

Once in the truck cab beside Uncle James, I looked back at Grampa's pig, nose busy, standing alone in the truck bed.

Grunt, grunt!

"Where're we going?" I imagined the pig said. At least, that's what I'd want to know.

Settled into my seat, I studied the headstones and mowed grass in the graveyard near the stop sign at the junction with 31W. I didn't want to think about how dead people looked in their coffins, but couldn't avoid it.

Uncle James slowed the pickup to a stop.

Ready to think about something else, I read the street sign at the stop, MAGNOLIA. *The Old Road had another name?*

With no sidewalks, no streetlights, no fire hydrants, no painted lines down the middle nor curbs, the road in front of Grampa's house never seemed like a street to me. And Upton felt as far away as the moon. At night the farm remained quiet and pitch-dark, except for the light from the house, stars, moon, and passing cars.

I expected we'd go right, but we turned left instead, away from Upton. And as soon as I'd adjusted to that, we turned left again.

"Here we are," Uncle James said.

Gravel, thrown up by the tires, clanked against the bottom of the truck as we bounced across a parking lot. A light-gray dust cloud followed us. Grampa's pig bumped about, nose busy, pushed and pulled in, out, in, out, in, out.

Grunt!

We stopped near the back of a large, corrugated metal building, overtaken by the dust cloud. A young man in a white full-length apron, blood-streaked from chest to knees, approached us. Looked like he could still be in high school.

"How can we help you?" he asked Uncle James in a strong accent.

Not from Louisville. Nobody I knew talked that way.

"We've got one pig to butcher," Uncle James told him.

When Uncle James and I skinned rabbits, we never needed aprons to avoid blood.

"You won't have to wait long. Back up to the shoot and lower your tailgate," the guy said.

Friendly. Straight to the point.

Grunt!

The young man shepherded Grampa's nose-snuffling pig into a shoot with a whack on the rump.

Squeal!

I figured the pig had said, "That hurt!"

Uncle James and I raised the tailgate, moved the truck, and returned to watch.

Two cows, white, brown, and black, both with short horns—regular cows to me—guided by a wooden fence on each side, stood in line ahead of Grampa's pig, though each separated by a gate.

The young guy worked quickly and quietly, prodding the first cow into the dead-end enclosure, where it could barely move. With quick aim of a .22-rifle—*Pop!*—the cow's skittishness ended with a shot to the forehead.

Just like that? No moo, no eye roll, no gasp, no twist or turn, nothing like bad guys shot in westerns. *Shot in the head. No anesthesia. No blindfold. Bam. Dead?* My heart raced and I couldn't spit, even if I'd wanted to.

The guy attached a rope to one of the cow's hind ankles, then hoisted her and pushed her along an overhead track into the building.

Just like that. A bullet in the head, upside down by an ankle, and into the building within the minute.

The second cow got the same treatment.

Pop!

How fast their situations had changed. Shot and moved into the building, hardly time for their hearts to stop, if their hearts had stopped. I didn't want to think that, but couldn't help myself. My ears pounded.

Grunt!

Grampa's pig suspect anything?

Pop!

Grampa's pig managed a brief squeal and collapsed in a heap.

"Aw," I whispered. I'd never heard an animal cry out in death before. *Felt the bullet? Prayed to a pig god for mercy?* I wanted to reach out to comfort Grampa's pig, but knew I couldn't.

"Let's go inside and watch," Uncle James said.

I wanted to cry. I wanted to focus on something different, anything not about death and killing. I didn't want to see Grampa's pig treated like a thing, like it didn't feel or didn't think. I didn't know if pigs had feelings or thoughts, but how could they not?

We entered the large building. Men talked and worked along a pulley assembly line, each wearing a bloodied knee-length apron.

Thwack! Thwack!

One guy had chopped off a cow's front leg. I guessed that was a cow, about the size and shape of one.

The warm, moist air inside reminded me of my sweaty shirt after I rode my bike fast on a summer's day. The heavy, thick, salty smell, different and stronger than a rabbit's, reminded me of dirty pennies I'd found. I wanted to hold my breath, but couldn't last more than a few seconds, before I gave up and breathed through my mouth.

Another man, maybe Dad's age, his voice raised to overcome the noise, said to us, "You're welcome to watch us butcher. I'll explain what we're doing."

With a glance I followed the overhead rail around three sides of the room to its end. Men focused on what hung in front of them, removed parts in assembly-line fashion. They pushed the remainder to the next guy. Everyone wore a plastic hat, goggles, gloves, and knee-high boots.

Too much to take in, I looked back at the older man.

"The animals come in there where we drain their blood." He pointed towards Grampa's pig hanging above a large vat of pooled blood collected from other animals.

And not just one animal with a throat cut, but many. Multiplied by ten, by a hundred, by a thousand?

A sharp knife sliced deep across Grampa's pig's throat.

Painful? I hoped not. *Dead meant the end of pain, didn't it?* I preferred to think that, anyway. I'd scraped my knee badly when I'd fallen with my bike a week ago. The pain hadn't started immediately. Instead, my brain had taken a second to get the message, and then I wanted to scream.

Blood from Grampa's pig splashed into the vat below.

Blood. Death. Bloody death.

When we skinned rabbits or squirrels, one, two, maybe three at a time, we didn't use a production line, unlike what surrounded me, a business, where people got paid to do it.

"Then, we dip them in boiling water to remove the hair and clean the hides."

I watched water vapor rising from several vats. Two men raised the first cow I'd seen shot from a hot bath, then lowered the second one in.

Good that those animals weren't in pain. At least there'd been some mercy. I recalled burning my finger on a hot skillet, and I cringed at the idea of getting boiled alive.

The guy turned to his right, pointed and said, "We remove the entrails over there."

Guts bulged, drooped, then dropped to the floor.

Plop!

Hadn't wanted to watch that either, but too late.

"Every man has a specific job and works their position by repeating the same procedure on each animal as it moves along."

How could those men work there every day? I understood animals needed to be processed to make them into hamburgers and pork chops, food for people. But around the last sounds of dying? The number of animals hung from the rail and cut open? The quantity and smell of blood and guts? All that knotted my stomach and left me frozen. Not able to run, not sure what to do, I could only look away when I caught myself staring.

Grampa's pig became less recognizable as it moved along the rail. First a pig, it became an animal, then parts found in grocery stores within an hour. They turned it into hams, pork chops, and sides of bacon, wrapped in paper and ready for the refrigerator.

I carried packaged parts of Grampa's pig to the truck, glad to be outside again. Hoped to erase what I'd seen.

Quiet on the drive back, I noticed the first road sign down Magnolia, CHILDREN AT PLAY. *Play, more fun than a visit to the animal death house.*

One sign near the rise before Grampa's farm read, SPEED LIMIT 50. I pictured the next sign, which displayed a bent arrow.

Past the farmhouse, past the dirt road to the two barns, over the rise, it stood adjacent to the lower end of the blackberry patch. Beyond, Mr. Cruz's farm spread out on the left side and the road curved right, into unknown territory to me.

Where did Upton end and Magnolia Street stop? Could be, Grampa's farm lay just beyond Upton city limits.

* * *

Gramma had laid the table for dinner.

"Well, what do you think?" Uncle James asked me.

"I'm not hungry," I said and went to sit alone in the living room.

A few minutes later, Mom insisted I come eat. "It'll be a while before we have supper," she said.

I understood Mom hadn't said that out of malice or a threat, but as a fact that general snacking between meals wasn't practiced on the farm, except for a tomato or watermelon off the vine now and then.

"Alright," I said. *I'll eat a little but not the fried pork chops.*

* * *

After dinner clean up, Mom said to Verlon and me, "Let's go gather some walnuts."

Fine by me. I needed a diversion from slaughterhouse scenes and Grampa's pig turned to pork chops.

"Put on your sweaters and bring a pair of gloves," she told Verlon and me. "You don't want to get stains on your hands. It'll take several days for that to wear off."

On the way, I studied the field of dried, broken corn stalks. Brown, shriveled leaves, scattered under the walnut tree, crinkled as we gathered nuts. A few nuts in the tree remained out of reach.

Grunt, grunt, grunt!

Grampa's pigs approached and gathered along the fence, one pig short.

Grunt, grunt, grunt!

I figured they begged, "Paalease feed us. Please, please, please."

No walnuts lay on their side of the fence. Eaten, no doubt.

I put on a pair of gloves, picked up several walnuts, their split dark-shiny husks like shriveled prunes, and threw them into the bag. They smelled musty, like the mud from the swampy part of the pond.

Mom must've noticed. "Take the husks off before you put the nuts into the bag."

"Okay," I said and happily tossed the mushy husks over the fence.

Grunt, grunt, grunt!

"Stop shoving. You can have the next one," one pig complained.

We gathered every nut we could find and removed and pitched the husks over the fence for the pigs.

My gloves, covered with dark-green stains, smelled of husks. "Store-bought walnuts never smell this good," I said.

"Let's take them to the screened-in side porch and spread them out on a table to dry," Mom said.

"Why can't we eat them now?"

"They need to dry out first."

"Then, when can we eat them?"

"They should be ready by Christmas."

"Won't they go bad by then?"

"If they're dried, they could last years."

Little mummies.

In You Go

November 1959

I hated our Fairdale neighbors, the ones who lived in the rear house on the property opposite the preacher. Didn't know why, just did. I never went to their house. I avoided stepping onto their graveled driveway, which separated our territory from theirs. I averted my attention from their house as much as I could. No kids my age lived there, but they owned a cat, which, as cats do, didn't respect any physical boundary.

* * *

By myself near the garage on that chilly day, I spotted their cat when it turned a corner of the garage and approached me.

Though the cat offered some resistance, I picked it up. *What to do?* I carried my captive into the garage, out of sight of spying eyes.

My prisoner hissed and squirmed as I constrained it.

What's with you?

The cat scratched me.

"Ow!" *Damn cat, I'll teach you.* I knew I was up to no good.

Find a piece of rope. I'll tie you up.

I used a rope pulled from under a work bench. Tied that around the cat's neck and to the staircase that led to the garage's second floor.

223

I watched the cat claw the air as it dangled at the end of the rope. *You're going to die, damn you.*

I couldn't have told you when I'd finalized my decision, perhaps, months or only moments beforehand. I'd hated that cat for quite some time. But as I'd tied the rope, I knew I shouldn't. But my anger welled up, as well as my fear of discovery, as the cat clawed the air and twisted at the end of the rope.

The cat struggled several minutes, then went limp.

My anger subsided as quickly as it had intensified, replaced by guilt and shame.

What to do with a dead cat? An answer and my decision? *Into the outhouse.*

With no one in sight who might watch, and so somewhat sure the coast was clear, I hurried to the outhouse with my victim, rope still around its neck.

I shouldn't have done that. Would I turn into Dad? Had I already?

At supper I resolved to hold my mud and never tell anyone.

* * *

Looking back on that act of cruelty, I've since learned that I was steeped in the process by which anger, without appropriate skills of expression, builds and erupts in violent ways. That's also how it gets passed to the next generation. But, as a kid, trapped in that cycle, I couldn't know a way out existed.

I've learned to like cats, encourage them to approach me and pet them when they're willing. I prefer to consider that as my way to make amends, though token.

How about Them Apples?

August 1960

We arrived for another visit to the country Friday evening. I was twelve years old and between the seventh and eighth grades.

"Well, hello, Son. Gramma's going to can those apples," she said, then wiped her hands on a white apron as she stood near a large tub on the electric stove.

"Hi, Gramma." I'd stopped at the open doorway of the screened-in side porch connected to the kitchen. I'd studied the shriveled apple pieces spread over two tables, drying there since we'd last visited several weeks before. "Can I have a piece of apple?"

"Yes, get you one," she said.

I hurried before Verlon could spot me and want one, too. During the long warm days and with the sun directly on them in the west-facing porch every evening, the apple slices had become chewy little chunks.

Mom, Verlon, and I pitched in to help Gramma. The house filled with the sweet smell of apple.

Once we'd completed Gramma's assembly-line canning job, we retreated to the living room. There, Mom, Dad, Gramma, Grampa, and Uncle James talked about grownup things, while Verlon and I haggled over couch space.

* * *

Didn't seem long before Gramma said, "I think the apples are cooled enough by now." She looked at me. "Will you help Gramma carry them to the root cellar?"

"I'll help, Gramma." *I could carry one box and handle myself, even if I saw a snake. Probably. Maybe.*

"What about me?" Verlon said.

"You can help me clean up," Mom told him.

I grabbed one box and pulled it off the edge of the table.

Heavy but manageable.

Unable to see my feet, I shuffled across the kitchen floor.

Gramma propped the screen door open while she held the other box. "It's okay to go slow."

My foot searched for the large stone landing while I looked at Gramma. "There it is," I said.

The distance to the tool shed had somehow grown, multiplied by the weight of my box. I waited at the top of the cellar steps, watched Gramma find a space on the cellar floor for her box before she talked me down. *That snake around? Maybe I'd stomp on it.* My box laid atop hers, I climbed the steps in front of Gramma.

* * *

The next morning, well after breakfast and bored, I passed through the hallway on my way to the front yard.

Gramma's singing greeted me. The ornate bedroom door stood open. I could see she faced the fireplace, but turned to look; she must've heard me at the door. "These are your Gramma's." She cradled a doll, brushed and straightened its clothing with one hand. She set the doll in an open spot on the mantle. Picked up another. Continued singing. She didn't sound embarrassed nor ever seem bothered about what lay beyond the glossy-white door that goes upstairs.

You'd never catch me touching Gramma's dolls. They creeped me out. *But why did Gramma have a collection? Mom didn't have one. Aunt Shirley didn't, not even Aunt Irene. Cousin Betty Jo, maybe one or two, tops.*

* * *

An hour later, tired and thirsty from my time on the front porch swing, I started into the house for a drink of water.

The ornate bedroom door still open, I peeked in. The room was lit by early afternoon sunlight unblocked by clouds and unfiltered by curtains. The glossy-white door waited in plain view. Gramma was not in sight.

More emboldened because Gramma didn't seem scared to be in there alone, I figured I could handle a ghost, if one was behind that door. I crossed the room, climbed the three painted steps, and gripped the doorknob. I took a deep breath and whispered, "Okay. If you're in there, I'm ready."

I leaned back and for the first time, pulled the mysterious door open.

The stairway, lit from somewhere above, turned as the steps led upwards.

So far, so good. No sounds of a ghost.

I leaned in. There appeared to be an open room at the top of the steep stairway, some twenty steps up.

What was up there? As long as I could see I'd be okay.

With each step up, I recognized more features of the room above, until my eyes rose above the last step. *I knew that room.* I'd slept there a few times. I'd always come and gone through the doorway on the opposite side, which led to the main hallway staircase. I'd never had cause to look down the secret passage.

Yay. I'd explored the secret passage, though in the light of day. But I had no guarantee there wasn't a ghost, so I cleared out before it might wake from a nap. Nighttime? That was another story. Any ghost would surely be out after dark. I shut the glossy-white door before I retreated to the hallway on my way to the kitchen.

As far as I knew, the stairwell remained unexplored by other cousins, so I'd keep my discovery to myself. And what lay behind the glossy-white door would remain *my* secret passage.

* * *

I'd joined Uncle James on the front porch in time to watch Uncle Joe slow his car—a new one I'd not seen—to a gentle stop near the oak tree in the front yard.

Every year, Uncle Joe traded-in his car for a newer model. Every year! We'd had our old car for a few years, and it wasn't new when Dad got it. I couldn't help but feel less than. *Dad's fault, all Dad's fault.*

Aunt Irene and my cousins, Jerry, Betty Jo, and Cathy, disappeared through the front door. Uncle Joe settled into one of the two metal chairs on the front porch.

"The field across the road looks good," he said. "I brought some softball equipment. Maybe, we should play a game tomorrow."

Got my vote. I'd brought my Tigers Little League baseball cap—named after the Detroit Tigers, I figured—as well as my glove and a ball, in case an opportunity to play arose. Even playing catch would've sufficed.

In the warmer months, Uncle Joe brought a ball, a bat, bases, and gloves to the farm when he visited. He delivered milk products to grocery stores on a route in Louisville. I thought him strange for putting butter in his coffee, rather than cream, until I learned he received that butter free.

"I just mowed that field yesterday," Uncle James said. "So it's perfect for playing."

* * *

News had gotten out.

After we'd eaten our Saturday dinner and Mom, Irene, and Gramma had cleaned up the dishes, Mom turned recruiter.

"Rene," that's what Mom called Aunt Irene, pronounced like the last syllable of marine, "do you want to play a game?" Then, cheerleader-Mom added, "Come on, everybody, let's play."

Most everyone decided to participate.

* * *

A few clouds drifted overhead, while the sun warmed everything. Surely, warm days had been created to play ball, although to me, any day not occupied by a blizzard served well enough.

We chose the flattest part of the open field across the road. Trampled the worst of the remaining weed-stubble to lay out an infield. We positioned everything a safe distance from the sinkhole, which would eat an errant ball in a heartbeat.

Uncle Joe and Uncle James served as captains and chose up sides. Everyone who wanted to play ended up on a team.

"Okay, your team can bat first," Uncle Joe told Uncle James. "Batter up."

We covered the field in turns, thick as ticks on a farm dog.

Off to the side, Dad chain-smoked cigarettes, his second favorite pastime right behind Friday beer-benders. I'd never seen him play ball, nor had he ever offered to play catch with me, so I figured he couldn't.

* * *

A couple of hours later the game ended in favor of supper, but since its preparation would take a while, Uncle Joe and I stayed behind to play catch.

"Want to see a knuckle ball?" he asked me.

"Yeah, I've heard of them but never seen one."

Uncle Joe wound up and let 'er rip.

The ball wiggled and danced towards me, though the seams hung in place.

Mantle reaches out with his glove to make the catch. The crowd roars! Thwack! I felt the sting. "How did you do that?" I asked as I threw the ball back.

"You hold it with your knuckles."

Thwack! Another sting.

"Show me how you do it," I said.

Uncle Joe held the ball with his knuckles, rotated his hand several times to give me a better look. "Hold it like that." He gave the ball a slight push as he straightened his fingers. "Release it like that."

"Okay." *I'd be the envy of all boys.* I tried to duplicate his pitch. Couldn't, my hand not big enough. Dad couldn't teach me that, or much else, except how to carry a shotgun, smoke a cigarette, or swing a hammer.

* * *

"Well, I guess we should be heading home," Dad said to Mom after supper.

Uncle Joe, with Aunt Irene and their three kids in tow, had high-tailed to Louisville ahead of us. Uncle Joe, a fast driver, would've arrived home within an hour. I couldn't imagine him not driving on the toll road every trip to and from Upton. With money for a new car each year, the toll would be of little consequence to Uncle Joe. And he'd drive over the speed limit, too. Dad, a cowpoke on the other hand, would take about two hours when he drove the entire way on 31W. When Dad did drive on the toll road, we were passed by most everyone going our direction. In the backseat, directly behind him, I'd repeat my mantra: Speed it up, Dad.

Mom packed up our things. "Cecil, take these out to the car."

Individuals said their goodbyes in random combinations as we moved towards the front door through the hallway.

Mom paused midway. "Which door did we come in? We have to go out the same door."

"Why is that important?" I asked.

"I just believe you need to come in and go out the same door. You'll have bad luck otherwise."

How did that work?

I recalled the time Dad had stopped our car when a black cat ran across the street in front of us.

"Why are you turning around?" I'd asked him.

"I'm not going to cross the path of a black cat," he'd said.

He'd driven down an alley to the next street in order to get home.

Superstition, smuperstition. I'd be logical, the one sure way I could, and would, be different from Mom and Dad. Maybe, I'd avoid their blind spots.

I knew then I needed to think for myself and made a promise not to copy their marital conflict. I didn't appreciate the difficulty of that, however.

Popularity

February 1961

I couldn't say who had started it or why. I could say it had started with one simple phone call.

Our party-line phone rang and Mom answered. "Some girl is asking to talk to you," she told me with a grin.

What? "Hello," I said.

"Can I interview you?" the girl asked.

"Yeah." *What else could I say?* Somebody, and in particular a young girl, had called and wanted to talk with me. Me!

I'd adopted the strategy not to pass up an opportunity when someone showed interest in me. I liked the idea of having friends, but hadn't always read situations well when I'd initiated contact.

A half-hour later, she completed her interview.

That one call would open a door to a greater degree of popularity at school for me, at least among some girls, though their faces would remain unknown to me. Heck, I couldn't even remember their names.

My name and phone number must've gotten on a Fairdale High sorority pledge list. Girls practiced their conversational skills and delved into the mystery of boys. I, at least superficially, practiced my skills of delving into the mystery of girls. I asked no whys or hows, instead considered myself lucky and wallowed in my notoriety.

My confidence in holding up my end of a conversation with a girl improved, well enough to avoid appearing a complete idiot.

An hour or so spent on our party line every few days, I wondered why Mom or Dad hadn't told me to get off the phone.

* * *

Sixth grade had been a mixed blessing for me. I'd liked Tracey, while Joyce had liked me. No secret to anyone in our class, I had a sixth-grade spurned-love chain going on. Joyce always picked me to read next in class. Hot on Tracey, I'd pick her, unless I was angry at her for picking Ricky the last round, then I'd pick Joyce. I worked to win over Tracey. I even visited her once at home the following summer, but that didn't impress her.

In seventh grade I more easily talked and joked with girls on a casual basis in class. I didn't have the wherewithal to suggest meeting with any after school, nor would I or could I broach the subject of my sexual interest in them. At least some girls liked talking to me, I could tell. I wondered if my willingness to be interviewed hadn't labeled me an approachable boy. Regardless, I was all in.

On the other hand, I shied away from school friend stay-overs. No way I wanted someone I knew to find out about my house and our use of a chamber pot. I worked hard to keep home life separate from school. Broke down once, though, and swapped stay-overs with a classmate, Dennis.

Run, Rabbit, Run

June 1961

I'd completed the seventh grade.

No one talked of Uncle Tunney and Aunt Betty at Gramma and Grampa's, though I missed Billy and frequently thought about what had happened.

Gramma, Grampa, and Uncle James had moved across the road, about a football field from the big house, and into one of two houses Grampa had had built a few years before.

I didn't like the cramped, tiny rooms with low ceilings of that single-level house. Its basement, though, another matter altogether, had a high ceiling and ample floor space. But other than a few boxes stored there, it remained empty.

I missed the high ceilings, the hideaways, the fireplaces, the front porch of the big house. I even missed the glossy-white door in the ornate bedroom to *my* secret passage that led upstairs. That ghost didn't scare *me* anymore.

* * *

"I want to sleep there," Verlon said.

"First come, first served," I replied. Without a word beforehand, I'd jumped into bed to claim the spot next to an open window.

"Everybody has a place to sleep," Gramma said. She'd put Mom and Dad in one bed, Verlon and me in a second, and Uncle James in a third. "I'll go to bed now. Good night."

Before Gramma had closed the bedroom door, all of us bid her good night, except Dad, who breathed heavily.

A few last-minute checks completed, Mom went to the light switch. "Everybody ready for lights out?"

"Whenever you're ready, Bea," Uncle James said.

"Okay, then." After a brief pause, Mom switched off the ceiling light. Her footsteps moved across the room, then her bed creaked and sheet rustled. Dad snorted.

I noticed my ears ringing.

The two raised windows helped little to circulate the stagnant, humid air, suffocating until it cooled in the early morning. Sleeping near a window provided some relief when a breeze pushed through the screens.

Not quite ready for sleep, I propped myself on one elbow and gazed out the window.

On-off, on-off. At regular intervals, silent individual fireflies signaled with their beacons. On-off, on-off.

The moon wouldn't rise for some hours. Stars in the clear sky provided enough light to see the ridge and two barns across the open field. Tiny flashes, on-off, filled the space between, near and far.

Fireflies lived only days, I knew. Anything less than decades deemed too short, I accepted they had no time to waste. I knew they would stop blinking as dawn approached. They would shelter until darkness returned. And they would continue night after night as long as they could. But I'd never seen that many fireflies. I'd never considered there could be so many, countless as stars in the sky. In the top bunk at home in Fairdale, beyond the city limits of Louisville, I had a limited view outside our bedroom window.

Closer flashes brighter than the farthest ones, each firefly blinked to some mysterious rhythm. Uncle James snorted and his bed creaked. Verlon's leg slid between the sheets, his body weight shifted and a foot came to rest against my leg, which I moved away.

I alone watched. Close, seemed I could reach out and touch the fireflies, as if in some way I'd joined their dance. I felt special.

* * *

No two summer nights are the same. None, ever.

Some weeks later, Mom, Dad, Verlon, Uncle James, and I again settled into the same beds. Covers rustled and bed springs squeaked as everyone sought comfortable positions.

Gramma gave us a soft warning with, "Lights out."

"Good night, Gramma," I said.

What little breeze entered through the nearest open window provided only slight, temporary relief. I anticipated the cool air of early morning.

With the moon somewhere high in the sky and out of my view, everything in the open field, and the ridge and two barns beyond, stood out in the pale, blue-tinted moonlight.

I'd heard crickets many times. I'd noticed their sounds as we prepared for bed, but given them little thought until the light went out and we quieted. The chorus of thousands of collective cricket calls grew louder until they seemed inside my head. Some chirped from far away, others from right outside and below the window. I imagined orchestra violinists synchronizing in a performance.

Chirp, chirp! One cricket in the bedroom tested its musical legs, tentative at first, as if tuning up, then joined the symphony in full force.

Chirp, chirp, chirp! "Hey, I'm in here," I imagined that cricket called.

No surprise, a cricket in the house. Often, one found a way inside. Spiders, flies, an occasional bee, too. I could handle critters in the house, but the mere thought of a mosquito made me itch.

The crickets' symphony, as if conducted by an unseen hand, provided a steady background noise, and except for the cricket inside, I detected no change in the chorus from one moment to the next.

Chirp, chirp!

Where was that little booger?

Verlon snorted and rolled over.

I recalled the fireflies, thankful that I witnessed this second special event. Amazed by the blinks of the fireflies, I was equally amazed by the chirps of the crickets. I listened to their individual sounds and combined effort, awed by their numbers, until at some point I drifted into sleep.

* * *

Summer advanced into August. Weeds had turned into dried-brown fire hazard.

"Do you want to ride on the tractor while I mow weeds?" Uncle James asked Verlon and me. "I'll be right back, I need to find a hat," he added.

"I'll go," I said as Uncle James left the room.

Riding on a tractor and mowing a field sounded fun, the nearest thing to a trip to Fountain Ferry that I'd get that day. Fountain Ferry, the amusement park in Louisville located next to the river, served as our local version of Disneyland.

When Uncle James returned with a hat, Verlon said, "Me, too."

"Wear your hats," Mom said.

Jeez. I grabbed my Little League Tigers cap.

* * *

Uncle James rigged the tractor, then tested the connection.

Clack, clack, clack!

Attached to the back, extended off the right side, the mower arm worked like a big hedge clipper that skimmed the ground, powered by the tractor's drive shaft.

Verlon and I climbed onto the tractor, and we claimed positions opposite each other against the back-wheel fenders with Uncle James in the driver's seat almost between us.

About a half-mile down the road towards Upton, Uncle James turned into a vacant field covered with chest-high weeds, perfect for hide-and-seek, though a tick-and-chigger heaven. Easy to spot, a large sinkhole occupied the middle of the field.

"Why are we coming here?" I said.

"This belongs to your grampa. He purchased this property as an investment," Uncle James said.

The sun's heat reminded me of the red glow of Gramma's potbelly stove.

We mowed our way across the field in rough parallel rows, except where we skirted the sinkhole.

Clack, clack, clack!

The faster Uncle James drove the tractor, the louder the clacking, and larger the swirl of dust and fragments of weed.

I thought about Grampa's two mules, John and Beck. "I can't imagine Grampa mowing weeds with mules," I yelled to overcome the racket.

"That's how he used to do it," Uncle James yelled back.

For an hour, back and forth, we laid waste to the weeds that had covered half the field. Fallen weeds lay flat and ordered in neat rows, like combed hair.

Verlon and I watched for large rocks or other things hidden in the brush that might damage the mower.

"Rabbit," Uncle James yelled, as he stopped the tractor.

An adult rabbit zigzagged over fallen weeds before it turned and disappeared into tall, uncut weeds.

Uncle James said, "Keep a close watch, we're likely to see more."

I wiped sweat from my forehead.

Clack, clack, clack!

When we returned to near the spot of our first sighting, Uncle James stopped the tractor again. "Rabbits," he said.

Several small rabbits scurried about, guided to seek cover somehow.

We must've wrecked their home.

"Catch 'em," Uncle James said.

Verlon and I jumped off the tractor and selected a moving target.

As best they could, they hopped over and through the fallen stalks of weeds, which now acted as a hindrance, rather than a safe haven.

I'd never run down a grown rabbit, but quickly closed in. It hunkered in the brush, using the best cover available. I feared getting bitten, but the little fellow quivered in my hands.

I formed a pouch with my shirt and tucked the baby inside. Snug against my warm body, the rabbit calmed. "Hold it like this," I yelled to Verlon.

Within several minutes we'd gathered six.

"Some of them are bigger than the others," I said.

"They're probably from the same litter, though," Uncle James said.

Our catch quite a haul, we hadn't thought out what we'd do next. Plentiful, everyone treated rabbits like they were a dime a dozen, although we never killed any just for a thrill.

* * *

"We caught some rabbits, Gramma. See?" I told her back at the house, and pulled out my shirt, careful not to encourage an escape.

"Do you have a box we can keep them in? I'll feed them until they're big enough to let go."

"Yes, Gramma will find you a box to put them in." She returned with a cardboard box and provided a few scraps of raw vegetable leaves.

Rabbits, food, and water inside, I closed the lid. Left the box outside near the kitchen door for the night.

* * *

The next morning, I checked on the brood. A quick count revealed three missing.

"Augh. Gramma, some of the rabbits are gone. Where'd they go?"

"I think the cats must have gotten them." She pointed towards the tool shed.

Mousers, as Gramma called her cats, kept the rodent population in check, a baby rabbit no different.

I spied a small clump of fur.

"How did they get out?" I said.

"I don't know, Son," Gramma said.

I looked into the box. Small shreds of cardboard lay in the bottom near a hole in one corner.

"Augh. They chewed their way out."

Too late for those gone, I blocked the hole to keep the three remaining captives inside, then went into the house for a hurried breakfast.

* * *

I picked up one, which squirmed and kicked its legs.

Let it go? No way to build a sturdy cage, I set the rabbit on the ground and released my grip.

The rabbit bounded off a short distance and stopped.

Unseen until then, one of Gramma's mousers appeared in a full-speed run directly for the rabbit. Closed in within seconds.

The young rabbit didn't move until the last moment, but the cat dispatched it with a bite to the neck before carrying off its fresh kill.

Aw. Damn you, cat.

I picked up another rabbit, biggest of the bunch.

"Stop kicking," I said, but that didn't help. "I'm trying to find a good place to let you go." I gave it a shake. "Quit."

The baby rabbit continued to squirm and kick.

"Stop it." *A karate chop to the neck might make you stop.*

The rabbit spasmed several times, then went limp.

Aw. I didn't mean to kill you, just wanted you to stop kicking.

I didn't dare look towards the kitchen door for fear someone would finger me as a killer. The limp rabbit lay on the ground near the tool shed, I slunk away and watched a few moments. Figured the cats would carry away the evidence of my crime.

Back at the box I looked at the remaining rabbit. *At least maybe that one would live. Could live. Might live.* Quivering in my hands, I carried it around the house, away from Gramma's cats' reach, I hoped.

Was releasing it the right thing to do? Would it survive without a mother? I doubted I could survive without Mom. *Could it feed itself? Find shelter?*

It probably would do better on its own than around me. Nothing I'd done had helped its litter mates. I bent down near a growth of grass under the spread of the black walnut tree.

One pig came running.

Grunt, grunt!

"Got something for me to eat?" the pig must've said.

I placed the rabbit on the ground and loosened my grip.

The baby rabbit hesitated, then took several hops after I gave it a nudge.

"I'm sorry. Go hide and be safe." I walked away and wanted to cry. *Had I redeemed myself by saving at least one baby rabbit?* I wished I could undo the last two days. Knew I couldn't.

Another Start

February 1962

Thirteen and mid-year eighth grade, I struggled with an experimental ninth-grade algebra class taught to eighth-graders, first time I'd had difficulty with a subject. My grades suffered as my teacher piled on homework every day.

Mom sprang the news on me. "We're moving back to Highland Park."

"Again?" I hated that idea. *Dad's fault, all Dad's fault.* In spite of my difficulty with algebra and Dad's continued drinking, some things had been looking up, particularly my popularity with girls.

We'd moved ten times before Fairdale from what I could count. Friendships short-lived, I never knew when another move would severe more of them, which left me hesitant to form any. I'd adopted a passive stance towards friendships. I waited for others to approach me, prepared to cut ties at a moment's notice, as if they were trees on a riverbank that I floated past.

Dad's continued periodic bingeing on Fridays had encouraged Mom, Verlon, and me to abandon our house those evenings in favor of the Community Center. Mom tended the concession stand there while Verlon and I skated. I'd developed a fancy for one girl. I could tell she liked me, too, but I couldn't overcome my hesitations to approach her. Besides, no way I wanted girls to find out about my family's poverty, Dad's drinking, and my secret angry thoughts.

Now another move would break my friendships at a time when my social life outside of school could lead to a one-on-one most-personal encounter with a girl. And I certainly wanted a physical encounter; thought about that daily.

With one fell swoop, I'd leave behind friends, Little League, roller skating, and a possible position on the Fairdale High School varsity football team, and I would enter a new school environment.

I blamed Dad.

* * *

We moved back to Highland Park, across the street from the house where we'd lived when Verlon was born.

With Freddie left behind, as well as all the girls who liked me and whom I liked, I started over. Despite my fear of losing another friend, a new neighbor, Roger, became my best friend in short order. That dye cast, I exercised my options to minimize time at home. Mom trusted me to track time, stay out of trouble, and return home when she expected. I stayed at Roger's house for hours daily, weekends, and after school, or played neighborhood football or baseball until Mom called me for supper. And I participated in the after-school sports activities of track and summer football clinics.

People liked me; I wondered why. I didn't try hard, but I smiled and presented myself as flexible and open. I certainly didn't blab my secrets. No way. My good looks didn't hurt my cause, I reckoned; girls' glances from about the sixth grade had made that clear. I didn't doubt one bit that Joyce had been hot on me.

As it turned out, however, I didn't recover my Fairdale glory days. I never regained that degree of popularity in school. I didn't play in Little League again. I didn't date, much less have a sexual encounter. I didn't attend my high school prom. I didn't make the varsity football team. Nor did I learn to drive. And I blamed Dad.

As my eight-grade year drew near a close, I focused on my high school elective classes, according to the urgings of my teachers.

Curious about things mechanical and intrigued with things technical, I'd been keenly interested in our space race with the Soviet Union since Sputnik. I couldn't get enough space-related news; I followed each public launch and could recite names of various satellites, astronauts, and some of the Soviet cosmonauts.

I aspired to become an astronaut, willing to take whatever the risks as I perceived them. But how could I get there? Many of the Mercury Seven had flown jet fighters. Some had tested planes. Seemed to me pilots had a leg up, or two, if they had a scientific background.

Debating and thinking, I asked Dad. Figured his opinion couldn't hurt.

"Engineers make good money," he said.

The synthesis of all my thinking? A pilot with an Aeronautical Engineer degree would be the ticket into the astronaut inner circle. And to boot, my new school, Durrett, had a teacher who taught German and Russian. Understanding German wouldn't be a disadvantage, but surely, knowing Russian could seal the deal.

I was in, all in. Set my sights on as many elective math, science, Russian, and mechanical drafting classes in which I could enroll. In the meantime, I had little use for other subjects.

Don't Let the Smoke Get in Your Eyes
June 1962

At the start of my three-month school summer vacation, I lounged in my freedom from homework and Mom's insistent early-morning intrusions on my slumber with her calls, "Reveille." I'd grown to hate that word, reveille. Seemed she said it to irritate me out of bed. Not that I minded going to school, I liked it, but I hated getting out of bed, as well as that word.

We'd packed the car when Dad got home from work late Friday afternoon and were on the road within an hour.

Gramma came out the front door to greet us as I got out of the car. The late-Friday-evening sun cast sideways shadows. Lazy, white smoke rose in the warm, humid air across the road where Uncle James worked. "What's he doing, Gramma?" I asked.

"He's burning brush to clear the field."

"I'm going to help," I said, though with no clue how I could. What I meant to say was, I'm going to watch, as if by watching I would be helping.

"Is there any poison ivy in that field?" Mom asked Gramma.

"Yes, there is, Bea," Gramma said.

"Be careful," Mom yelled. "Don't touch the poison ivy."

Halfway across the road, I yelled back, "I won't." No strangers, poison ivy and me, I'd suffered bouts.

Verlon stayed behind at the house.

* * *

"Hi, Uncle James," I said.

"Well, hello there," he said and raked a pile of burning brush. *Crack! Pop! Sizzle!*

Smoke, blown by shifts in the gentle wind, engulfed me, which I attempted to avoid, though couldn't. Within an hour darkness crept in around us.

"It's getting too dark. I can't see," Uncle James said. "I'm going to quit for now and finish this tomorrow."

We left the pile to smolder overnight.

* * *

Scratch! "I'm itchy, Mom." I knew she'd seen me in spite of her conversation with Gramma. *Scratch, scratch!* I recognized the familiar itch. *Scratch!* I knew I shouldn't scratch the red welts on my arms, hands, face, and neck. *Scratch!* I guess I hadn't avoided the poison ivy after all.

"Stop scratching it," Mom said. "You'll just spread it around."

"But I can't help it."

"I have some calamine lotion we can put on it," Gramma said.

Mom swabbed on layers of the off-flesh-colored goop. "Let it dry. If you don't stop scratching, we'll have to wrap you up in bandages," she said. "I had a case of poison ivy so bad once that Mom and Dad wrapped me up and tied me down. I was miserable for a week."

Tied down for a week? Hardcore, no pussy-footing, a side of Gramma and Grampa I hadn't seen. *Whose idea was that?* I guessed they'd resorted to a common treatment of that time, calamine lotion not in the picture. *Best to be careful scratching around Mom.*

Repeated coatings, dried and caked on my skin, announced my plight to everyone. I fancied myself a primitive, young native, covered in special mud for a rite-of-passage.

I endured the rest of the weekend with my itch-mania. And since I didn't want to be wrapped like a mummy, I avoided scratching, within sight of Mom anyway.

Where was she?

Scratch!

Tallulah Street

July 1962

Aside from the house, the property we rented had two other buildings, a larger one with two rooms and a smaller one-room playhouse, both suitable for sleepovers. A large backyard also served as an excellent place to seek privacy from Dad and Mom, as my cohorts and I, sometimes with Verlon tagging along, pursued our teenage male interests. Girls didn't figure into the mix, which frustrated me to no end.

* * *

Perhaps, consuming beers with Carl at his house during our Friday evening visits fulfilled Dad's drinking needs. And though Mom and Dad continued to argue, his physical abuse of Mom had diminished. Epithets about each other's families, my grandparents mostly, as well as their political leanings—Mom, a Republican, and Dad, a Democrat—peppered the air. Their digs at each other and family, all people I loved, wounded me, and provided me more incentive to seek distance from them.

Time spent with Roger fit the bill, served as an escape from home, as well as same-age male friendship and potential clues to the mysteries of girls.

* * *

Dad drove us to Florida for our first family vacation. We'd rendezvoused with Beulah, Carl, and their boys along the way. Within several days we'd arrived in New Smyrna and rented the upstairs of an old house together.

For about a week, we hung out on the beach every day, until I heard Dad say to Carl, "I think we'll start back home tomorrow."

"Why?" Carl replied.

"My dick is getting hard," Dad said.

Ooh. I'd never heard Dad say anything like that before and be so blunt in my presence. Maybe, Dad and Mom still had sex after all their years of conflict. I hadn't given the idea much thought, but figured they must've, now and then.

* * *

About a week after our return home, I suffered appendicitis, and spent seven days in a hospital bed, while subjected to penicillin injections every several hours.

I soldiered on, as best I could, my spirits lifted when candy stripers, many about my age, delivered a soft drink or juice order I'd requested. I broke down completely after five days, however, and I cried to Mom, "I want to go home." I couldn't help it. I'd had enough of being poked every few hours around the clock.

Once home, I returned to usual activities as quickly as possible.

* * *

My neighborhood cohorts and I gravitated toward small construction projects.

I don't remember who'd brought up the idea. Short of building our own tree house, which required a tree that wasn't available, we dug an underground bunker with a short tunnel. Seemed the next best thing to serve as a boys-only sanctuary. Our nightly consumption of Vietnam War newscasts had introduced us to the idea of VC tunnels and the US Army tunnel rats who entered them.

So, a handful of us built a hideout on a nearby abandoned lot. We dug one main room and an entrance tunnel. Covered those with plywood and excavated dirt.

Not long afterward, Roger, Verlon, and I dug a second, ill-fated one in my backyard. A heavy summer rain flooded it a few weeks later. We attempted to dry it out by burning gasoline. That didn't work, so we abandoned our dugout and gave up on any further underground constructions.

Our interests moved on to exploring nearby storm-drain sewage tunnels. When a neighbor, Gary, caught hepatitis, we abandoned that as well.

Later still, when Roger met a neighbor down the street who owned a car, our interests morphed into unsupervised spelunking in areas around Upton, where caverns littered the landscape. I dared not go near Gramma and Grampa's farm though. Those weekend outings served as opportunities to carouse and drink, usually presented to our parents as going fishing.

Puff, Puff, Puff that Cigarette

March 1963

Not allowed to do much with my Christmas BB gun at home, I brought it to the country. There I shot frogs, trees, and signs. Because I had a gun and they were there.

The first bird I'd shot, a robin, fell off its branch.

Heck of a shot. Still alive?

The robin had offered no resistance when I picked it up, just blinked an eye. I noticed a tiny blob of blood on each side of its head.

Aw. Why had I done that?

Lifted back to a branch, it regained a perch.

I decided it time to put my gun away.

When I returned to check a few minutes later, the robin had disappeared, no signs of feathers anywhere.

Flown away? Shooting birds wasn't all that fun.

* * *

I'd concluded that cigarette smoke didn't smell that great, though cigar smoke smelled better. But, I still loved the smell of fresh tobacco.

A local farmer, Floyd, and his son, Floyd Jr., had dropped by for an afternoon visit.

Mom and Gramma stayed in the kitchen. The rest of us men—Grampa, Dad, Uncle James, Floyd, his son, Verlon, and me—gathered around the warm, potbelly stove in the living room. We warded off the winter chill, even though a recent snow melted under bright sun and turned bare spots in the front yard to mud.

Floyd Jr. produced cigarettes from his coveralls pocket, pulled one out of its pack, and lit it. About my age and size, he was a country boy and I wasn't. Even though we visited Gramma and Grampa often, I knew I only tasted country life while Floyd Jr. lived it.

I didn't envy his country life, but I did envy his cigarette. I pictured the Marlboro Man. Confident, he was an outdoorsman with a wide-brimmed hat, leather vest, and a colorful neckerchief. He sat on a horse, held out his chin that announced to everyone, I'm a man and I know what I want. A deep male voice encouraged, "Enjoy the great taste of a Marlboro cigarette." Music, similar to the *Bonanza* theme song, played. Thin towers of rock stood in the background against a red-orange sunset.

Floyd Jr. saw me eyeing his cigarette and grinned.

I looked at Dad. "Can I smoke, too?"

"No," he replied.

I stared at the stove.

No stranger to holding a cigarette, I knew how to smoke, with sufficient examples provided daily. Most adults I knew smoked regularly, some constantly. I'd never smoked a cigarette in the presence of adults that knew me, but inhaling unavoidable secondhand smoke proved close enough.

I'd had opportunity on a limited basis, when I'd attended Louisville Colonel's Minor League Baseball games at Kentucky Fairgrounds Stadium with several of my older cousins.

With a cigarette lightly pinched between a forefinger and thumb near the butt end, I took a short dainty draw. Tasted momentarily before a purse of lips, I exhaled a stream of smoke. I fancied my choreographed routine an act of maturity. Better yet, I was in public. I'd wondered if Mom or Dad might see me on TV, since the games were televised. But I'd played the odds they wouldn't be watching. Dad had never shown interest in baseball, much less any other sport, nor had I reason to think Mom would watch.

Nothing said by either of them about my behavior afterwards, I'd figured I calculated correctly.

Dad had smoked free cigarettes given to him by the navy in WWII. At least, that's what he'd told me. But how old was he when he'd started smoking?

I looked at Dad again, then at Floyd Jr., who took another drag from his cigarette. "Why not?"

"Because, I said so."

"But I want to smoke, too." I couldn't say I hoped for his affirmation of me by welcoming me into the men's smoking club.

"I told you, 'No.'"

Why won't you let me be a grownup? Not fair, no way, no how. Not fair.

Seemed to me Dad and Floyd Jr., a younger, coveralls farm version of the Marlboro Man, were deliberately torturing me with their smoking.

Defeated, I studied Floyd Jr's shoes. Clodhoppers, clumped with dried mud around the edges. With quick glances I could see that he gloated as he enjoyed his cigarette.

But I got nicer shoes than you.

The Wrong Path?

June 1963

Though Dad wouldn't approve of me smoking, his refusal didn't deter my further exploration anyway out of a sense of rebellion, though only in a token fashion.

Roger had the wherewithal to obtain cigarettes, if not by the pack, at least as singles, not that cigarettes were highly regulated or guarded. I suspected he liberated them from packs his sister left around her house. She lived in a smaller house on the same lot as Roger's parents.

Roger produced a cigarette. "Want some?"

"Sure," I said.

To decrease the odds of detection by our parents, we strolled the few yards to the end of Tallulah. Then, we turned left and walked to the farthest end of the open field to within a rock's throw of Watterson Expressway.

We'd incorporated tobacco into our daily rituals for a few months, perhaps. I don't recall how long, before the proverbial electric oscillator redistributed the excrement.

Home from work, Dad approached me straightaway with a severe expression. Then, in a stern voice, he said, "Don't let me catch you smoking again."

Catch me again? I hadn't been aware he'd caught me a first time.

But that was all he said and turned away.

He must've driven by on the freeway on his way home and seen Roger and me in the field. Had to have, no other possibility.

Dad, putting the fear of God in me, had excised my fun of smoking. The risk no longer proved worth his potential wrath.

* * *

My reach within the neighborhood expanded.

I joined Roger and John, who Roger had met not long beforehand. John, about our age at fourteen, lived nearby on an adjacent street, almost directly behind Roger's house. Neighborhood fences provided no obstacle to us when we wanted to get from place to place. We hung out in John's backyard around the old cars that his Dad bought and scrapped for money.

One Friday night, John said, "I think my uncle will buy us some alcohol, if we give him money."

"How much money?" Roger said.

"Enough to buy him some, too," John replied.

"We could get together enough for a half-pint, maybe even a pint, and offer to buy him one," Roger said.

"I'm in," I said.

When we arrived at John's uncle's house about a mile away, his uncle agreed with one stipulation: "Just don't get me into trouble over this."

"We won't," John said.

"We'll be careful," Roger said.

"Oh, no," I said. I'd have promised almost anything.

Within an hour we'd established a weekend booze connection and scored our own pint of sloe gin.

Didn't take long once we'd returned to John's backyard to polish off the contents. One swill at a time, we passed around the bottle, all without adult interference.

256

The slurring of speech, fuzziness of thinking, unsteady gate and balance, all new sensations, as well as the thrill of engaging in adult behavior, propelled me forward. I wanted to explore this liquid tool and the realm of sensations it created. I wanted to understand the hoo-ha surrounding Dad's consumption of booze, though I fully understood potential dangers existed.

Was I prepared to pick up the mantle where Dad left off? At least, now, I could appreciate to some degree alcohol's allure for Dad as I enjoyed the buzz and temporary euphoria. I'd known long beforehand that I needed to exercise vigilance, maintain self-control. Without that I might end up at the bottom of a booze bottle. Instances of that played out with several of Dad's brothers. Reports of fighting, job problems, a near-fatal auto accident, and more than one divorce, peppered their histories. One neighbor, a painter by trade, exhibited drunken tirades on a regular basis, his tirades inside and outside his house impossible to escape.

At the same time, I understood I needed to let go of my vigilance regarding Mom as my independence grew. Mom had married Dad and chosen to live with him, I hadn't, and she was my mother, not my wife.

* * *

The following summer, we moved again and to a house across the street and two doors down. Nothing else changed though; Dad continued to drink and argue with Mom. On the plus side, I wouldn't need to change school again or lose my friends.

I didn't find out the reason for that move, but supposed it boiled down to money. I couldn't be bothered. My thoughts focused on girls, time with Roger, and neighborhood football, which we played in the open field at the end of Tallulah and in plain sight of the airport's terminal and control tower.

Seemed, since my early years, Mom and Dad circled some magnetic pole centered near the dead-end of Tallulah.

Take Steady Aim

May 1965

I expected we'd pull into the driveway of the little house that Saturday morning. Instead, Dad parked next to the oak tree in front of the big house.

"Why are we parking here?" I said.

"They've moved back into the big house," Mom said. "Your Gramma told Rene last weekend that she missed being here."

Yay!

I checked the closest of Gramma's two rain barrels as I passed by. *More empty than full.*

Within the hour, Mom and Gramma had laid the supper table and we gathered around.

Once Grampa had finished grace, he started, "I went out on the front porch yesterday with my .22-rifle," then he put a piece of warm cornbread on his plate and selected the neck from the remaining pile of Gramma's fried chicken.

The sight of a gun, even the mere mention of one, would make me uneasy, and the memory of Uncle Dave, or Uncle Tunney and Aunt Betty, would come to mind.

I bit into the leg I'd selected. *Wasn't Grampa's grace a funeral service for the sacrificed hen? Hadn't thought of it that way before.*

I'd learned that Indians thanked an animal's spirit when they killed it, a far cry from the killings I'd done, though. Seemed the Indians had it right. Maybe, I should change my ways, be more like them, not kill anything except as food. Maybe, I should be respectful, humble, and appreciative of the sustenance animals provided.

Grampa went on, "I sat down on a porch chair to watch the sinkhole across the road. I've seen a groundhog show himself there several times lately."

Easy to see from the front porch, the sinkhole appeared ready to swallow me up, if I got too close, so I'd steered clear.

"How big is the groundhog, Grampa?" I asked.

"Pretty good size. Looks fat to me. Good eating. Well, I didn't wait long before he showed himself. I raised my rifle, took aim, then shot. Looked like I missed. He went back into his hole, but I'll get him next time."

Grampa would eat almost anything.

* * *

When we finished supper, Dad said to me, "We're going hunting. You can carry my .410 shotgun."

"Okay." I'd never carried a real gun, not even an unloaded one. *Dad treating me more like a grownup at sixteen.*

"We'll go over to the Cruz farm," Uncle James said.

"I haven't hunted there in a while," Dad said.

It only took Dad a minute to drive us the half-mile east along the Old Road, over the gentle rise, past the blackberry patch, and then left into the gravel driveway of Mr. Cruz's farm.

Shotguns in hand, Dad and I stopped at the bottom of the porch steps while Uncle James continued to the open front door.

A thin-framed man in coveralls approached from the kitchen with a slight limp. His face weathered, he appeared a hundred years old.

"Well, hello, James," he said in a cheery, soft-spoken voice.

"Mr. Cruz, is it alright for us to hunt on your farm today?" Uncle James asked him.

"Sure, James, you can hunt here anytime you want," Mr. Cruz said.

I liked him right off.

* * *

"Let's go that way," Uncle James suggested by pointing his shotgun.

I hefted the single-shot .410 several times. *All right. The big game hunter walks across the grassland for a trophy kill, a lion, perhaps hidden in the brush. He keeps a sharp eye for anything lurking behind that small cluster of trees, like an elephant or rhino, that if startled, might charge in a panic.*

"Pay attention and stay in line with us," Dad said to me. "Face forward and keep your finger off the trigger until you see something."

"Okay." Less nervous that I had control of the gun's trigger and direction it pointed, compared to someone else, I knew the damage from a .410 shotgun far outweighed that of a .22-caliber rifle. If the .410 went off in the direction of Uncle James, Dad might never trust me again. If it went off in Dad's direction, maybe he'd beat me within an inch of my life.

On a random route, we worked our way through fields of high weeds, into and out of woods, and crossed fence lines. We checked for squirrels in high branches of trees. We scanned for rabbits that might jump from clumps of brush in the fields. I knew other small animals inhabited the woods and fields, like raccoons and opossums, but didn't expect to see them in broad daylight.

Several small birds took flight.

"Uncle James, have you ever shot a turkey?" I asked.

"No, but I see one around every once in a while."

"How about a deer?"

"No. People have scared them off or killed them all, I reckon."

I expected we'd flush a rabbit any second, instead, a flock of geese took flight from several tall trees in the woods ahead.

Honk, honk, honk, honk!

I imagined they screamed an alarm, "Danger, danger, fly away!"

"They're probably out of our range," Uncle James said, referring to his sixteen-gauge and Dad's fourteen-gauge shotguns.

Honk, honk!

I imagined that one asked, "Where's Mildred?"

"Yeah, you're right," Dad agreed, "but we might hit one with the four-ten."

Honk, honk!

"I'm right behind you," another said.

The graceful geese gained altitude and distance from us. I couldn't help but envy their ability to fly.

"They're probably out of range now, anyway," Dad added.

Good. I didn't want to shoot one.

If I took a shot at anything, I'd get one chance. The worn ejection pins in Dad's .410 usually left the shell in the chamber when the bolt was pulled. Any animal not killed on a first shot might die of fright or old age before a second shot could be taken. I could probably do more damage with a muzzle-loaded musket, like the ones Davy Crockett and Daniel Boone had carried.

* * *

After we'd wandered in a loop and neared his house again, Mr. Cruz, who must've spotted us, met us outside.

"Get anything?" he asked.

"No, not this time, Mr. Cruz," Uncle James said.

The conversation ranged to other topics before it settled on an empty fifty-five-gallon drum nearby.

"I've been thinking about slaughtering a pig," Mr. Cruz said. "It wouldn't be hard to boil one in that barrel."

"Dad hasn't slaughtered a pig in a while," Uncle James replied.

I couldn't help but recall the sights, sounds, and smell in the slaughterhouse.

* * *

Upon our return to Gramma's house by the back door, Mom asked, "Did you get anything?"

"Not a thing," Dad said.

"Have you checked for chiggers and ticks?" Mom said to me.

"No," I said.

"Well, we'd better do that. Stand still."

Mom parted my hair with her fingers looking for tiny, crawly bugs.

We'd found ticks on Ring, our dog, several days after the last time we'd brought him to the farm. We'd named him Ring after the black hair around his right eye, which stood out on his white face, recognizable a mile away. By then the ticks on him had grown big and fat, like brown peas with little waving legs.

Verlon and I had mashed them, once we'd pulled them off, just to see the smear of blood.

"Take your shirt off and turn around," Mom said. "I don't see any on you, but you'll have to check your waist and legs."

I didn't mind Mom checking my public parts. But I examined my private areas alone. I discovered none, though the chiggers, tiny bright-red slow-moving dots, were almost impossible to find. Usually one or two would be overlooked.

* * *

The next morning, I woke up to an itch at my waist. The raised, red spot, smaller than a mosquito bite, looked familiar.

In the kitchen and ready for breakfast, I said, "Mom, I think I got a chigger."

"Let me see."

I pulled up my shirt with one hand and pulled down the waist of my pants with the other.

"Yeah, that looks like a chigger, alright," she said. "Mom, do you have anything to put on it?" she asked Gramma.

"We can mix some salt with lard and smear that on or you can cover the bite with nail polish."

"I'll put some nail polish on it," Mom said. "Wait here," she told me.

Mom produced a bottle of ruby-red polish, her favorite color, and painted the spot. "Let that dry."

I tried to blow on the polish to speed the drying, but that didn't help much. Although the nail polish felt strange on my skin, the itching soon stopped.

"It'll be gone when the polish wears off in a couple of days," Gramma said.

* * *

Aunt Shirley and Uncle Walt had arrived Saturday mid-morning.

Everything was about usual until that afternoon when Uncle Walt or I—I don't remember who—mentioned the pond. Or frogs. Or frog legs.

"Have you eaten frog legs before?" Uncle Walt asked me.

"Yeah, they taste like chicken." I'd gone frogging with Roger on fishing trips.

"Do you know how to clean them?" he asked.

"Yeah, I've cleaned a few."

"We could probably catch a bunch at the pond," he said.

The more we talked, the better frog legs sounded.

"Let's go see if we can catch some," Uncle Walt suggested.

Uncle Walt, a country boy, mild mannered and quick to smile, had grown up in those parts, Bonnieville, not far from Upton.

Dad had never offered to go frogging with me.

Uncle Walt and I set out with a burlap sack and two flashlights, prepared to nab frogs at the pond's edge as the evening's light dimmed.

* * *

Ribbit! Ribbit!

"We have to be quiet," Uncle Walt said.

We approached the pond like two thieves raiding a hen house.

Ribbit! Kneedeep!

Flashlights led our search through the tall grasses. "There's one," Uncle Walt whispered, light held steady on a frog. "Sneak up on it."

The frog jumped as I closed in. "I'll get the next one."

Ribbit, ribbit! Croak!

With each attempt, my technique improved.

Ribbit, ribbit!

The chorus quieted where we approached, but started again, first tentative, then full-throated, when we remained motionless a few moments.

"They're not very smart, are they?" I said. "You try to catch a few, Uncle Walt."

He handed me our squirming sack.

A few captured, and not sure when one would attempt escape, I kept the bag closed with a tight grip.

Kneedeep! Ribbit, ribbit!

We each took a short turn, maybe fifteen minutes or so.

"How many we got?" I asked.

"About a dozen. That ought to be enough, don't you think?"

Croak!

"Yeah." Not the catch I'd hoped for, but hungry, I said, "I'm ready to quit."

"We still need to dress the legs before we can eat," Uncle Walt said.

* * *

On the large rock at the back door, careful not to let them escape, we took one frog at a time from the sack and removed its hind legs with a sharp knife.

Uncle Walt had pointed away from the house. "Throw them over there, out of the way."

I'd flung each frog, still alive, a few feet away. Unseen in the dark, one frog added at a time, they must've littered the ground in a loose, unplanned formation. "The cats will probably get them," I said, not proud of treating frogs like they were worthless.

The skin peeled off the legs in a slow process without major effort, we carried our haul into the kitchen on some newspaper Gramma had provided. She'd mixed a bowl of flour and placed a skillet on the stove for us, too.

Uncle Walt and I coated the legs in flour and laid them into the hot skillet. Well, mostly Uncle Walt did. Gramma and Mom sat at the kitchen table. I guessed they feared Uncle Walt and I might burn the house down, if we were left unsupervised.

The sizzle increased my hunger. The batter turned a crusty deep brown, but my portion of legs looked meager, indeed, even appeared to shrink as they fried.

"Anybody want a taste?" Uncle Walt asked.

"No, none for me," Mom said.

"No, you go ahead and eat them," Gramma said.

I noticed thin dark lines that snaked through the meat as I brought one leg to my mouth and held my lips wide apart to avoid burning them. *Blood vessels, had to be.* "Yep, a light chicken flavor."

"Well, was it worth killing those frogs?" Mom asked.

"Yeah," I said. *But was it?* I'd disliked watching the helpless frogs after they'd been cut, knowing they would die and wondering if they had a clue.

I never succeeded in killing an animal with a shotgun. I couldn't hit anything seriously on the move. Frogs, on the other hand, could be gathered with a bare hand or the swing of a stick. The whole killing and dying issue wasn't a simple matter. I could see both sides of the issue. But I never got comfortable about killing an animal.

For the Sake of You

June 1965

Dad's rampages had eased by the time I turned sixteen. He'd still come home drunk Friday evenings, as unpredictably as ever, and Mom and Dad would argue over household finances. He had stopped pounding on Mom, which was a good thing. Maybe, due to the fact that Verlon and I would stand up to him.

I continued to seek escape away from home with friends, mostly Roger.

One afternoon, mid-week, while Verlon and I ate breakfast before heading off to our outdoor adventures of the day, Mom asked, "Why do you think your daddy spends his paychecks in beer joints?"

I'd wondered that many times, never arriving at a satisfactory answer. I gave her the only response I could think of, one I'd harbored some time, grown from a seedling into a fully-formed opinion. "I don't know, but you should leave him, if you're not happy." I'd said it before, though not with the same conviction.

"Yeah," Verlon said.

"I don't know what I'd do," she replied.

"I'll go with you," Verlon said.

"I will too," I said, if there was any question in her mind. Me, a protector of Mom, and at the same time, a traitor to Dad. *How would he manage?* My words seemed a betrayal of Dad, worse, a betrayal of myself. I loved him, no question, but the hurt from their arguments and his treatment of Mom had piled up. I leaned towards what seemed the lesser of two evils. I wanted to reduce our collective pain, willing to chance the unknown of their separation. I couldn't imagine how Mom remaining with Dad would be better. At the same time, I didn't want to find out if Dad could be pushed into something far worse, like Uncle Tunney. Aunt Aileen, one of Dad's sisters, had left her husband, Tyke, and then he'd drank himself to death.

Mom responded, "I don't think I'd be able to work. I was a nervous wreck when I worked at the Dobbs House."

Now a plea, Verlon said, "Leave him."

"I don't think I can. I don't know how we'd live," she said. "I've stayed with your daddy for your sakes."

How had that helped us? I couldn't read Mom's mind. I had a hard time understanding my own. I couldn't earn money to live on. I could encourage, plead, beg, but I couldn't make the decision for her to abandon Dad. *Her decision, hers alone.* I'd determined separation, a retreat from the battlefield, served as an option exercised to avoid all-out loss in a no-win situation. Mom couldn't face the financial uncertainty of separation and I had to settle for knowing she had her weaknesses. Even Superman had Kryptonite.

Imminent Demise

June 1965

A few weeks later, the warm air on that cloudless Friday had cooled slightly, when we arrived for another weekend visit and encountered Grampa on the front porch swing.

No sooner had we exchanged our hellos, and Mom had gone into the house, Grampa started in, "The road workers drove a spike in that tree over there." He pointed to the maple tree. "They're trying to kill it." He shook his head. "Law. I heard them doing it. When I gave them a what for, they claimed they can take part of my farm through eminent domain, as long as they pay me a fair price."

Why that tree?

Construction of the toll road from E-town to points south had arrived.

"Let me show you," he said.

Dad, Verlon, and I followed Grampa to the maple, smaller than the bigger oak and off to one side of the front yard.

The tree in the picture I'd seen of Mom with the overcoat and standing in the snow.

"There," Grampa said and pointed.

A railroad spike, identifiable by its offset head, stuck out several inches from the base of the tree, which appeared to have suffered no ill effects, yet, anyway.

I remembered how Billy, his brother and sisters, Verlon, and I had played in the yard with the winged seeds from that tree. We called them helicopters. They'd swirl down in the warm, late afternoon, loosened by gusts of gentle breezes. We'd picked them up, re-launched them as high as we could, and watched them turn.

One time, Aunt Betty, on the front porch, had watched us play until she interrupted us, "Let me show you something."

We'd gathered around her. She pulled several small branches from the tree and separated the stems from the leaves. Using the stems, she pinned the leaves together in a long string. "I used to do this as a young girl. Turn around, Billy."

Billy turned and stood, not like a soldier ordered to attention, but more like a slouch.

"Hold still," Aunt Betty told him. She wrapped the string of leaves around his head like a wreath and pinned them tight. She fashioned a string of leaves at the back to form a tail.

"Make one for me," we all said.

Aunt Betty fashioned several more, then said, "Now, you know how to make your own."

Soon, all of us wore our own wreath with a tail.

Billy and I had run around in a small circle. We'd whooped and hollered our Indian war cries as we prepared for battle, but sunset and supper had interrupted us and prevented any major hostile action.

Then I recalled the fun time when Billy and I had played in the fruit tree across the road. I missed Billy as I turned to look at the tree.

The fruit tree not in sight. *What happened?*

I walked over for a closer examination.

Where it once stood, I discovered a shallow hole. I'd known I'd lost Billy, but hadn't realized I'd lost that tree, too. Silent, I examined the hole, thought about loss. I took a deep breath, checked the Old Road in both directions, and re-crossed.

As I approached Dad, Grampa, and Verlon, who had moved to the front porch, I heard Grampa. "They come around here anytime they want, all hours, driving stakes with ribbons into the ground," he said. "And now they're trying to kill my maple tree. It's not right."

Doesn't seem right.

Grampa went on, "I told them, 'I'm not going to sell my property.' They're not willing to pay me a good price," he explained. "The government shouldn't be able to take a man's land and give him what they decide is a fair price."

Parts of it. They didn't want the whole thing, just parts. Yeah, like somebody could buy parts of my bike and tell me what they'd pay for the front wheel or chain.

* * *

The next morning, Saturday, Dad, Mom, Verlon, and I followed Uncle James to the line of flag markers in the ground. We paused near where the Old Road crossed the ridge going east.

"I guess, this is where the toll road is coming through," Uncle James said.

A long line of orange ribbons flapped in the breeze, leading the eye to cuts through the bedrock of the ridges to the north and south. They provided evidence that the road ran on a collision course with Grampa's farm, a slow chilled-syrup version of the train that had run over Mr. Johnson.

"It looks like they're going to take the barns and pond," Uncle James went on.

* * *

The next morning, Sunday, I overheard Grampa and Uncle James talk of Mr. Cruz' death.

Aw. Mr. Cruz? They'd always spoken highly of him and I remembered his gentle, friendly voice.

I'd never learned if Grampa and Mr. Cruz had slaughtered and cleaned any pigs in that fifty-five-gallon drum.

* * *

At each visit, Grampa grumbled about the highway's approach as he fought a losing battle against the progress of eminent domain.

Adhering to the line of ribbons, work crews felled a wide swath of trees. After that, bulldozers demolished the pond, tore down the two barns with their haylofts, stalls, and one corn crib, then scraped away the topsoil. Then, dynamite subdued the gentle ridge across the Old Road and carved the highway's path deep through limestone bedrock. Other farms were subdued, as well, everything affected for a mile in both directions, straight from one ridge to the next.

* * *

The next spring, after the highway's completion, Grampa, Dad, Verlon, and I congregated on the porch after dinner.

Grampa pointed south, towards the smallest parcel of his divided farm. That piece lay across the Old Road, beyond the sinkhole, and beyond a new access road that ran from the toll road to 31W and Upton. "They asked me if I wanted an access built for that piece of property when they were paving that road. The only chance I'd have for them to build it, they said. I told them, 'No.' Now, it's too late, they won't build an access. I can't get to that parcel because of the fence, and the neighbor there doesn't want to buy it. I can't do anything with that land now."

A no-man's land. I guessed Grampa had a stubborn streak and didn't always make the best decisions.

The maple tree, which looked healthy, didn't seem damaged by the spike still in it. A small victory for Grampa, at least. Had planners wanted to use the Old Road for access to Upton? Probably. If so, Grampa's single-handed resistance movement must've forced a shift in the location of the on/off ramps several hundred feet farther south and away from his house. Another victory for him, of sorts. Partial victories better than nothing, I supposed.

The Old Road, which now dead-ended on the largest remaining parcel of the farm, created a semi-private driveway for the house and a newer barn. Grampa had sold a third parcel, southeast of the house, where a gas station and a Stuckey's Restaurant appeared. The fourth parcel lay east of the house across the toll road and adjacent to the Cruz farm. Access to that piece required a round-about drive over the highway interchange. May as well be another no-man's land.

From that time forward when we visited Gramma and Grampa, we used the toll road and exited using the ramp at their farm. The highway's smooth pavement, and almost straight path, created the convenience of high-speed travel, bypassing Shepherdsville, Lebanon Junction, and E-town.

Wasn't progress wonderful? But I knew something most travelers on the toll road didn't. Nor likely, I guessed, ever bothered to think about. Progress didn't feel wonderful to those of us who'd known Gramma and Grampa's farm. Didn't feel wonderful to those who'd walked the fields, cultivated the crops, fished the pond, and hunted the woods. The highway robbed the country of charm, chopped Gramma and Grampa's farm into four unequal pieces, and destroyed the continent of my childhood explorations.

Transitions

Summer 1966

I'd graduated high school that May at seventeen.

We moved, again, in early summer. We moved back to Harding Avenue about two hundred yards from the house Dad had built. Our new house near the corner and stone's throw from the mom-and-pop basement store, now closed, that I'd ridden my bike to and from years before.

Mom and I secured part-time jobs at Park Aerial Survey, which was next door. Mom had an in, as Mr. Park owned the house we'd rented.

Then, Mom coached me to get my learner's driving permit using our Chevy station wagon, though we still only had one car.

Based on reports I'd heard from fellow classmates in high school, I'd memorized the final driver's road-test route, held at the Kentucky Fairgrounds parking lot. Things proceeded perfectly, I thought, even the parallel parking, which surprised me, until the highway patrol officer said, "Turn right."

Instead, I turned left.

"Pull over," he said.

Damn. We weren't supposed to turn left there.

A few weeks later, I avoided a repeat of that mistake and got my license.

* * *

In September I started engineering courses at Speed Scientific School at the University of Louisville. I continued to live at home, about a four-mile drive. I couldn't provide myself transportation, so I bummed rides from Mom and classmates.

Dad continued to mellow. Apparently, he'd abandoned Friday evening beer-benders in saloons. I couldn't help think that Verlon and I growing older had eased Dad's parental burden. Sharing more frequent beer-drinking rituals with Carl had helped, perhaps.

I witnessed far less arguing between Mom and Dad. My growing independence resulted in spending more time with Roger and company and less time at home, particularly Friday and Saturday evenings, which provided Mom and Dad ample opportunity to clear their systems. Mom seemed less in need of confiding to me about her difficulties with Dad. She certainly didn't mention knock-down-drag-out battles, nor did I observe bruising on her face or arms.

A Genteel Visit

October 1966

With some weeks' experience as a full-fledged licensed driver, I drove Mom and myself for a visit with Gramma and Grampa.

After Friday evening's supper, Mom suggested, "Let's go visit Tunney's kids. I haven't seen them since before Tunney died."

Grampa could no longer drive. Gramma had never gotten a driver's license.

"I feel nervous about driving that far," Mom said to me. "Will you drive us there for a visit?"

"Sure." My stomach knotted. I hadn't seen Billy for years, either.

* * *

The next afternoon, I drove as Mom provided directions to Billy's maternal grandparents' farm.

Billy, Bobby, and their two sisters met with us in the living room while their other grandparents presided over the meeting.

Everyone maintained a pleasant demeanor. Our conversation remained subdued. Seemed to me, though, a lumbering elephant squatted in the room. I wanted to talk about what had happened. I figured their maternal grandparents would do anything to avoid the subject. I wanted to blurt out how I'd missed Billy and wished things hadn't changed. But, I didn't dare. Instead, I worked to appear calm while I screamed in silence from the hurt.

When the time came to leave, everyone smiled, said goodbye in pleasant voices, and waved as we drove away. My sadness welled. I couldn't say that, either, not even to Gramma, Grampa, or Mom.

Had we acted normal? Any of us? I didn't think so, but I wasn't sure what normal meant, anyway.

* * *

The details of Aunt Betty and Uncle Tunney's marital difficulties and deaths, as I know them, haven't changed over the years. My appreciation of navigating marital relationships has, however. I've learned that marital conflict is inevitable, that disagreements, though not violence, are necessary to maintain a healthy relationship. I've learned that some marriages take a turn for the worse and become irreparable.

Doors Close

1975 and Beyond

Years had rolled by. I'd settled into my life in California and had precious little means to visit Kentucky on a whim, so my visits became infrequent.

Even before Uncle James married and moved away, a large portion of the farm nearest the house had fallen unattended, the remaining pieces nearly all but forgotten. Gramma and Grampa never believed in hired help. Gramma's chicken brood had shrunk, and the fewer flowers that she planted were nearer the house, while Grampa's scarred leg and poor hearing hampered him to near invalidity.

Then, when Grampa's health faded to the point that he needed twenty-four-hour nursing care, the family moved him to a facility in Louisville. Although still spry, Gramma abandoned the farm to be nearer Grampa, when she moved in with Uncle Clifton, who by then was divorced from Aunt Roselee.

Another door to my past had shut. The farm, acting as collateral for their nursing care, remained idle, like some dust-covered jar of Gramma's canned fruit in the far corner of the root cellar.

Grampa, in his early nineties and three years older than Gramma, died first; news I hadn't wanted to get, though I understood the inevitability. Another door had closed.

Gramma followed him several years later; additional news I hadn't wanted to get, which felt more ominous. Another door had shut and I had to own up to myself that I felt fonder of Gramma.

And, so, after some fifty years of occupation and use by Gramma and Grampa, the farm changed hands.

* * *

For one of Dad's few visits to California, and the one which would be his last, he traveled with Mom by plane.

A thought occurred to me to share a little with each of them while they visited. I hadn't thought it through beforehand, but didn't want a full-on review of our mutual past. I didn't want to open wounds, but wanted to acknowledge something with each I'd always held secret. I wanted to close the loop and say what I'd needed to say all those years ago.

"You were an alcoholic when I grew up," I told Dad.

"I didn't know you thought that about me," he replied.

I understood, according to his definition, he thought I considered him no different than a derelict bum on skid row. I didn't mean that at all, though I didn't elaborate. In retrospect, I wished I had. I'd meant that his drinking resulted in untold damage to all of us, in ways we couldn't fully appreciate, nor ever would.

I told Mom, "I was angry with you growing up." Not for her confronting Dad, but for tolerating his years of abuse.

A tear came to her eye.

I should've added that I felt proud that she'd stood up to Dad and argued for what she believed, but that didn't occur to me.

Regardless, in some sense, I'd put to rest demons shouldered since childhood, said without fanfare, though time had ushered me down a long road.

Though incorporated into my bones at an early age—which I couldn't articulate until years later—the depth of Mom's willingness and capacity to endure suffering in her marriage, also contributed to my lack of preparedness for healthy relationships. Turned out my deficiencies developed as a result of Dad and Mom's unintended dysfunctional team effort. In a sense, I enjoyed the best of both, and the worst.

During our next phone call after their return home, Mom told me, "Your daddy wouldn't get up to go to the restroom on the plane. Had me hold up a blanket while he peed into a bottle."

When Dad got on the phone, he told me, "I won't fly on a plane again."

I had no doubt he meant that.

"Well, you actually flew six times on your trip, three here and three home," I pointed out, though I didn't think that changed his mind on the subject.

Janet, my wife, and I laughed ourselves silly when I told her about Dad using a bottle during the trip home. Yes, I'd married in spite of Dad's proclaimed wishes to me years earlier that I not do so. And I'd done it three times to boot.

That was the only time I knew Dad traveled by plane, and I considered it a miracle, close though not quite on par with Jesus walking on water. His trip reinforced my notion that some old dogs can do new tricks, though limited. It also reinforced the realization that Dad did love me, though that leaked through his protective veneer in dribs and drabs.

I'd concluded Dad's emotional stunting was directly affected by his own traumas, and for that matter, those of his father as well. Beyond that, so was mine, though to what degree I'll never fully know. For sure, I've worked at not letting my fears hold me back to the same degree as Dad.

* * *

The Marlboro Man, whom I'd seen in all those TV cigarette commercials, died of smoking-related cancer. And for a few years, packs of cigarettes had included the Surgeon General's warning about the dangers of smoking, but that hadn't slowed Dad's habit.

When Mom informed me that Dad had been diagnosed with lung cancer, I wasn't completely surprised. He'd already had a cancerous lesion removed from his lip several years prior to that.

I kept in closer phone contact with Mom and Verlon, interspersed with brief talks with Dad. As days passed, I calculated when best to visit—I might get only one shot—when it would do the most good for Dad, Mom, Verlon, and me.

"Connard, I visited your dad and talked with his doctor at the VA," Carl William told me. "Things don't look good. You should plan to go see him soon." He went on, "It was pretty bad when my dad died of cirrhosis."

I couldn't figure which was better, lung cancer or liver failure, both were bad, neither anything to wish for. And though Carl hadn't been a raving lunatic when he drank, as far as I knew, his alcohol consumption hadn't done him any favors, nor had it for Beulah, Carl William, and Gerald.

When I'd decided to visit, Dad remained hospitalized after he'd undergone a round of radiation treatment.

Mom, Verlon, and I met the oncologist who informed us that Dad's radiation treatments hadn't stemmed the tide and his tumor had metastasized. Though the oncologist was prepared to continue the battle with chemotherapy, he added, "The prognosis isn't good. I haven't told him. I don't want to take away his hope."

I appreciated the doc's sensitivity to Dad's emotional process. I'd long ago accepted that as we humans give up the illusion of control over our lives, we cling to hope and desire to be treated with dignity.

I visited Dad daily and, at one point, when the two of us were alone, he confided, "Jesus came to me. He motioned and said, 'Come on, it'll be okay.'"

To me that meant Dad had accepted the inevitable. I almost burst into tears, though didn't. I felt grateful. My hope soared, though not for a reversal of fortune, about which I harbored no magical thinking. Instead, my hope soared that Dad would achieve peace of mind.

And when an uncle visited later, I encouraged Dad with, "Tell Uncle Clayton what you told me." I figured Dad's re-telling would help him. I believed Uncle Clayton, one of Mom's older brothers and familiar with the Bible, would interpret Dad's story as I did. I didn't share my interpretation, however. I kept that secret.

A few days had passed since my arrival, when Mom, Verlon, and I met again with the oncologist. "I'm recommending that we transfer Mr. Hogan to a hospice," he told us.

Mom, Verlon, and I concurred.

* * *

After his move, Dad appeared somewhat subdued, though not despondent.

Mom, Verlon, and I visited daily and various members of our extended family visited occasionally.

Everyone chatted about daily routines, weather, food, and meals with Dad. Frequently, someone asked about his comfort and offered their assistance to reposition his head or adjust his bed. Nothing negative was mentioned that might undermine Dad's hope or create a needless upset. Talking points exhausted, we sat in the silence of one another's presence. All of us, even Dad, conspired in an acceptance of the inevitable.

I boiled it all down to saying, I love you, anyway. What else needed to be said?

* * *

Dad sported whiskers several days old, when he asked, "Will you shave me?" as he produced a disposable razor.

"Do you have any shaving cream?" I asked.

"No, but it's okay. A dry shave will be okay. I've done it before."

A chance to do what I'd watched Uncle James do for Grampa years before. I thought a moment. I wanted to say yes, but instead said, "But I don't want to cut you." I meant that. A nick, caused by my hand, would've tortured me. Strangely, it never occurred to me to ask for shaving cream from the nursing station or use a wet bar of soap.

"I'll do it myself," he said.

I watched and listened as he'd scraped his dry face with the razor, amazed he'd avoided cuts. He appeared not to mind I hadn't shaved him, but I felt sad that I'd missed a golden opportunity to express my love non-verbally. Because, despite everything and maybe because I'd come to accept that I understood what made Dad tick, I did love him.

No do-overs. Though we get chances to make amends in other ways, we get no do-overs.

The inevitable was close at hand. But my timing had been off. My job in California called me home.

I began my goodbye to Dad, knowing the end would come soon. "I don't know if we'll," my voice broke momentarily, "get to see each other again."

Dad must've missed my drift. He didn't mention death or dying. If he had caught my point, he didn't say.

But in deference to him, I didn't, either. Instead, I said, "I love you."

"Me, too," he said.

Still allergic to that word, Dad?

* * *

Mom called about a week later. "He hasn't been taking ice chips or had a drink of water in three days. He's not very responsive to anyone and has been calling your name."

"Mom, that's not good. People can't live more than three days without water," I told her. I felt prepared to be there at his last breath, though that would be painful, but it looked unlikely I'd get to him in time.

Mom, Verlon, and I had already agreed to a "Do Not Resuscitate" order based on the doctor's recommendation. Resuscitation would only prolong the physical agony for Dad, and couldn't, wouldn't reverse the outcome one iota.

I phoned Verlon to provide my best assessment of the situation.

"I've been thinking I'll start a vigil," he said.

"You should do that right away. People can't live without water for more than about three days," I told him.

I requested more time off work and began making flight arrangements.

The next day Verlon called to say, "Dad passed away in the early morning."

I believe I'd already known that in my bones.

Another door had shut.

Mom, Verlon, and I agreed, after I told them I wanted to give Dad's eulogy, that I should be honest about his drinking. No BS, just the unvarnished truth and without hysterics. I'd lay it out in a matter-of-fact manner without the blow-by-blow details. Not that Mom, Verlon, or I wanted to make Dad out to be an ogre. But Dad's drinking was no big secret to anyone; we figured honesty was our best way to share our love for him. Seemed only appropriate to be honest about the damage done by alcoholism. After all, Dad had been a victim, too.

Though I couldn't appreciate all of Dad's qualities as I'd grown up, I'd learned patience for a story, both received and given, along with a dry sense of humor. By observing Dad's fear of heights, I learned to challenge my own. I'm sure I absorbed his stubbornness, a mixed blessing. And though I've never relished work, I learned considerable carpentry skills from him, which I put to use on jobs around the house and my arts and crafts projects. Come to think of it, I'd probably absorbed my dislike of work, seeing it as just for the sake of money, from him as well.

Perhaps, I hadn't rolled far from that apple tree, either.

From Mom I learned to appreciate music and the more creative part of myself, as well as the willingness to venture. Mom demonstrated sensitivity to and caring for others, though with a thin self-protective shell. She'd turned martyr and suffered for the sakes of Verlon and me in her relationship with Dad. But she helped soften the rougher edges of what I'd learned from Dad.

* * *

Maybe, I'll pay the farm a visit someday and ask to look around the house. Or maybe, I'll just pull off the toll road, now a free interstate highway, and look at the house from a distance. Though, if I do visit, I suspect it will pale in comparison to my memory, changed into something I no longer recognize.

But Frank and Ada Riggs? They will remain unchanged in my heart, accompanied by childhood warm-blanket feelings. And I will always know them as Gramma and Grampa.

Afterword

Dad's bouts of drinking during my childhood had seemed to slacken after I'd been drafted into the US Army and left home at age twenty.

Mom's reports, and the few visits I'd had, indicated that both she and Dad had mellowed. She'd overcome her personal prohibition to alcohol and consumed mixed drinks. They socialized at a local Eagles Club on the weekends. Her way of moderating Dad's behavior by keeping him in her sight, my bet.

I couldn't help but believe that the worst bouts of Dad's drinking had somehow related to me and Verlon, as we'd grown up. Not that I thought either of us had done anything in particular, but that, instead, Dad didn't know how to relate to us as sons and couldn't handle the responsibility of his early fatherhood. As I mulled over the bits and pieces of wreckage, and learned about Grampa Hogan's drinking, I'd concluded Dad didn't know how to act any other way. And Mom had tried the only way she knew to intervene in Dad's drinking. Of course, codependent by the standard definition, she hadn't succeeded in changing his drinking. Given Dad's strong stubborn streak, I imagined that sometimes he'd done things even to spite Mom with the mantra: You're not telling me what to do!

When I've thought of my visits to the farm over the years, my interactions with everyone and everything I experienced there, my memories circle back to Gramma. Several decades passed after she'd died before I realized that Gramma's unbounded kindness had acted as my emotional anchor, around which all else hinged.

And it's not as if my Gramma and Grampa Hogan didn't love me. I had no doubt that they did. I loved them both, even after the early rift I'd felt between Gramma Hogan and myself. My mental gravitation towards my maternal grandparents rested more upon the fact that they'd stayed put, lived on one farm. Gramma and Grampa Hogan owned no farm or property where they'd settled. They moved much like Dad had moved us, on what seemed a random basis. And without a fixed, permanent place where I could root my hopes and dreams when I visited my paternal grandparents, I relied upon Gramma and Grampa Riggs' farm to fill that need. The familiarity of their farm, and the history I built there, helped me navigate my struggle and create balance, as best I could, without fully appreciating that at the time.

In addition, I've learned that recovery from trauma is not an event, but a lifelong process. I've learned that physical escape, or a geographic cure, is nowhere near the end of the recovery process, though in some cases is a necessary first step. I've realized my experiences on the farm proved invaluable in my survival of Dad's bouts of drinking and his fights with Mom. I've learned to put their relationship into a healthier perspective and overcome my fear of the raging bull of alcoholism. I've come to appreciate that every family member provided me something of value.

My recovery, as yet unfinished, continues. In the meantime, I'm nourished by childhood memories of little things. I relish the memories of Mom's laughs, her playing piano and accordion. I appreciate recalling Dad's stories, and yes, his joking and laughs at those times when he wasn't in a drunken rage.

I cherish most of my childhood memories, particularly those on the farm and not just Gramma's smiles and gentle manner. I cherish those of play with cousin Billy, my soulmate, and piles of broken Easter-egg shells scattered across the front yard. I cherish those of warm tomatoes off the vine, cornbread soaked in a glass of cold fresh milk, and watermelon consumed on the front porch.

As I continue to mull my painful memories over time, my mental tapestry shifts. The worst memories lose their power and fade, like grime cleansed by detergent. Those memories that remain are the better ones, the best ones, the important ones to caress. Memory is that way, strange and wonderful.

CPSIA information can be obtained
at www.ICGtesting.com
Printed in the USA
BVHW041345250322
632310BV00005B/11